THE CRIMINOLOGY SERIES

EDITED BY

W. DOUGLAS MORRISON

I.

THE FEMALE OFFENDER

The Female Offender

BY

PROF. CÆSAR LOMBROSO

AND

WILLIAM FERRERO

WITH AN INTRODUCTION

BY

W. DOUGLAS MORRISON

HER MAJESTY'S PRISON
WANDSWORTH

ILLUSTRATED

Fred B. Rothman & Co.
LITTLETON, COLORADO
1980

ISBN: 0-8377-0807-9

THE FEMALE OFFENDER

BY

PROF. CÆSAR LOMBROSO

AND

WILLIAM FERRERO

WITH AN INTRODUCTION

BY

W. DOUGLAS MORRISON
HER MAJESTY'S PRISON
WANDSWORTH

ILLUSTRATED

LONDON
T. FISHER UNWIN
1895

INTRODUCTION.

It is generally recognised that the supreme if not the exclusive object of criminal law and penal administration is the protection of society. Unfortunately it cannot be said at the present time that either criminal law or penal administration is fulfilling this object. In a recent comprehensive survey of criminal problems, Professor von Liszt, a distinguished German jurist, felt himself compelled to admit that our existing penal systems are powerless against crime. Similar expressions of opinion are of frequent occurrence among eminent specialists in France, Italy, and elsewhere; and it is only because the question of crime has recently fallen into the background in Great Britain that the same confession of failure is not heard with equal emphasis among ourselves.

In order to be satisfied that these grave allegations are resting upon solid grounds of fact we have only to look at the increase of criminal expenditure and the growth of the habitual criminal population among all civilised communities. As far as Great Britain and the United States are concerned, the annual official expenditure in connection with crime amounts to an enormous sum. In Great Britain this expenditure reaches a total of at least ten millions sterling per annum, and according to a recent report of the Ohio Board of State Charities, the citizens of the United States spend an annual sum of fifty-nine million dollars on judiciary, police, prisons, and reformatories. What is the result of this vast annual drain on the resources of the nation? Are the people getting an equivalent in the shape of a diminution in the numbers of the criminal classes? According to all the evidence we possess, it is to be feared that this is not the case. Here are the words of General Brinkerhoff, President of the National Prison Congress, as to the condition of affairs in the United States: "Other questions which agitate the public and divide parties are doubtless important. But the country can live and prosper under free trade or protection, under bimetallism or monometallism, under Democracy or Republicanism, but it cannot survive a demoralised people with crime in the ascendant. That crime is on the increase out of proportion to the population is indicated in many ways, but for the country as a whole, the United States census is the most reliable guide. Let us look at it by decades:

Year.	Prisoners.	Ratio to population.
1850	6,737	1 in 3,442
1860	19,086	1 in 1,647
1870	32,901	1 in 1,171
1880	58,609	1 in 855
1890	82,329	1 in 757

This rate of increase in a few states, we are glad to note, has not been maintained, and in one or two, for the higher crimes, it has even decreased a trifle; but, upon the whole, the swell has been continuous like a tide that has no ebb."

In the United Kingdom it is impossible to estimate the movement of the criminal population by a reference to the number of persons detained in prisons and convict establishments on a given day. Owing to the growing practice of committing juveniles to industrial institutions of all sorts; owing to the substitution of fines for imprisonment; and owing to the shortening of sentences, the prison population of Great Britain has not increased in the same manner as in the United States. But when the value of existing methods of penal administration is tested by the growth of the habitual offender we are confronted with a similar record of disastrous failure.

Why are our penal methods so helpless and discomfited in face of the criminal population? Why do the combined efforts of legislators, judges, police, and prisons produce so few practical results? Is it because the social disease with which these agencies are grappling is beyond the reach of human skill, and will continue to rage with unabated virulence so long as social life exists? This deduction is hardly warranted by the facts. The failure of existing methods of criminal legislation and administration is not to be accepted as a proof that the organised forces of society are face to face with an incurable disease in the body politic. All that the failure of our present methods succeeds in establishing is the immediate and imperative necessity of placing our whole penal system upon a more rational foundation.

The collapse of penal legislation is to be accounted

for on the ground that it proceeds upon principles which are not resting on the facts of social experience. It is assumed, for instance, in every criminal code that the only remedy, or almost the only remedy, against the criminal population is the fear of punishment. As far as the average member of the community is concerned, it is not to be denied that the fear of penal consequences may exercise a salutary effect on his impulses and resolves at some critical moment in his career. To what extent the dread of coming into collision with the criminal law determines the course of human action is in the nature of things impossible to estimate. In any case it may safely be accepted that the ordinary man—that is to say, the man who habitually lives under ordinary social and biological conditions—is on critical occasions deterred from entertaining certain kinds of anti-social ideas by an apprehension that the practice of them will be followed by public indignation and public punishment.

If the criminal population was composed of ordinary men it is possible that the purely punitive principles on which the penal code reposes would constitute an efficient check on the tendency to crime. But is it a fact that the criminal population is composed of ordinary men? Is there any evidence to show that the great army of offenders who are passing through our prisons, penitentiaries, and penal servitude establishments in a ceaseless stream is made up of the same elements as the law-abiding sections of the community? On the contrary, there is every reason to believe that vast numbers of the criminal population do not live under ordinary social and biological conditions. It is indeed a certainty that a high percentage of them live under anomalous biological and social conditions. And it is these anomalous conditions acting upon the offender either independently or, as is more often the case, in combination which make him what he is.

Penal laws pay exceedingly little attention to this cardinal and dominating fact. These laws assume that the criminal is existing under the same set of conditions as an ordinary man. They are framed and administered on this hypothesis; and they fail in their operation because this hypothesis is fundamentally false. It is perfectly evident that a legislative and administrative system which is drawn up to meet one set of conditions will not be successful if in practice it is called upon to cope with a totally different set. A patient suffering from an attack of typhoid fever cannot be subjected to the same regimen, to the same dietary, to the same exercise as another person in the enjoyment of ordinary health. The regimen to which the patient is subjected must be suited to the anomalous condition in which he happens to be placed. Criminal codes to be effective must act upon precisely the same principle. They must be constructed so as to cope with the social and individual conditions which distinguish the bulk of the criminal population, and it is because they are not constituted upon this principle that these enactments are so helpless in the contest with crime.

The impotence of criminal legislation is also due to another circumstance. It follows from the fallacious principle that the offender is an ordinary man, that each offender must be dealt with on exactly the same footing if he has committed the same offence. On this principle all offenders convicted of the same offences must be subjected to the same length of sentence, the same penal treatment, the same punitive regulations in every shape and form. This idea finds expression from time to time in popular outcries against the inequality of sentences. It is seen in the newspapers that one person is sentenced to six months' imprisonment for an offence of the same nature and gravity as another person who is only sentenced to six days. The offences are in all essential respects the same, but the sentences are absurdly different. It is immediately assumed that there has been some miscarriage of justice, and a great deal of popular indignation is the result. In many cases there can be no doubt that the popular instinct is right. Existing methods of penal treatment do not admit of the application to any great extent of sentences of unequal length for offences of a similar character. Our penitentiary systems are based upon the principle of uniformity of treatment for all offenders. In this respect they resemble our penal laws and are like them equally barren of good results. As long, therefore, as we have almost exactly the same kind of prison treatment for all sorts and conditions of offenders, so long will public opinion be to a large extent justified in protesting against the unequal duration of sentences for offences of a similar nature and gravity.

But, apart from the considerations which have just

been mentioned, the principle of equality of sentences, as far as their mere duration is concerned, is fundamentally erroneous. The duration and nature of sentences, as well as the duration and nature of prison treatment, must be adjusted to the character of the offender as well as to the character of the offence. In other words, judicial sentences and disciplinary treatment must be determined by the social and biological conditions of the offender quite as much as by the offence he has committed. In certain cases this principle is acted upon now, but if penal methods are to be made of greater social utility, it is a principle which must be much more extensively applied.

The principle of adjusting penal treatment to the social and biological condition of the offender is acted on, for instance, in the case of children. A theft committed by a child of twelve is not dealt with by our judges and magistrates in the same manner as a theft of precisely the same kind by a person of mature years. In the one case the juvenile is perhaps dismissed with an admonition, or if his parental conditions are defective, he is ordered to be detained in an industrial or reformatory school. In the other case the offender of mature years is usually committed to prison. But according to the maxim that the punishment should be adjusted to the crime, both these offenders should be sentenced to exactly the same form of penal treatment. Again, in the case of offences committed by adults, if the one offender is a man and the other a woman the sentences are not the same, although the offence may be precisely the same. Or again, in the case of offences committed by men the sentences are not the same if the one is discovered to be feeble-minded and the other is in possession of his senses. In all these instances justice works upon the maxim: *Si duo faciunt idem, non est idem.* It sets aside the notion that two offences of equal gravity are to be dealt with by awarding the same amount of punishment to both. In such circumstances equality would be gained at the expense of justice.

The principle that punishment should be adjusted to the condition of the offender as well as to the nature of the offence is distinctly laid down by Bentham. "It is further to be observed," he says, "that owing to the different manners and degrees in which persons under different circumstances are affected by the same exciting cause, a punishment which is the same in name will not always either really produce, or even so much as appear to others to produce, in two different persons the same degree of pain. Therefore, that the quantity actually inflicted on each individual offender may correspond to the quantity intended for similar offenders in general, the several circumstances influencing sensibility ought always to be taken into account." As he says elsewhere, "These circumstances cannot be fully provided for by the legislator; but as the existence of them in every sort of case is capable of being ascertained, and the degree in which they take place is capable of being measured, provision may be made for them by the judge or other executive magistrate to whom the several individuals that happen to be concerned may be made known." In both these passages Bentham makes it perfectly plain that in penal legislation and administration other circumstances must be taken into account besides the actual offence; and the circumstances to which he alludes are what we have already described as the social and biological conditions of the offender.

The question therefore arises, What are these conditions, and how are they to be ascertained? What these conditions are and how they can be ascertained can easily be got at by an examination of the delinquent population in our penitentiary establishments of various kinds. Let us look first at social conditions. In the sixteenth Year Book of the New York State Reformatory a very excellent account is given of the social antecedents of the inmates. According to the returns 2,550, or 52·6 per cent., of the inmates came from homes which were positively bad, and only 373, or 7·6 per cent., came from homes which were positively good. It is also stated that 1,998, or 41·1 per cent., of the population left home before or soon after reaching the age of fourteen, and in a total population of 4,859 it is recorded that only 69, or 1 and a fraction per cent., were surrounded by wholesome influences at the time of their lapse into crime. When we come to look at the social condition of juveniles committed to Reformatory Schools in England we are confronted with a very similar set of results. According to the returns for 1892, in a total of 1,085 juveniles committed to these institutions, only 425 were living under the control of both parents. All the others had only one parent, or had one or both parents in prison, or had been deserted by their parents altogether. The social condition of the juvenile population in the prisons of our large cities is equally as bad. In a high percentage of cases they have either no homes or no parents, and are without skilled occupation in any shape.

Instances such as these—and they might be multiplied a hundredfold—make it quite plain that it is useless attempting to deal with the offence without looking at the same time at the social conditions of the offender. In the majority of cases the offence is the natural and almost inevitable product of these social conditions. Up to the age of sixteen the magistrates and judges in England are empowered by law to take these adverse circumstances into account, and to send the offender to a school instead of committing him to prison. But after the age of sixteen has been passed our penal legislation makes absolutely no provision for the unhappy juvenile bereft of paternal support and paternal counsel at the most critical period of his existence. Imprisonment is its only remedy. But as imprisonment does nothing to remove the adverse social circumstances which have turned the juvenile into a criminal, it has absolutely no effect in preventing him from continuing to pursue a career of crime. As long as the conditions which produce the offender remain he will continue to offend, and as long as Penal law shuts its eyes to this transparent fact it is doomed to impotence as a weapon against crime.

The criminal, as we have said, is a product of anomalous biological conditions as well as adverse social circumstances. Dr. Lombroso's distinctive merit consists in the fact that he has devoted a laborious life to the examination of these biological or, as he prefers to call them, anthropological anomalies. Criminal anthropology, as he has termed his investigations, is really an inquiry on scientific principles into the physical, mental, and pathological characteristics of the criminal population. The present volume is an example of the method in which these inquiries are conducted. It is a translation of that portion of Dr. Lombroso's *La Donna Delinquenta* which deals with the female criminal. Dr. Lombroso had predecessors in France in such men as Morel, Legrand du Saulle, Brierre de Boismont, and Prosper Despine; and in England in Pritchard, Thomson and Dr. Nicolson. But he has surpassed all these writers in covering a wider field of investigation, in imparting a more systematic character to his inquiries, and in the practical conclusions which he draws from them. Dr. Lombroso proceeds from the principle that there is an intimate co-relation between bodily and mental conditions and processes. In accordance with this principle he commences with an examination of the physical characteristics and peculiarities of the criminal offender. As a result of this examination he finds that the criminal population as a whole, but the habitual criminal in particular, is to be distinguished from the average member of the community by a much higher percentage of physical anomalies. These anomalies consist of malformations in the skull and brain and face. The organs of sense are also the seat of many anomalies, such as abnormal development of the ear, abnormalities of the eye and its protecting organs, abnormalities of the nose, such as a total absence or defective development of the bony skeleton; abnormalities of the mouth, such as hare-lip, high palate, and malformations of the teeth and tongue. The criminal population also exhibits a considerable percentage of anomalies connected with the limbs, such as excessive development of the arms or defective development of the legs. We have also sexual peculiarities, such as femininism in men, masculism in women, and infantilism in both. Where a considerable number of deep-seated physical anomalies are found in combination in the same individual, we usually see that they are accompanied by nervous and mental anomalies of a more or less morbid character. These mental anomalies are visible among the criminal population in an absence of moral sensibility, in general instability of character, in excessive vanity, excessive irritability, a love of revenge, and, as far as habits are concerned, a descent to customs and pleasures akin in their nature to the orgies of uncivilised tribes. In short, the habitual criminal is a product, according to Dr. Lombroso, of pathological and atavistic anomalies; he stands midway between the lunatic and the savage; and he represents a special type of the human race.

It is almost needless to remark that Dr. Lombroso's doctrine of criminal atavism and the criminal type has provoked a considerable amount of opposition and controversy. It is impossible in the space at our command to examine the question in detail. The most weighty objection to the doctrine of a distinctively criminal type is to be found in the circumstance that the mental and physical peculiarities which are said to be characteristic of the criminal are in reality common to him with the lunatic, the epileptic, the alcoholic, the prostitute, the habitual pauper. The criminal is only one branch of a decadent stem; he is only one member of a family group; his abnormalities are not peculiar to himself; they have a common origin, and he shares them in common with the degenerate type of which he furnishes an example.

Let us give a few instances of the ratio of degeneracy among the criminal population of Great Britain and the United States. Among the inmates of the New York State Reformatory 12 per cent. were descended from insane or epileptic parents, 38 per cent. were the children of drunken parents, and 4 per cent. were the children of pauper parents. In England suicide is five times more prevalent among the prison population than among the general community, insanity is twenty-eight times more prevalent. According to a census taken of the English convict establishments in 1873 it was found that 30 male convicts per thousand were suffering from weak mind, insanity, or epilepsy. It was also found that 109 per thousand were suffering from scrofula and chronic diseases of the lungs and heart, and that 231 per thousand were afflicted with congenital or acquired deformities and defects. In Scotland 33 per cent. of the cases of insanity occur among offenders who have been in prison before, and in England 41 per cent. of the cases of suicide occur among offenders who have been in prison before. More minute investigation into each individual case would undoubtedly heighten all these percentages. But as they stand they are sufficiently striking, and they establish beyond the possibility of a doubt that the criminal population exhibits a high percentage of defective biological conditions.

In what way do our existing methods of penal law and administration attempt to deal with the offender exhibiting these anomalous conditions? Do we act upon the principle so clearly enunciated by Bentham of adjusting our methods of penal treatment to the nature of the offender as well as to the nature of the offence? On the contrary, as far as adults are concerned, the existence of this principle is practically ignored. It is assumed that all offenders are the same, and are therefore affected in exactly the same way and to the same extent by penal discipline. And what is the result? A steady and uninterrupted increase of recidivism; a failure of penal law and penal administration as instruments of social defence, a constant augmentation of expenditure in connexion with the repression of crime.

What are the best means of mitigating this unsatisfactory state of affairs? In the first place penal law must be constructed with a view to cope with the conditions which produce the criminal population. At present the principal office of a criminal court is to ascertain whether a person under trial for a criminal offence is innocent or guilty; if he is found to be guilty the sentence is almost entirely determined by the character of the offence. Except in glaring cases of lunacy the court takes little or no cognisance of the individual and social conditions of the offender. The sentence is not adjusted to contend with these conditions. In fact it is often calculated to aggravate them, and in such instances is worse than useless as a weapon against the tendency to crime. It should be made the business of a criminal court to inquire not merely into the alleged offence, but in cases of conviction into the conditions of the offender who committed it; and the duration and nature of the sentence must be determined by the results of this inquiry quite as much as by the nature of the offence. It may be said that this proposal is throwing new and unaccustomed functions upon courts of justice, and to a certain extent this is no doubt the fact. But it is also to be remembered that as social organisation increases in complexity, the machinery of government must be adapted to these new conditions. The judicial machine is at present of too primitive a character: in order to do its work efficiently it must be reconstructed, its functions must be enlarged.

In the next place penal establishments must be placed upon the same basis as penal law. In other words, they, too, must be classified and administered with a view to deal with the conditions which produce the offender. At present these establishments are all of practically the same type; they are all administered on the same lines. Except in extreme cases the same kind of penal treatment is meted out to all classes of offenders. Uniformity of penal establishments and uniformity of penal discipline rest upon the assumption that all offenders are of the same type and are produced by exactly the same conditions. A practical acquaintance with the criminal population shows that this is not the fact. The criminal population is composed of many types. It is composed of casual offenders who do not differ to any great extent from the ordinary man; it is composed of juvenile offenders; it is composed of insane, weak-minded, and epileptic offenders; it is composed of habitual drunkards, beggars, and vagrants; and finally there is a distinct class consisting of habitual offenders against property. It is useless applying the same method of penal treatment to each and all of these classes of offenders. The treatment must be differentiated, and determined as far as practicable by the kind of criminal type to which the offender belongs. In order to effect this object, penal establishments must as far as possible be classified. Where classification of penal establishments is impossible, and where, in consequence, offenders of various types have to be incarcerated in the same establishment, these offenders should be classified in accordance with the type to which they belong, and subjected to a regimen adapted to their class. If these principles of penal treatment were applied to the criminal population it is certain that recidivism would diminish; it is certain that the habitual criminal would become a greater rarity, and, most important of all, it is certain that society would enjoy a greater immunity from crime.

W. D. M.

CONTENTS.

CHAPTER I.
    PAGE
THE SKULL OF THE FEMALE OFFENDER . . 1

CHAPTER II.
PATHOLOGICAL ANOMALIES OF THE FEMALE OFFENDER 27

CHAPTER III.
THE BRAINS OF FEMALE CRIMINALS . . 36

CHAPTER IV.
ANTHROPOMETRY OF FEMALE CRIMINALS . 45

CHAPTER V.
FACIAL AND CEPHALIC ANOMALIES OF FEMALE CRIMINALS . . . 76

CHAPTER VI.
FURTHER ANOMALIES 82

CONTENTS.

CHAPTER VII.
PHOTOGRAPHS OF CRIMINALS AND PROSTITUTES . 88

CHAPTER VIII.
THE CRIMINAL TYPE IN WOMEN AND ITS ATAVISTIC ORIGIN 103

CHAPTER IX.
TATTOOING 115

CHAPTER X.
VITALITY AND OTHER CHARACTERISTICS OF FEMALE CRIMINALS 125

CHAPTER XI.
ACUTENESS OF SENSE AND VISUAL AREA OF FEMALE CRIMINALS 134

CHAPTER XII.
THE BORN CRIMINAL 147

CHAPTER XIII.
OCCASIONAL CRIMINALS 192

CHAPTER XIV.
HYSTERICAL OFFENDERS . . . 218

CHAPTER XV.

CRIMES OF PASSION. 244

CHAPTER XVI.

SUICIDES 269

CHAPTER XVII.

CRIMINAL FEMALE LUNATICS . . . 289

CHAPTER XVIII.

EPILEPTIC DELINQUENTS AND MORAL INSANITY . 298

LIST OF ILLUSTRATIONS.

1. SKULL OF CHARLOTTE CORDAY (3 plates). *Facing page* 34

2. OLD WOMAN OF PALERMO . ,, 72

3. PHYSIOGNOMY OF RUSSIAN FEMALE OFFENDERS (4 plates) . . . *Facing page* 76

4. GABRIELLE BOMPARD . . ,, 96

5. THOMAS . . . . ,, 98

6. MESSALINA . . . ,, 98

7. MARGHERITA. LOUISE . . ,, 100

8. PHYSIOGNOMY OF FALLEN WOMEN, RUSSIAN (4 plates) . . . *Facing page* 100

9. PHYSIOGNOMY OF FRENCH, GERMAN, AND RUSSIAN FEMALE OFFENDERS (5 plates). *Facing page* 102

10. NEGRO. RED INDIAN . . ,, 112

11. FIELDS OF VISION OF F. M., IN EPILEPTIC ATTACK AND TRANQUIL STATE (2 plates). *Facing page* 142

12. FIELD OF VISION OF FEMALE OFFENDER (2 plates) . . . *Facing page* 144

CHAPTER I.

THE SKULL OF THE FEMALE OFFENDER.

WHEN one of the present writers began his observations on delinquents some thirty years ago, he professed a firm faith in anthropometry, especially cranial anthropometry, as an ark of salvation from the metaphysical, *à priori* systems dear to all those engaged on the study of Man.

He regarded anthropometry as the backbone, the whole framework indeed, of the new human statue of which he was at the time attempting the creation; and only learnt the vanity of such hopes and the evils of excessive confidence when use, as is usual, had degenerated into abuse.

For all the differences between the authors of this work and the most authoritative modern anthropologists—all of them in reality professors of anthropometry—arise precisely from the fact that the variations in measurement between the normal and the abnormal subject are so small as to defy all but the most minute research.

One of the writers had already noted this fact as his work "The Criminal Man" was reaching its second and third editions; and only became still more convinced of it when Zampa's observations upon the crania of four assassins in Ravenna disclosed an exact correspondence between their measurements and those found in an average taken upon ten normal Ravennese. And while the anthropometrical system failed thus to reveal any salient differences whatever, anatomico-pathological investigation, on being applied to the same crania, proved the existence in them of no less than thirty-three anomalies.

But unfortunately the attention of inquirers had been diverted from the anatomico-pathological method to anthropometry, with the consequence that the former came to be rashly abandoned. And as one result of this we may mention that Topinard and Manouvrier, being deficient in anatomico-pathological knowledge, failed to detect the immense anomalies existent in certain crania of assassins which they were examining; and because there were no salient anthropometrical differences in these skulls and the skull of Charlotte Corday, they rejected the theory of anomaly altogether.

We must not, however, be understood to advocate the total abandonment of measurements. On the contrary, we would retain them as the frame, so to speak, of the picture; or, rather, as the symbol, the flag of a school in whose armoury numbers furnish the most effective weapon; and we would recommend such retention the more, that whenever a difference does result on measurement, the importance of the anomaly is doubled.

The study of female criminology was undertaken by Messrs. Bergonzoli, Soffiantini and myself, with the help of 26 skulls and 5 skeletons of prostitutes in the possession of Signor Scarenzi. Messrs. Varaglia and Silva[1] made notes on 60 criminal subjects who died in the prisons of Turin; while 17 others who died in Rome were investigated by Mingazzini[2] and Ardù[3]; the proportion of offences being: Prostitutes, 4; infanticide, 20; complicity in rape, 2; theft, 14; arson, 3; wounding, 4; assassination, 10; homicide, 15; poisoning, 4; abortion, 1. As regards race, 11 were Sicilians, 6 Sardinians, 31 Neapolitans, 7 natives of the March and Umbria, 2 Venetians, 4 Lombards, 4 natives of Emilia, 3 Tuscans, 3 Ligurians, and 6 Piedmontese.

I. Cranial Capacity.

Beginning with cranial capacity, we have the following:—

Capacity.	26 Prostitutes.	60 Criminals.	Normal Females observed by Amadei.	Morselli.	Female Lunatics.	Papuans.
1,000 to 1,100 c.c.	3·8	1·72	2·73	1·1	2·50	4·0
1,100 ,, 1,200	15·3	19·1	6·45	9·2	7·47	12·0
1,200 ,, 1,300	42·3	46·3	21·8	29·9	21·78	38·0
1,300 ,, 1,400	23·0	22·5	30·9	30·1	37·12	24·0
1,400 ,, 1,500	11·5	8·6	15·45	13·7	25·35	8·0
1,500 ,, 1,600	3·8	1·72	10·90	12·6	4·64	2·0
1,600 ,, 1,700	—	—	1·82	2·3	—	2·0
1,700 ,, 1,750	—	—	0·91	1·1	1·07	—

The lowest capacity in the 60 criminals is 1,050; the highest 1,630 (a poisoner). Among the prostitutes the smallest is 1,110; the highest 1,520.

---

[1] Varaglia and Silva, "Anatomical and Anthropological Observations on Sixty Crania and Forty-two Encephali of Italian Female Criminals."

[2] G. Mingazzini "On Thirty Crania and Encephali of Italian Criminals."

[3] Ardù, "Notes on the Biangular Diameter of the Mandible" (*Archivio di Psichiatria*, 1892).

The average among the first named is 1,295 with respect to 13 brachycephalic crania, and 1,266 with respect to 45 dolichocephalic crania, the latter being, as Calori had already remarked, always of inferior capacity.

Among female criminals we find the smaller capacities to be more common in the serial averages than among normal subjects, while the larger capacities fall off more than one half.

Arithmetically speaking, the average of criminals (1,322) is higher than the average shown by prostitutes (1,244), and is a little even above the normal (1,310—1,316).

But according to Mingazzini, who is a far better and more trustworthy observer, the average cranial capacity is 1,265, a very inferior average to that furnished by normal Italian women, for whom the figure found by Nicolini is 1,310, and by Mantegazza and Amadei, 1,322.

And there is much importance in the fact that he observed a capacity inferior to 1,200 in 20 per cent. of these criminals, and in only 5 per cent. a capacity above 1,400; while among the normal women noted by Amadei and Morselli, only 14 per cent. fell below the former figure and 29 per cent. rose above the latter: a result which establishes the inferiority of criminals.

Coming now to separate delinquencies, we find the figures of highest capacity to be under the different heads as follows:—

Poisoning 1,384		Wounding 1,314
Arson 1,328		Infanticide 1,280

And of lowest capacity:—

Theft	1,261	Homicide	1,238
Assassination (murder)	1,253	Rape	1,180
Prostitution	1,244		

The capacity again varies geographically, as under:—

Sicily	1,226	The Marches	1,340
Sardinia	1,248	Tuscany	1,268
Calabria	1,280	Emilia	1,257
Neapolitan Territory	1,260	Piedmont	1,285
Lombardy	1,250	Liguria	1,289
Venetia	1,506		

When these figures are compared with those known in regard to normal females and female lunatics—for instance, with the Tuscans of Chiarugi and Bianchi—the average is notably lower.

II. ORBITAL CAPACITY.

The maximum orbital capacity among the 60 female criminals was 62, the minimum 44, and the medium 52·76 c.c.

For the series we have the following figures:—

44 c.c.	1 cranium	=	1·66	per cent.
46 ,,	2 crania	=	3·33	,,
48 ,,	7 ,,	=	11·66	,,
50 ,,	16 ,,	=	26·66	,,
52 ,,	9 ,,	=	15·00	,,
54 ,,	5 ,,	=	8·33	,,
56 ,,	10 ,,	=	16·66	,,
58 ,,	5 ,,	=	8·33	,,
60 ,,	2 ,,	=	3·33	,,
62 ,,	3 ,,	=	5·00	,,

In these series we have a predominance of the high capacities of 50 and 56 c.c., and the average is 52·76.

The distribution according to crime was:—

Poisoning	57	Rape	53
Assassination	54	Infanticide	52
Homicide	53	Theft	52
Wounding	53	Arson	51

The high capacities predominate in the gravest forms of crime.

Among 26 prostitutes of Paris the average was 43·5, showing an extraordinary inferiority to the remainder. The minimum was 30, and the maximum 69; the last being presented by a woman formerly a teacher and notorious for her profligacy.

III. Area of the Occipital Foramen.

Inferior to 600	2 =	3·33	per cent.
Between 601–650	4 =	6·66	,,
,, 651–700	11 =	18·33	,,
,, 701–750	18 =	30·00	,,
,, 751–800	13 =	21·66	,,
,, 800–850	12 =	20·00	,,

The minimum area is 580 mm.q., the maximum is 850, the average is 731. The larger areas, between 721 and 740 mm.q., predominate.

The distribution according to crime was:—

Arson	790	Infanticide	733
Wounding	767	Homicide	728
Poisoning	767	Rape	710
Theft	748	Prostitution	705
Murder	739		

IV. Cephalo-Rachidian Index.

The predominant figures are between 15·01 and 19; the minimum is 14·58, the maximum 21·69, the average 17·72.

The distribution as regards crime is:—

Poisoning ... ... 18·04	Homicide ... ... 17·06
Prostitution ... ... 17·85	Murder ... ... 17·03
Infanticide ... ... 17·61	Arson ... ... 17·77
Theft ... ... 17·57	Complicity in Rape ... 16·64
Wounding ... ... 17·40	

V. Cephalo-Orbital Index.

The predominant figures are between 22 and 26; the minimum is 18·46, the maximum 30·90, the average 24·64.

Distribution according to crime:—

Arson ... ... 26·1	Prostitution ... ... 23·0
Wounding ... ... 25·1	Murder ... ... 23·0
Infanticide ... ... 24·9	Homicide ... ... 23·0
Poisoning ... ... 24·3	Rape ... ... 22·0
Theft ... ... 24·3	

VI. Facial Angle.

The minimum angle is 69°, the maximum 81°. The general average is 74·2° (according to Mingazzini it is 83°), the serial average is 74° to 76°.

Distribution according to crime:—

	Maximum.	Minimum.	Medium.
Poisoning	75°	80°	76·2°
Wounding	75°	78°	76°
Arson	71°	79°	75°
Theft	78°	72°	76·9°
Infanticide	79°	70°	74·9°
Murder	77°	71°	74·3°
Homicide	81°	69°	72·9°
Rape	73°	72·5°	72·7°

Among prostitutes the maximum was 82°, the minimum 72°, and the average 74·6°.

VII. Horizontal Circumference and Curves.

	Proportion per cent. Criminals.	Prostitutes.
Between 460 and 470	6·66	—
,, 470 ,, 490	43·33	42·1
,, 490 ,, 510	33·33	49·71
,, 510 ,, 520	20·00	12·5
,, 520 ,, upwards	7·6	1·66

Whence it appears that prostitutes do not reach either the highest or the lowest figures.

The maximum circumference was found in a poisoner of Verona (535), and in a woman guilty of infanticide (530).

The predominating circumferences among criminals are between 470 and 490; among prostitutes, between 490 and 510; while among 52 per cent. of normal subjects, at least according to Morselli, the prevailing figures are between 501 and 530.

The average presented by criminals—492 (Mingazzini gives it 490·2), is inferior to the normal average of Parisian women (498), and of the ancient Roman women (505), but is equal, indeed superior to the average among modern Italian women, which is 491.

Curves.—An examination of the proportions of the various parts of the fronto-occipital curve (reduced to 100), and of the anterior horizontal line (putting at = 100 the total horizontal curve), we obtain, in common with Varaglia and Silva, the following results:—

Horizontal Anterior Curve	46·14
Sub-cerebral Anterior Curve	4·50
Frontal Curve	29·7
Parietal Curve	34·4
Occipital Curve	31·0

These figures demonstrate that the asserted increase in the sub-cerebral curve of the criminal does not exist.

As regards the anterior horizontal curve, we find a large development in Venetia (48·06) and in Umbria, and a small one in the Marches and in Latinia (45·31).

The figure given for Sardinian women, 45·74, differs notably from that of the modern women of the same region, and approximates to the figure presented by the ancient Sardinian females, which was 46·94.

The medium anterior horizontal circumference is 227.

VIII. Cephalic Index.

Among 60 criminals we find 13 brachycephalic and 47 dolichocephalic crania. Among 26 prostitutes we observed 3 sub-dolichocephalic and mesocephalic crania (75 to 80), 17 brachycephalic and sub-brachycephalic, with a minimum of 68 and a maximum of 82.

Mingazzini among 17 criminals found an average of 73·35, which shows a larger number of cases of dolichocephalic skulls than among the male criminals whom he examined, where the average was 77·81, and this fact corresponds to the normal. In the 10 dolichocephalic skulls he found an average of 7·26, and in the 8 brachycephalic an average of 80·65.

The average index among the 13 brachycephalic skulls is 84·41; among the 47 dolichocephalic it is 74·58. Calori gives 84 as the average cephalic index among Italian brachycephali, and 77 among Italian dolichocephali. In the 26 prostitutes, all from Paira, the average is 74·6, with a minimum of 68 and a maximum of 82.

Among the Tuscans, 2 are dolichocephalic, with an index of 76·77, and one brachycephalic female had the ancient Etruscan type.

Of 4 crania belonging to natives of Emilia, 2 are dolichocephalic, with an average of 78, and 2 brachycephalic crania have an average of 85, which is a higher number than the average of the Bolognese brachycephali. There are 20 crania from the Neapolitan territory.

I. Crania from the Abruzzi, Molise, Avellino, Benevento, Basilicata. Average index, 75·93; vertical, 73·87.

II. Crania from Naples and Salerno. Average cephalic index, 78·28; vertical, 75·01.

III. Crania from Pughi. Average cephalic index, 76·10; vertical, 72·74.

These are consequently all dolichocephalic, with a minimum of 67·03 (in a poisoner), and a maximum of 79·31 (in a murderess—assassin), and a general average of 75·48. Calori found in the Neapolitan provinces 52 per cent. dolichocephalic, with a cephalic index of 76.

Among Sardinian women we have an average of 70·9, with a minimum of 68·27, and a maximum of 74·28 (the subject was a thief). All these cases are dolichocephalic to a higher degree than was observed by Calori, who found 6 per cent. of brachycephali, with an average of 74 among the dolichocephali, and 81 among the brachycephali.

Zannetti found a minimum cephalic index of 65·07 and a maximum of 76·08, with an average (among 6 women) of 72·36; which is a higher figure than that obtained by us. The cephalic index of the ancient Sardinian women is 74·81, while 71·64 represents that of modern Sardinian males, and 71·68 that of the ancient male inhabitants. Our figure consequently approaches that of the actual Sardinian males, and differs from that of the present Sardinian females.

The average vertical index of our female criminals (71·22) is higher than that of the modern Sardinian women (68·98), but lower than that of their ancient progenitors (77·05), and approximates more nearly to that of the Sardinian males, both modern (71·86) and ancient (72·34). The Sardinian female criminal more nearly resembles the contemporary male type than the type of the woman of her epoch.

Sicilian Females. — According to Morselli the measurement for normal females is 70·6, and for normal males 74·5.

The ancient Corsican women had an index of 78·26, as against 73·53 among the men, showing a difference of 4·73 in favour of the females.

This difference, which up to now remains insufficiently proved, results as reversed in 8 Sicilian female criminals with a minimum index of 68·2, a maximum of 77·19, and an average of 73·65, which is much nearer to the male average (74·9) than to that of the women of the Sicilian provinces.

Offences.—After this there is little importance to be attached to the distribution according to crime.

Among prostitutes we find an average of 74·6. The other results are as under:—

	Average.	Average.	Average.
Infanticide	74·0	73·3	81·2
Complicity in Rape	77·29	67·6	89·9
Theft	79·8	76·8	84·1
Arson	80·3	78·0	85·0
Wounding	75·4	72·4	84·2
Murder	75·4	73·3	83·8
Homicide	76·1	74·5	83·0
Poisoning	74·2	76·2	—

IX. VERTICAL INDEX.

The average among the 60 female criminals is 79·9, according to Mingazzini 71·5, while among the males it is 74·8.

The highest index is 82·53; the lowest 65·62, in a woman of Cosenza who had committed infanticide, and 61·6 in another criminal of the same class observed by Mingazzini. Now it is to be remarked that the Calabrian crania are among the most platycephalic in Italy.

Among the modern Italian women, as among those of ancient Rome and Etruria, the larger number of crania have an index of 71 (Morselli), just as with our female criminals; the average being 72·31 for 56 Italian women of every race, while that of 99 male crania is 73·85 (Mantegazza). These results differ but little from ours.

The distribution according to crime is as follows:—

Complicity in Rape	80·18	Homicide	73·10
Arson	78·51	Murder (assassination)	71·34
Prostitution	76·61	Infanticide	71·09
Theft	74·54	Poisoning	70·44
Wounding	73·95		

X. Minimum Frontal Diameter.

Between 81· 55 ... 1 = 1·66 per cent.
   ,,   86· 90 ... 17 = 28·33 ,,
   ,,   91· 95 ... 27 = 45·00 ,,
   ,,   96·100 ... 12 = 20·00 ,,
   ,,   101·105 ... 3 = 5·00 ,,

The minimum frontal diameter among the 60 female criminals is 85 mm., the maximum is 102. The average is 93 mm.; and the predominating figures are between 86 and 100; and especially between 91–95.

Among prostitutes the minimum is 85, the maximum 100, and the average 89.

XI. Coronal Diameter and Index.

The minimum coronal diameter is 97, the maximum 131, the mean 113 mm.

The prevailing figures are 106–120.

Among prostitutes the maximum is 126, the minimum 110, the mean 117.

The smallest coronal index is 75·42; the highest reaches 97·02.

The prevailing measurements are between 75·01 and 90, 80·01 to 85 being especially frequent. The general mean is 82·94.

But these figures correspond more to the geographical origin of the respective criminals than to their crimes, and the predominating numbers are usually low. For the rest we generally find the smallest frontal and coronal indices in the female subject, owing to the lesser development in her of the minimum frontal and coronal diameters and to the larger development of the maximum antero-posterior diameter.

XII. Minimum Frontal Index.

The smallest frontal index is 59·85, the largest 88. The general average is 69·97; and the predominating numbers are between 65·01 and 75, especially 65·01 and 70.

Between	55·01–60	... 1 = 1·66	per cent.
,,	60·01–65	... 2 = 3·33	,,
,,	65·01–70	... 30 = 50·00	,,
,,	70·01–75	... 22 = 36.66	,,
,,	75·01–80	... 3 = 5·00	,,
,,	80·01–85	... 1 = 1·66	,,
,,	85·01–90	... 1 = 1·66	,,

The distribution as regards crime was:—

Complicity in Rape	... 75·43	Murder (assassination)		68·87
Infanticide	... 71·47	Wounding	...	68·70
Homicide	... 70·39	Prostitution	...	67·97
Poisoning	... 70·28	Theft	...	67·76
Arson	... 67·18			

XIII. Nasal Index.

The smallest nasal index is 36·53, the largest is 56·42. The average measurement is 46·25 (according to Mingazzini, however, 48·09), showing narrowness of nostril. The maximum is 56·4, and the minimum 36·5.

The distribution as regards crime is as follows:—

Poisoning	48·65	Arson	45·69
Wounding	47·50	Complicity in Rape ...	45·08
Infanticide	46·97	Murder...	43·88
Homicide	46·27	Prostitution	42·92
Theft	46·14		

XIV. Palatine Index.

General average 82·03 (but according to Mingazzini 79·5), which is inferior to the male's (78·7). The maximum is 100, and the minimum 68·08.

The distribution as regards crime is as below:—

Complicity in Rape	...	87·23	Homicide	83·37
Poisoning		85·63	Arson	82·75
Wounding		85·33	Infanticide	82·70
Theft		84·70	Murder...	81·74

XV. Orbital Index.

Among 17 female criminals the mean found by Mingazzini was 87·6 on the right side, and 87·35 on the left.

Among 60 of the same class, Varaglia found 22 with an orbital index of over 89; 26 in whom the figures were between 83 and 88·99; and 12 who only reached 82·96. The general mean was 87·26. The maximum (found by Mingazzini) was 102 in an infanticide, while two other infanticides showed the minimum of 74·66.

The distribution as regards crime was as follows:—

Wounding	89·70	Complicity in Rape	...	85·98
Poisoning	89·69	Arson		85·18
Homicide	88·93	Prostitution		85·02
Murder...	88·25	Infanticide		84·75
Theft	86·04			

XVI. Facial Index.

The minimum is 49·18, the maximum 77·87; the general average is 66·99.

The prevailing figures are 65·01–70.

The distribution as regards crime is as under:—

Homicide	... ...	68·91	Murder	65·88
Infanticide	... ...	67·98	Prostitution	64·92
Wounding	... ...	67·80	Poisoning	64·59
Complicity in Rape	...	67·49	Arson	58·09
Theft	... ...	66·01		

XVII. TOTAL HEIGHT OF FACE.

Between 56– 60 ... 1 = 1·66 per cent.
,, 61– 65 ... 1 = 1·66 ,,
,, 66– 70 ... 3 = 5·00 ,,
,, 71– 75 ... 3 = 5·00 ,,
,, 76– 80 ... 13 = 21·66 ,,
,, 81– 85 ... 26 = 43·33 ,,
,, 86– 90 ... 11 = 18·33 ,,
,, 91– 95 ... 1 = 1·66 ,,
,, 96–100 ... 1 = 1·66 ,,

The minimum height is 60 mm., the maximum 99.

The prevailing numbers are between 81–85, and then between 76–80 and 86·90.

The distribution as regards crime is as follows:—

Wounding	... ...	83	Theft	80
Infanticide	... ...	83	Murder	80
Complicity in Rape	...	81·5	Prostitution	78
Poisoning	... ...	81	Arson	75

XVIII. BIZYGOMATIC BREADTH.

	Criminals.		Prostitutes.
Between 111–115 =	8·33 per cent.	...	— per cent.
,, 116–120 =	28·33 ,,	...	26 ,,
,, 120–125 =	46·66 ,,	...	42 ,,
,, 126–130 =	8·33 ,,	...	23 ,,
,, 131–135 =	6·66 ,,	...	17 ,,
,, 136–140 =	1·66 ,,	...	— ,,

The minimum breadth is 111 mm., the maximum 138 mm. The prevailing figures are between 121–125, and then between 116–120.

Among prostitutes the average is **123**, the maximum is 130, and the minimum 118.

The distribution as regards crime is as follows :—

Arson	**128**	Infanticide		**122**
Poisoning	**126**	Theft		**121.5**
Wounding	**123**	Rape		**121.5**
Murder (assassination)	**122**	Homicide		**120**

XIX. Weight of the Lower Jaw.

A special—virile—characteristic of the lower jaw among the 26 prostitutes is its greater weight relatively to the cranium.

Weight of Jaw.			Weight of Cranium.
65·9 on an average	...	...	507
35 minimum (in syphilitics)	...	...	287
90 maximum	...	...	728

The average of 65·9 is really equal to the general average, but if the two, absolutely abnormal minima, of 35·33 are set aside we get an average of 70·5 ; and in any case the weight relatively to that of the cranium is 12·0, which is the same as in the male.

Mingazzini found the average weight of jaw among 17 female criminals to be 79·1, and that of the cranium 599·5.

Ardù, examining 20 crania of female criminals and 20 crania of normal women, obtained the following :—

	Weight of Lower Jaw.			Weight of Cranium.	
	Crim.	Norm.		Crim.	Norm.
Maximum	87	95	...	831	850
Minimum	54	43	...	466	313
Difference	33	52	...	365	537
Relation	82·4	45·2	...	56·0	36·8
Total average	68·2	63·0		586·2	516·5

The highest figure among criminals does **not**

reach that presented by the normal woman, but the minimum is superior to the minimum of the latter. The difference (between jaw and cranium) is notably smaller, and the average being higher, it follows that the lower jaw of criminal women weighs more and varies less than the corresponding feature among normal women. The series of the crania is regular.

XX. CRANIO-MANDIBULAR INDEX.

Out of 20 crania Ardù obtained the following results:—

	Index. Criminal.	Normal.
Maximum	15·64	19·7
Minimum	7·34	9·0
Divergency	8·30	10·7
Relation	48·5	46·5
Total average	11·54	13·7

Here the maxima and minima do not reach in the criminal the same figures as in the normal woman, and the average of the criminal is lower. This is owing to the fact that while the criminal has a heavier jaw and skull, the proportion between them is not the same as in the normal subject:—

Weight of Cranium in Criminal : ditto in Normal : 100 :: 85
   ,,   Jaw   ,,   : ditto   ,,   : 100 :: 92

The cranium, that is to say, is heavier in proportion.

Among the 17 criminals mentioned by Mingazzini, however, the index is 13·2, and 12·0 in 60 of the same class observed by Silva; and this yields an average equal or superior to the male.

XXI. Bigonial Diameter.

According to observations made by Ardù upon 17 criminals their average is superior to that of normal women, and even of the male, while the minima do not fall to the figures shown by either; that is to say, the mean oscillates between higher limits:—

	17 Criminal Women.	Normal Women.	Normal Males.	55 Male Criminals.
Maximum	112	105	105	117
Minimum	89	84	92	89
Divergency	23	21	13	28
Relation	79·4	80	87·5	76·1
Total average	97·2	90·7	94·1	100·1

By analysis of the series we find:—

Under 80	0	=	·0 per cent.
Between 81–90	3	=	17.6 ,,
,, 91–100	13	=	76·4 ,,
Above 100	1	=	5·8 ,,

Mingazzini found the least breadth (79·5) in a husband-murderer, while a woman guilty of homicide showed the maximum of 116.

I obtained the following among—

	57 Criminal Women.	26 Fallen Women.
Between 81–85 =	12·28 per cent.	7·6 per cent.
,, 86–90 =	29·82 ,,	15·3 ,,
,, 91–95 =	36·84 ,,	42·3 ,,
,, 96–100 =	21·08 ,,	34·5 ,,

The maximum breadth is 105, the minimum 81; and the predominating figures are between 91–95 and then between 86–90.

The highest figures for the jaw, taken serially, are found in Sicily, and the lowest in Sardinia.

Fallen women furnish the maxima among the highest figures.

The distribution per crime is as follows :—

Arson	96	Complicity in Rape	91
Wounding	93	Theft	91
Homicide	93	Murder (assassination)	90
Prostitution	91	Poisoning	90
Infanticide	91		

XXII. Symphitic Height.

Between				
12–15	...	1	=	1·75 per cent.
16–19	...	0	=	0·00 ,,
20–23	...	4	=	7·01 ,,
24–27	...	21	=	36·84 ,,
28–31	...	21	=	36·84 ,,
32–35	...	9	=	15·78 ,,
36–39	...	1	=	1·75 ,,

The figures which predominate are between 24–31, he minimum height is 15, and the maximum 36.

The distribution per crime is :—

Complicity in Rape	31	Arson	27
Infanticide	30	Murder (assassination)	27
Prostitution	29	Homicide	27
Theft	28	Poisoning	27
Wounding	27·5		

Among the female criminals observed by Mingazzini, he medium height of the symphisis was only 28·8, while among males it is 31.07.

XXIII. Length of the Branchial Arches.

The predominant numbers are between 56–60, and again between 51–55 and 61–65 ; the least length is 46, and the greatest is 76.

Distribution per crime :—

Complicity in Rape	63	Theft	56
Poisoning	60	Wounding	55
Assassination	59	Arson	54
Homicide	58	Prostitution	52
Infanticide	56		

Conclusions.—As we expected, and as we found already during our researches into the male criminal,[1] the conclusions to which the above data lead us are but few.

The most important are those which relate to the cranial and orbital capacity, and to the weight and diameter of the jaw, to which add observations on the cheek-bones.

It is clear, indeed, that fallen women have the smallest cranial capacity of all, and up to 1,200 a scanty cranial capacity continues to be noted in prostitutes and criminals alike; while among normal women, even those whose cranial capacity is small and those who approximate to the average, the superiority to the other two classes of their sex persists up to the limit marked 1,300, and offers more analogy to the mentally afflicted than to the sane.

In average capacity and in capacity above the average, women of good life and even lunatics surpass both criminals and the fallen class.

In great cranial capacity the better class of women surpass, five or six times over, criminals, prostitutes, and lunatics. Also in this respect prostitutes are slightly superior to criminals; and among the latter the highest are the poisoners.

As a whole prostitutes are more remarkable than criminals for smaller as well as for larger cranial capacity, although when compared with women of good lives, they rank below lunatics—a peculiarity

[1] "Uomo Delinquente," vol. i. 3rd ed.

which they share especially with thieves among male criminals.

The maxima and minima among prostitutes more nearly resemble those of Papuan women than of normal females. With regard to size of orbit the maximum is reached by poisoners and murderesses generally, who in this respect resemble the male. The minimum is found among thieves and unchaste women, especially prostitutes.

It is curious, however, that the average size of orbit presented by normal women, which is 47, and even by lunatics, whose average measure according to Peli is 51, should be surpassed, as in the case of males, by almost all criminal women, especially those guilty of the graver crimes, such as poisoning, assassination, and homicide. To this rule prostitutes are an exception. The occipital region of female criminals surpasses to a great degree the average in the case of women of good lives, as given by Mantegazza; but here the maximum is not furnished by murderesses, but by women guilty of arson and of wounding, while prostitutes offer the minimum. The cephalo-rachidian index in criminals is but little below the normal average, 18·1, which is, if anything, somewhat higher than the average supplied by poisoners, while the minimum here again is found among women who have committed arson and rape. The cephalo-orbital index is very much below the normal female average of 28·4, and there is but little difference in this respect between women guilty of arson and wounding; but the lowest figure is reached by those whose offences have been homicide and rape.

THE SKULL OF THE FEMALE OFFENDER.

The facial angle is found largest in the lists of poisoning and wounding, lowest in those of arson and rape, and of medium size among thieves and cases of infanticide.

The horizontal circumference of prostitutes, both as to maxima and minima, is lower than among criminals, but the medium measurement in both cases is equal to the normal average, and the curves of the cranium furnish no data. This last is true also of the cephalic index, except that in some places, and especially in Sicily, the measurement approximates to that of the male, and, what is more curious, of the males of antiquity, both with respect to the curves and to the vertical index.

The average of the antero-posterior, the transverse (maximum), the vertical, and the frontal (minimum) diameters, is as under :—

Among Sardinian female criminals	178	127	128	92
,, Modern Sardinian females (Zannetti)	180·67	143	124·67	91·5
,, Ancient ,, ,,	176·50	132	136	92·5

It will be seen that the figures given for the criminals approximate to those of the ancient Sardinian women, with the exception of the vertical diameter, which is larger in our women (Italians of the Peninsula) than among the modern Sardinians, but less than among the ancient Sardinians. The transverse diameter is less among our women, while the longitudinal and frontal minimum occupies a middle position between the measurements of the ancient and modern Sardinian females.

The following is a table of the cranial curves:—

	Bi-auricular Curve.	Occipito-frontal Curve = 100.		Horizontal Curve = 100.	
		Ante.	Post.	Ante.	Post.
Ancient Sardinian females...	292·50	33·53	66·47	49·26	50·74
Modern ,, ,,	303·17	29·95	70·05	50·36	49·64
Sardinian female criminals...	281	33·61	66·39	45·73	54·27

By this it will be seen that Sardinian women approximate more to their ancient than to their modern prototypes; and as regards the anterior portion of the whole horizontal curve, the figures given are nearer to those of the ancient Sardinian males (46·94) than to any others.

And when it is considered that the figure 33·81 stands for the anterior portion of the occipito-frontal curve of the ancient Sardinian males (which is very near the 33·61 of our modern women), it is evident that we have here two other peculiarities beyond those above noted, in which female criminals resemble males, and males of ancient days.

Zannetti's great work on the modern Sardinians supplies us with further conclusions, for he has shown that modern females differ more from modern males than did ancient females from ancient males.

The bizygomatic diameter in Sardinian women is on the average 120, 111·50 for the moderns and 116·00 for the ancients. For the males the figures are: 116·77 (moderns) and 115·75 (ancients), which prove that here again the modern women approximate more to the ancient females, and still more to the males. The longitudinal diameter of prostitutes is usually the shortest; and the longest is shown by criminals; the exact contrary is the case with the transverse diameter, prostitutes possessing the highest, and criminals the lowest measurements. But here the ethnical element has to be taken into account, and obscures all conclusions.

The frontal diameter is larger in prostitutes than in criminals. Females guilty of rape and infanticide have the highest frontal index, and thieves and prostitutes the lowest.

The same is true in great part of the coronal index. The nasal index is inferior to the average of 48, especially among prostitutes, thieves, murderesses, and incendiaries.

The largest facial index is found in the lists of infanticide and homicide, the smallest in those of poisoning and arson; the length of the face is greatest among those guilty of wounding, and least among those guilty of arson.

But it is especially as regards the diameters of the cheeks and cheek-bones, and in the weight of the jaws, that figures come to be of great importance. Prostitutes are wider across the cheek-bones than criminals in the proportion of 36 to 16 in all the higher numbers, and are inferior to the same class in all the lesser figures.

The bigonial diameter of female criminals is much greater than in women and men of moral lives; but the higher average is distinctive of the male criminal, who, while surpassing his female prototype in this respect, does so less markedly than the normal woman surpasses the normal male. The maximum like the minimum of male criminals is more remarkable than in the female. Finally, when the extreme figures at either end among criminals of both sexes are compared, it is to be observed that, although the man's maximum is higher than the woman's, the same fails to hold good of the minimum. The divergence in the case of the male is greater, and begins consequently *at a higher* level. We are here in presence of a *sexual peculiarity*, persisting among criminals as among normals.

The bigonial diameter of prostitutes exceeds that of criminals among the higher series (of figures) as 34 is to 21 per cent. The maxima of the criminals are to be found among the women who have committed homicide, wounding, or arson.

The lower jaw of female criminals, and still more of prostitutes, is heavier than in women of moral lives, and the measure of skull and jaw is nearly always as virile as the weight.

The maximum measure of symphisis is found under the heading of rape, and the minimum under that of poisoning.

The length of the branchials is greatest among women who are guilty of rape and poisoning, and least among prostitutes.

CHAPTER II.

PATHOLOGICAL ANOMALIES OF THE FEMALE OFFENDER.

As we have already said, cranial anomalies yield far more striking differences than cranial measurements. In order to economise space, we append a table of anomalies prepared according to their percentages (*see* p. 29).

It is evident from this table that if anomalies be frequent in the crania of female criminals (and especially of murderesses), they are less so than in the males of a corresponding class. The difference is smaller especially in the median occipital fossa; in the nasal cavity (33 to 48); in irregularity of the occipital region (where the divergence is three times less); in the lower jaw (one-half less); in the plagiocephalon, in the sclerosis, and in the frontal sinuses (also one-half); finally, in the absence of subscaphocephali, oxycephali, and epactal bone (of which latter there is only one). The female criminal exceeds the male only in the greater number of wormian bones, in the simplicity of her sutures, in anomalies of the palate, and of the atlas.

Nevertheless a comparison of the criminal skull with the skulls of normal women reveals the fact that female criminals approximate more to males, both criminal and normal, than to normal women, especially in the superciliary arches in the seam of the sutures, in the lower jaw-bones, and in peculiarities of the occipital region. They nearly resemble normal women in their cheek-bones, in the prominence of the crotaphitic line, and in the median occipital fossa. There are also among them a large proportion (9·2 per cent.) of virile crania.

The anomalies more frequent in female criminals than in prostitutes are: enormous pterygoid apophisis; cranial depressions; very heavy lower jaw; plagiocephalia; the soldering of the atlas with the occiput; enormous nasal spine; deep frontal sinuses; absence of sutures; simplicity of sutures; wormian bones.

Fallen women, on the other hand, are distinguished from criminals by the following peculiarities: clinoid apophisis forming a canal; tumefied parietal prominences; median occipital fossa of double size; great occipital irregularity; narrow or receding forehead; abnormal nasal bones; epactal bone; prognathous jaw and alveolar prognathism; cranial sclerosis; a virile type of face; prominent cheek-bones.

As to the principal anomalies I proceed to give the average frequency with which they are severally found in normal female subjects, in female criminals, and in prostitutes; but it must be remembered that it is not always possible to deduce an average from

PATHOLOGICAL ANOMALIES.

	Criminals out of 66.	Women.	Thieves out of 12.	Infanticides out of 11.	Homicides out of 24.	Total out of 55.	observed by Mingazzini out of 17.[1]	out of 47.
Enormous pterygoid apophisis	12%	—	15%	18%	4%	12.6%	—	6%
Clinoid apophysis forming canals	—	—	8	9	8	10.8	10	16
Largely developed parietal and temporal prominences	43	—	—	—	4	1.8	—	6
Largely developed occipital and temporal prominences	—	—	—	—	8	3.6	—	—
Frontal crest	—	—	16	27	44	34.2	—	41
Cranial depressions	14	0.5	16	9	8	10.8	—	10
Anomalous teeth	16	3.4	8	—	4	5.4	15	51
Occipital fossa	21	2.7	16	27	28	2.7	15	17
Deep canine cavities	10	—	—	—	—	3.6	10	—
Very irreg. occipital foramen	—	10	—	9	8	5.4	10	23
Receding or narrow forehead	36	16.5	16	9	4	18	—	16
Very large under jaw	37	—	8	18	4	—	—	—
Anomalous nasal bones	—	—	—	—	—	3.6	—	3
Porosity of bones	—	6.8	—	—	—	1.8	—	19
Epactal bones	9	10	—	—	4	1.8	—	—
Prominent (prognathous) jaw	34	17.2	32	54	30	32.4	—	3
Plagiocephalic	42	—	3.2	18	44	28.8	—	36
Platycephalic	—	—	—	—	—	—	25	22
Anomalous palate	3	—	—	—	—	1.8	—	—
Soldering of atlas with occiput	—	—	16	9	4	3.6	—	3
Enormous nasal bone	—	19	24	18	4	10.8	15	3
Developed frontal sinuses	62	17.2	24	36	8	23.4	—	16
Cranial sclerosis	31	10	8	9	16	16.2	15	22
Frontal suture	12	—	—	9	4	5.4	—	—
Absence, total or partial, of sutures	37	13.3	18	9	16	18	—	16
Simple sutures	—	—	32	27	24	27	—	16
Virile type of face	—	—	—	—	4	1.8	—	3
Wormian bones	59	20	56	54	76	64.8	—	26
Prominent cheek-bones	30	6.9	8	—	—	1.8	—	16

[1] Including 3 incendiaries and 5 poisoners, here not considered separately.

the observations made by different authors, for the reason that some of these pay but little attention to certain peculiarities. For instance, if Messrs. Varaglia and Silva do not make mention of platycephali among female criminals, or if Mingazzini omits to speak of cranial depressions or prognathous features or cranial sclerosis, we may, with the utmost probability, conclude that the reason of such omissions lies in attention not having been paid to those particular points.

Anomalous teeth, present in only 0·5 per cent. of normal subjects, are to be found in 10·8 per cent. of criminals and in 5·1 per cent. of prostitutes.

The median occipital fossa is existent in 3·4 per cent. of normal subjects, in 5·4 per cent. of delinquents, and in 17 per cent. of prostitutes, which is a figure exceeding that of male criminals (16).

The narrow or receding forehead is found in 10 per cent. of normal women, in 8 per cent. of criminal women, and in 16 per cent. of prostitutes. Prognathism distinguishes 10 per cent. of normals, 33·4 per cent. of criminals, and 36 per cent. of prostitutes.

Plagiocephali exists in 17·2 per cent. of normal subjects, in 28·8 per cent. of delinquents, rising to 44 per cent. among homicides, and in 22 per cent. of prostitutes.

This is an anomaly much more frequently observed among male criminals, where it is found in a proportion of 42 per cent.

The soldering of the atlas with the occiput is never observed in normal women, but exists in 3·6 per cent. of female criminals and in 3 per cent. of prostitutes.

Cranial sclerosis is present in 17·2 per cent. of normal women, in 16·2 of the criminal class, and in 22 per cent. of prostitutes. This peculiarity resembles plagiocephali in being much more frequent among male criminals, where it reaches the proportion of 31 per cent.

The wormian bones are found in 20 per cent. of normal subjects, in 64·8 per cent. of criminals, rising in homicides to 76 per cent., and in 26 per cent. in prostitutes.

The cheek-bones are prominent in 3·9 per cent. of normal women, in 1·8 per cent. of criminals, and in 16 per cent. of prostitutes.

Occipital foramen.—A curious fact is the irregularity of the occipital foramen, where in two cases we find the atlas soldered with the occiput (being 3·3 per cent.), and in seven other cases (or 11·6 per cent.) different irregularities of the following sort: Articular fossa of the basion, owing to dental apophisis (twice); porosity of surrounding bone (once); an offshoot of bone extending from the basion to the centre of the foramen (twice); incipient process of division of the occiput (once); marked asymmetry (once).

The sum shows 15 per cent. of irregularities among criminals, 23 per cent. among prostitutes; while in male lunatics the proportion was 0·5 per cent., and in male criminals 10·5 per cent.

Signor Legge, among 1,770 crania in Camerino, found occipital fusion with the atlas in 12 per cent., with median condyles and basilar tubercles in 2·5 per cent. In 76 out of 4,000 crania Tafani found either a third occipital condyle or protuberances representing it.

A basilar area with a double aperture was found once only (by us). Legge observed it twice in 1,770 crania from Camerino and the neighbourhood.

In the crania of certain prostitutes from Pavia (where idiotcy is common) were found two instances of a horizontal basilar bone, together with indications of imbecility.

Frontal suture.—Three instances: once in a parricide of Benevento, aged 54; once in a Piedmontese thief, aged 30; and once in a Florentine infanticide, aged 28. Here the proportion is 5·1 per cent.: inferior to the same in healthy males, where I calculate the peculiarity to exist in 8 to 9 per cent. Mingazzini, however, found it in 15 per cent. of female criminals.

Proportion of anomalies.—The very much larger number of anomalies in prostitutes than in criminals may be demonstrated by the fact that in 51·5 per cent. of prostitutes more than 5 anomalies will be present, whereas the same number is only found in 27 per cent. of criminals. The mean among prostitutes is 5 anomalies per cranium as against 4 among criminals.

First after prostitutes, whose anomalies are as 5·5, come thieves (4·2); then homicides (4·1); and lastly infanticides (4·0); although the latter are typically superior to the other two classes, as 27 to 24 per cent.

But all these figures sink into numerical insignificance when compared with male crania,[1] where the average of anomalies is three and four times higher (being 78 per cent.) than in the case of female delinquents and prostitutes.

It will have been remarked how many abnormal characteristics of the crania of female criminals, such as frontal sinuses and projecting cheek-bones, are normal in the male; and this must be held to reduce the average.

Political criminals (female).—Not even the purest political crime, that which springs from passion, is exempt from the law which we have laid down. In the skull of Charlotte Corday herself, after a rapid inspection, I affirmed the presence of an extraordinary number of anomalies, and this opinion is confirmed not only by Topinard's very confused monograph, but still more by the photographs of the

	50 Male Delinq.	Female Thieves.	Infanticides.	Homicides.	Total.	Prost.
[1] 2 Anomalies	0	8	18	12	12·6	6·5
3 ,,	8	48	18	20	27	16
4 ,,	0	16	36	40	32·4	26
5 ,,	2	24	—	12	12·6	1·6
6 ,,	4	—	18	8	7·2	9·5
7 ,,	78	—	9	4	7·2	26
Typical (5 and more anomalies)	84	24	27	24	27·0	51·5
Average of the anomalies per cranium	11·4	4·2	4·0	4·1	4·0	5·5

In their observations on 19 crania of male criminals Roncoroni and Ardù found—

1 Cranium with 23 anomalies.	2 Crania with 16 anomalies.
2 Crania ,, 22 ,,	1 Cranium ,, 15 ,,
2 ,, ,, 21 ,,	2 Crania ,, 14 ,,
1 Cranium ,, 19 ,,	1 Cranium ,, 13 ,,
1 ,, ,, 18 ,,	6 Crania ,, 12 ,,
1 ,, ,, 17 ,,	7 ,, ,, 11 ,,

cranium which Prince R. Bonaparte presented to the writers, and which are reproduced in Figs. 1, 2, 3.

The cranium is platycephalic, a peculiarity which is rarer in the woman than in the man. To be noted also is a most remarkable jugular apophisis with strongly arched brows concave below, and confluent with the median line and beyond it. All the sutures are open, as in a young man aged from 23 to 25, and simple, especially the coronary suture.

The cranial capacity is 1,360 c.c., while the average among French women is 1,337; the shape is slightly dolichocephalic (77·7); and in the horizontal direction the zygomatic arch is visible only on the left—a clear instance of asymmetry. The insertion of the sagittal process in the frontal bone is also asymmetrical, and there is a median occipital fossa. The crotaphitic lines are marked, as is also the top of the temples; the orbital cavities are enormous, especially the right one, which is lower than the left, as is indeed the whole right side of the face.

On both sides are pteroid wormian bones.

Measurements.—Even anthropometry here proves the existence of virile characteristics. The orbital area is 133 mm.q., while the average among Parisian women is 126. The height of the orbit is 35 mm., as against 33 in the normal Parisian.

The cephalic index is 77·5; zygomatic index 92·7; the facial angle of Camper, 85°; the nasal height, 50 (among Parisians 48); frontal breadth, 120 (among Parisian women 93·2).

Pelvi.—Out of 5 of these organs, all belonging to prostitutes of Pavia, two measure on an average 135

SKULL OF CHARLOTTE CORDAY.—(FIG. 1)

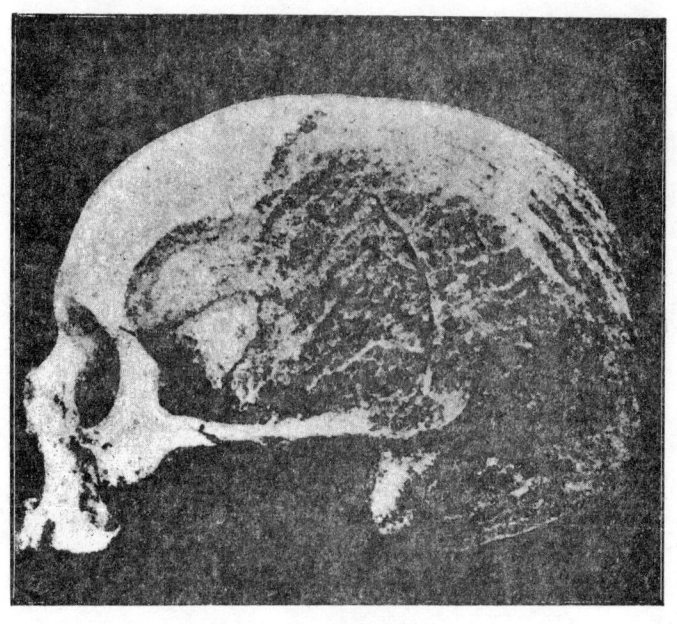

SKULL OF CHARLOTTE CORDAY.—(FIG 2.)

To face page 34.]

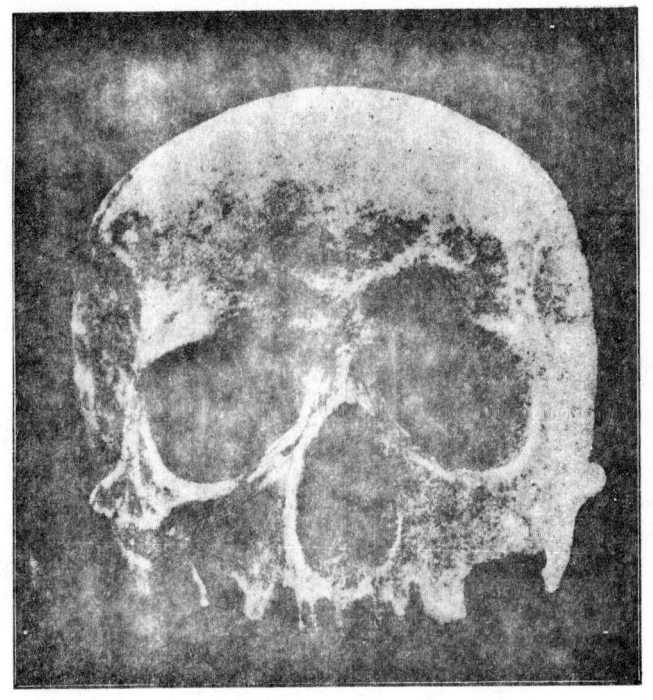

SKULL OF CHARLOTTE CORDAY.—(FIG. 3).

transversely and 123 obliquely, which is shorter than the average of 5 normal women (150–128). Two presented a virile appearance, and in one there was complete flattening of the right side of the pubes. In all 5 the channel of the sacrum was quite open, while in 5 normal women no such aperture existed.

CHAPTER III.

THE BRAINS OF FEMALE CRIMINALS.

1. *Weight.*—The average weight of the encephali of 42 Italian female criminals, according to Varaglia, and Silva, was 1,178 grammes.

The heaviest, belonging to an infanticide, was 1,328 grs.

Out of 17 brains of criminals Mingazzini found 4 sub-microcephalous, the weights being 1,006, 1,021, 1,056 in infanticides, and 1,072 in a matricide: the general average of the 17 was 1,146·76, or 108 grs. below the masculine standard. In 120 normal women the maximum weight found by Giacomini was 1,530 grs.; and the minimum, 929, was in a woman of 77 years whose intellectual faculties remained intact; while among the total number all were inferior to 1,400. Pfleger and Wechselbaum, out of 148 normal women, aged from 20 to 59 years, and of whom the average height was 1 m. 56, found an average weight of brain of 1,189 grs.; and in 377 women, of ages ranging from 20 years to senility, 1 m. 55 in height, the mean was 1,154.

Tenchini discovered an average weight of 1,194 in

167 encephala of Brescian women aged from 15 to 60 years.

If these results be compared with the weights of the 43 criminals it will be seen that the maximum of healthy women is higher than that of criminals, and the minimum is lower. The average weight of criminals falls by 16 grs. below the average of Tenchini, and by 12 grs. below the first mean obtained by Pfleger and Wechselbaum, but is 11 grs. above the second average of those writers.

In the matter of cranial types, we found among 31 dolichocephali an average weight of 1,162 (as against 1,136 in the normal), and among 11 brachycephali an average weight of 1,198 (Calori gives 1,150 for the normal). This proportion holds good also in respect of cranial capacity: thus showing that among criminals as well as normals there is a balance in favour of the brachycephalic.

Varaglia and Silva found that in 20 out of 42 encephala of criminals the left hemisphere weighed from 1 to 5 grs. more than the right; while in 18 cases the contrary was the case to the amount of from 1 to 6 grs. In 4 instances the two hemispheres were equal, and this proportion corresponds pretty nearly to Giacomini's observations on the normal subject.

In one instance only among the criminals was there a difference of 51 grs.

The average weight of the cerebellum, the pons, the peduncles, and bulb was as 155·42 (or according to Mingazzini 153·14), which was higher than the figure (147) exhibited by 16 normal Piedmontese women, but very inferior to the mean of the male (169).

2. *Anomalies.*—As to anomalies of the convolutions they are very rare, certainly rarer than in the case of male criminals; and it is precisely because he observed only the brains of female criminals that Giacomini had so few exceptions to record. For while Mingazzini, Willyk, and Tenchini found the occipital operculum in 4 per cent. of male criminals; in 33 per cent. a deepening of the second annectant convolution (very rare in normal subjects); in 6 per cent. separation of the calcarine fissure from the occipital (observed in 10 per cent. of normals); and in 5 per cent. superficiality of the *gyrus cunei;*—Giacomini observed in female criminals only a slight increase in the number of convolutions especially on the right side, and a greater scarcity of sulci.

Mingazzini, however, gives, as the result of wider investigations into 17 brains of female criminals, absence of the r. vertical anterior fissure on the left side in a sub-microcephalic homicide; deepening of the first annectant convolution on the right in two criminals, and on the left in one; division of this same convolution into two branches terminating in the occipital lobe in one case; superficiality of the gyrus cunei in two; rudimentary median frontal gyrus joining itself immediately to the superior frontal gyrus (the subject, an infanticide).

From the deep upper side of the latter a fold started, continuing laterally in a transverse direction until it joined the anterior portion of the lower frontal gyrus. In the left hemisphere of the same brain, the median frontal gyrus was interrupted in the posterior portion by a frontal arrow-shaped furrow, and in the anterior part the three gyri were almost entirely fused.

In another cerebrum, this time of a matricide, the left postcentralis is complete and independent; behind is a transverse furrow, really the prolongation of the left calloso-marginalis, and yet again behind is the left interparietalis arrow-shaped. In the right hemisphere of a woman guilty of corrupting morals, the left interparietalis is represented by a cruciform furrow dividing the superior parietal lobule from the lower, the two lobules being united behind by an anastomatic transversal fold, followed by a sulcus in front of the first external annectant convolution. In this same cerebrum the ascending parietal gyrus on the left was divided transversely into two secondary gyri by means of a convolution bifurcated on its higher side and exactly parallel to the sulcus of Rolando.

In two cases the left superior temporal convolution communicated with the incisura occipitalis; and in one instance after sending a spur in a downward direction it continued uninterrupted to the free margin of the malleus. In one case the calcarine fissure communicated with the collateralis; and in another the lower bifurcation of the same fissure joined the left extremus.

From all this it is clear that if the external superficies of the hemisphere is the same in criminals as in normals, nevertheless the signs of degeneration are more frequent among the former class.

Mingazzini satisfied himself that the whole cerebral

hemisphere is less extensive in women than in men, whether the women be normal or criminal; and if we cannot maintain with Hüschke and Rudinger that the parieto-occipital lobe is larger in females, it is yet true that the frontal lobe in men predominates over the other to a greater degree than in women.

Mingazzini also found that the absolute length of the sulcus of Rolando is often greater on the left than on the right, and that this occurs more frequently in women (18·34) than in men (7·26).

The morphological anomalies found among criminals of the two sexes were: 13 men, 19; 17 women, 19—so that in every brain the proportion of anomalies is 1·46 among males to 1·11 among females, thus showing a notable excess among males.

Some female criminals, however, show a number of anomalies.

Ferrier, for instance, relates the case of a woman whose right hemisphere was smaller than her left, as 510 grs. to 550, and in whom, moreover, the fissure of Rolando was interrupted by a deep annectant convolution following on the ascending frontal fold, which, in addition to being atrophied, was crossed in the middle by two sulci. The ascending parietal convolution was similarly divided, and the second frontal had the same peculiarity.

In the third frontal convolution he observed a depression, at the bottom of which were folds of smaller size and firmer substance than the usual annectant convolutions, which he attributed to inflammatory processes.

The malformation of the fissure of Rolando struck

him as extremely rare: he had, in fact, encountered it only twice in his examination of 800 normal brains.

Flesch, in a female thief, found pachymeningitis and interruption of the ascending frontal convolution on the left; also a real median lobe on the cerebellum, formed, as in many mammiferi, by two sulci beginning in the median fissure, diverging in front, and crossing the horizontal convolutions of the median lobe throughout the whole length of the hemispheres.

3. *Pathological anomalies.*—More important still are the pathological anomalies. Out of 33 female criminals, a post-mortem examination revealed in 11 grave macroscopic lesion of the central system and its involucra, such as: dilatation of the lateral ventricles; multiple sub-arachnoid hæmorrhages of the frontal region in both hemispheres; thickening of the spinal dura mater, both cervical and dorsal; abscess on the cerebellum in connection with the left median cerebellary peduncle; meningo-encephalitis; cerebral apoplexy; hæmorrhage in the lateral ventricles; syphilis; two transparent rounded vesicles adhering to the peduncle and on the lower side of the chiasma of the optic nerve under the arachnoid; broad furrows; abundant sub-arachnoid liquid; endo-cranial abscess; luxation of the odontoid; paralysis for a month previous to examination of all the extremities; meningitis of the base in connection with the pons and medulla oblongata; cerebral œdema and suffusion into the ventricles; humid mother-of-pearly tumour under the arachnoid, between third and fourth pair of nerves (origin evident).

Hotzen, in the "Archive of Psychiatry" (1889), relates the case of Maria Köster, who, at the age of 18, after having until then appeared of a quiet and industrious disposition, killed her mother with sixty blows of a hatchet, only to obtain possession of a scanty sum; kept a diary of her impressions; was in domestic service; then a typographer; then a needlewoman; and who presented only asymmetry of the face and of one pupil. She had hysterical attacks after puberty, which in her case only declared itself at 19, but often feigned these attacks. After her death she was found to have phthisis, traces of adherence of the dura mater and of hæmorrhagic pachymeningitis, besides true atrophy of the cerebral cortex.

Her central anterior convolution was crossed by fissures between the third median inferior convolution and its termination in the fissure of Rolando. The central posterior convolution was divided by a furrow into two halves, so that the parietal and rolandic sulci communicated.

The fissure of Rolando did not terminate in the fissure of Sylvius; both the paracentral convolutions were between the third superior convolution and the median, and traversed by a deep and yawning fissure, which brought the interparietal fissure into direct communication with the first frontal sulcus.

Here, then, is a case of atrophy, congenital and hereditary atrophy, of the cerebral cortex, characterised by insufficiently developed frontal convolutions, especially of the occipital lobe, by small convolutions, incomplete enclosure of the cerebellum by the large hemispheres, and by abnormally numerous segmentations of the cerebral cortex, amounting to positive aplasia.

Such furrows are not products of superior evolution ; no new cerebral substance is laid down in their neighbourhood, and they constitute, in fact, a case of atrophy of the cerebral matter.

Lambl, in "Westphal's Archiv. für Psychiatrie" (1888), gives the history of Marianna Kirtexen, who, under maternal guidance, gave forth oracles, and was consulted by peasants, and even by persons of high rank, showing much ability in guessing at their maladies and prescribing strange remedies, for which she was extravagantly paid. She was, in short, a clever swindler, although only 12 years old. She was lame, squint-eyed, and left-handed, her right arm being, indeed, almost paralysed. She was fluent, well-mannered, gave very correct replies, and had a real curiosity—passion even—for seeing and treating the sick.

She died of consumption, and autopsy revealed a long-standing porencephalia in the left hemisphere of the brain, forming a large clepsydral-shaped cavity, of which the middle part or isthmus consisted in an elliptic horizontal fissure 4 mms. long in the white substance. The wider base, rounded and 5·4 centimeters in breadth, lay towards the outside and terminated in the arachnoid, while the small end, measuring 2·8 centimeters, opened into the external wall of the left lateral ventricle. Into the upper segment of the cup-shaped fossa on the outer surface of the left hemisphere ran the lower part of the precentral (frontal ascendant) gyrus, and into the anterior segment a portion of the superior frontal gyrus entered, also the lower part of the same, and the posterior portion of the median frontal gyrus. In the lower segment the posterior portion of the inferior frontal gyrus and the gyri of Reil's island were found; while into the posterior segment entered the anterior portion of the first temporal gyrus, and the lower part of the retrocentral (ascending parietal) gyrus, together with the operculum. There was consequently partial destruction of the frontal ascending convolution, but the cortex had remained intact. On the internal surface of the hemispheres were other anomalies due to pressure of the ventricular fluid. The corpus callosum and fornix were atrophied. The gyrus fornicatus was flattened in the median portion, and the horns of the lateral ventricle were dilated and rounded. The internal ganglia were normal.

Microscopic examination of the grey cortex in the diseased parts revealed a fluted striated substance, mixed with round cells enclosing nuclei (evidently a thickening of the neuroglia).

Other cells mixed with the above had flattened edges, a transparent protoplasm, and in the centre two or even three simple nuclei. These cells were surrounded by dark, granular, nucleated matter, and had the appearance of cartilaginous fibre.

The convexities of the pia mater and arachnoid enclosed a large number of Pacchionian granulations such as are found in the aged, and were notably darkened and thickened.

CHAPTER IV.

ANTHROPOMETRY OF FEMALE CRIMINALS.

1. *Authors and the cases they studied.*—In the list of those who have recently made a study of the characteristics of female criminals, we must include—

Marro,[1] who investigated 41 cases; Troisky,[2] 58 cases; Lombroso and Pasini,[3] 122 cases; Ziino,[4] 188 cases; Lombroso, 83 photographs; Varaglia and Silva,[5] 60 crania; Romberg,[6] 20 cases; and recently Salsotto,[7] 409 cases; Madame Tarnowsky,[8] 100 female thieves; and Roncoroni,[9] who studied 50 normal women.

[1] Marro, " I caratteri dei delinquenti." Bocca, 1889.
[2] Troisky, "Cephalometry of Criminals with reference to some Symptoms of Physical Degeneration," Journal of Charkow, Russia, 1884.
[3] Lombroso and Pasini, " Archivio di psichiatria," 1883.
[4] Ziino, " Fisiopatologia del delitto," 1881.
[5] Varaglia and Silva, "Note anatomiche ed antropologiche su 60 cranii e 46 encefali di donne criminali italiane." "Archivio psichiatria," vol. vi.
[6] Romberg, " 101 Cefalogrammi." Berlin, 1889.
[7] Salsotto, " La donna delinquente. Rivista di discipline carcerarie," 1887.
[8] Tarnowsky, " Étude anthropometrique sur les prostituées et les voleuses." Paris, 1887.
[9] Roncoroni, " Ricerche su alcune sensibilità nei pazzi. Giornale della R. Accad. di Med.," 1891 ; " I caratteri degenerativi su 50 donne e 50 nomini normali : l'olfatto, il gusto e l'udito in 35 normali." "Arch. di psichiatria," 1892.

The characteristics of prostitutes, which we cannot study separately from those of female criminals, were investigated by Scarenzio and Soffiantini [1] in 14 crania; by Andronico [2] in 230 subjects; by Grimaldi [3] in 26; by De Albertis [4] in 28; by Tarnowsky in 150; by Bergonzoli and Lombroso [5] in 26 crania; while Berg [6] lately made researches into the tattoo marks on 804. Gurrieri examined into the sensibility of 60 cases, and Fornasari gave the anthropometry of a similar number.[7] Riccardi [8] and Ardù [9] made notes on the weight, height, &c., of 176.

We also published in the "Giornale della R. Accademia di Medicina," of Turin, Nos. 9 and 10, 1891, and in the "Archivio di psichiatria," vol. xiii., fasc. vi.," observations on characteristics of degeneration in 200 normal women, in 120 Piedmontese female thieves, and in 115 prostitutes of Turin. We also studied, synthetically, the type of the criminal in 300 women (234 of whom were in the female penitentiary, and 56 in the prison of Turin), as well as in 69 Russian female criminals and 100 prostitutes of the same

[1] Scarenzio e Soffiantini, "Archivio di psichiatria," 1881, vol. vii. p. 29.
[2] Andronico, "Prostitute e delinquenti." "Arch. di psichiatria," 1882, vol. iii. p. 143.
[3] Grimaldi, "Il pudore. Il manicomio," vol. v. No. 1, 1889.
[4] De Albertis, "Il tatuaggio su 300 prostitute genovesi. Archivio psich: scienze pen: ed antrop: crim.," vol. ix., 1888.
[5] Bergonzoli e Lombroso, "Su 26 cranii di prostitute," 1893.
[6] Berg, "Le tatouage chez les prostitueés Danoises." "Arch. psich.," vol. xi. fasc. 3 and 4, 1891.
[7] Gurrieri e Fornasari, "I sensi e le anomalie nelle donne normali e le prostitute." Turin, 1893.
[8] Riccardi, "Osservazioni intorno una serie di prostitute," 1892, Anomalo Nos. 8 and 9.
[9] Ardù, "Alcune anomalie nelle prostitute." Turin, 1893.

nationality, in which we collaborated with Madame Tarnowsky and with Ottolenghi.[1]

This constitutes a total of 1,033 observations on female criminals, 176 observations on the skulls of female criminals, 685 on the skulls of prostitutes, 225 on normal women in hospitals, and 30 others also normal.

2. *Weight and height.*—The net result of the data furnished by Salsotto and Madame Tarnowsky on weight and height (*see* Tables, pp. 51-2), is to show that 45 per cent. of infanticides and 29·6 per cent. of murderesses are of weight below the normal; while 50 per cent. of infanticides and 44 per cent. of murderesses are beneath the normal stature.

On the other hand, only 15 per cent. of poisoners were of lower weight, and only 25 per cent. of lower stature than the normal: facts which can be referred to the circumstance that poisoners do not generally belong to the poorer classes.

According to the data of Madame Tarnowsky 19 per cent. of prostitutes and 21 per cent. of female thieves are below normal weight, the figures for peasant women being 20 per cent., and for women of education 18 per cent. Height was less than the normal among 28 per cent. of prostitutes, 14 per cent. of thieves, 7 per cent. of peasant women, and 10 per cent. of educated females.

Salsotto gives 37 per cent. of infanticides, 70 per cent. of poisoners, and 52 per cent. of murderesses as

[1] Ottolenghi e Lombroso, "La donna delinquenti e prostituta." Turin, 1892.

of normal weight, and 38 per cent. of infanticides, 50 per cent. of poisoners, and 48 per cent. of female assassins as of normal stature.

Madame Tarnowsky's data are the following: Normal weight, 56·7 per cent. of prostitutes, 51 per cent. of thieves, 46 per cent. of peasant women, and 58 per cent. of educated women. Normal stature, 61·3 per cent. of prostitutes, 62 per cent. of thieves, 64 per cent. of peasant women (of good lives), and 74 per cent. of educated women.

Salsotto found, on the other hand, that 18 per cent. of infanticides, 15 per cent. of poisoners, and 21·6 of female assassins exceeded normal weight; and Madame Tarnowsky's figures in the same respect are 22·9 of prostitutes, 28 of thieves, 34 of peasant women (of good lives), and 24 of educated women.

As to height in Russia the normal was exceeded by 14 per cent. of prostitutes, 24 per cent. of thieves, 19 per cent. of peasant women (of good conduct), and 12 per cent. of educated women. Salsotto gives as of height above the medium, 11 per cent. of infanticides, 20 per cent. of female poisoners, and 10·4 per cent. of other murderesses.

To sum up, weight appears more often equal to or above the medium in thieves and murderesses, but especially in prostitutes: more rarely is this the case in infanticides.

3. *Medium height.*—This, on the contrary, appears to be rarer in all female criminals and prostitutes than in moral women. Here are the tables :—

ANTHROPOMETRY OF FEMALE CRIMINALS.

	Salsotto.				Tarnowsky.				
	Infanticides.	Poisoners.	Other murderesses.	Medium height in Italy.	Prostitutes.	Thieves.	Assassins.	Peasants of good lives.	Educated moral women.
Med. weight	55·1	57·7	58·5	55	55·2	56	58	56·4	56·4 kg.
„ height	1·52	1·53	1·53	1·55	1·53	1·55	1·56	1·56	1·54 m.

Marro found that the average height for women of good lives is 1·55, and for criminals 1·52, with a medium weight for moral women of 57, and for female criminals of 53.

Riccardi gives as the medium height of 42 Bolognese fallen women 1·52, with a maximum of 1·67, and a minimum of 1·43. Riccardi, who studied the question of stature in relation to age and social condition among the Bolognese, found the following data ("Statura e Condizione sociale, studiate nei Bolognese, 1885"):—

Normal (Riccardi).

Age.	Easy circumstances.	Poor.	Averages.	Normal.	Prostitutes.
17	156·6	150·4	153·3	153·3	158·7 c.
18	156·5	152·9	154·0	162.0	155·0
19	155·9	155·0	155.0	150·0	—
20—25	156·8	154·1	155·2	154·0	153·7
26—35	155·3	152·3	154·3	152·1	163.0

Whence it results that at the age of 25, which was that of almost all the twenty Bolognese prostitutes measured, they were of shorter stature than the average, not only of women in easy circumstances, but even of poor women.

4. *Medium weight.*—As to weight, from the averages furnished by Salsotto and Madame Tarnowsky, murderesses and female poisoners appear, as we

already remarked, to be above the average of moral women.

If we now follow Fornasari in a comparison of the respective weights of prostitutes and moral women in relation to age and height, as in the following tables:—

	27 Prostitutes.			26 Normals (Fornasari).	
Age.	Wgt. (kgms.)	Height.	Age.	Wgt. (kgms.)	Height.
27	44·300	1,445	15	42·000	1,445
22	45·000	1,415	31	43·000	1,500
24	48·150	1,523	25	47·500	1,540
24	48·200	1,510	26	48·000	1,450
22	52·000	1,604	30	51·500	1,544
24	52·000	1,580	22	52·400	1,540
26	58·000	1,500	19	55·200	1,500
20	59·000	1,584			
30	67·000	1,690			

it will be seen that height and age being equal, the weight is greatest among prostitutes.

Fornasari demonstrated this even better by the results of twenty more weight-takings, which gave him an average weight of 58 kilogrammes, with a maximum of 75 kilogrammes and a minimum of 38, these being figures above the average of normal women.

This greater weight among prostitutes is confirmed by the notorious fact of the obesity of those who grow old in their vile trade, and who gradually become positive monsters of adipose tissue. We could cite not a few who attain the weight of 90·98, and even 130 kilogrammes.

But this stands out still more clearly when, in conformity with a formula obtained by means of thousands of measurements taken by one of the writers [1] in order to find the relation of weight to

---

[1] Lombroso, "Sulla Statura degli Italiani," Milan, 1873.

TABLE II.

	No.	HEIGHT							WEIGHT						
		Inferior by 15 centi- meters and more than the average. p.c.	Inferior by 10 to 14 centimeters. p.c.	Inferior by 5 to 9 centimeters. p.c.	Correspondent to the normal average. p.c.	Superior by 5 to 9 centimeters to the average. p.c.	Superior by 10 to 14 centimeters. p.c.	Superior by 15 centi- meters and more. p.c.	Inferior by 15 kilogrammes to the average. p.c.	Inferior by 10 to 14 kilogrammes. p.c.	Inferior by 5 to 9 kilogrammes. p.c.	Correspondent to the normal average. p.c.	Superior to the average by 5 to 9 kilogrammes. p.c.	Superior by 10 to 14 kilogrammes. p.c.	Superior by 15 kilogrammes and more. p.c.
FEMALE CRIMINALS OBSERVED BY SALSOTTO.															
Infanticides	100	—	18 / 18	33 / 33	38 / 38	11 / 11	—	—	9 / 9	10 / 10	26 / 26	37 / 37	11 / 11	7 / 7	—
Poisoners	20	1 / 5	2 / 10	3 / 15	10 / 50	2 / 10	2 / 10	—	—	—	3 / 15	14 / 70	2 / 10	—	1 / 5
Assassins	128	1 / 0.8	12 / 9.6	42 / 33.6	60 / 48	13 / 10.4	—	—	2 / 1.6	25 / 20	10 / 8	65 / 52	9 / 7.2	7 / 5.6	10 / 7.2
Total	248	2 / 0.8	22 / 8.8	78 / 31	108 / 43	26 / 10.4	2 / 0.8	—	11 / 4.4	35 / 14	39 / 15.6	116 / 46.6	23 / 9.2	14 / 5.6	10 / 4
FEMALE CRIMINALS OBSERVED BY MADAME TARNOWSKY.															
Prostitutes	150	1 / 0.66	32 / 21.3	40 / 26.4	61 / 3	11 / 7.2	3 / 1.98	1	1 / 0.66	11 / 7.2	17 / 11.2	57 / 86.6	22 / 14.5	8 / 7.8	1 / 0.66
Thieves	100	—	2 / 2	12 / 12	62 / 62	20 / 20	3 / 3	—	3 / 3	3 / 3	15 / 15	51 / 51	15 / 15	8 / 8	5 / 5
Moral peasant women	100	—	2 / 2	7 / 7	64 / 64	21 / 21	3 / 3	—	2 / 2	3 / 3	15 / 15	46 / 46	16 / 16	14 / 14	4 / 4
Educated women	50	—	1 / 2	4 / 8	37 / 74	7 / 14	2	—	2 / 2	3 / 6	10 / 5	29 / 58	6 / 12	4 / 4	4 / 4
FEMALE CRIMINALS OBSERVED BY MARRO.															
Thieves	19	—	4 / 20	3 / 15	8 / 40	5 / 20	—	—	1 / 5	2 / 10	2 / 10	7 / 35	3 / 15	2 / 10	2 / 10
Offenders against nature	8	—	—	—	—	—	—	—	—	—	—	—	—	—	—
Various	84	1 / 1.2	1 / 1.2	4 / 4.8	3 / 3.6	5 / 20	—	—	7 / 3	1 / 1.3	2 / 2.4	4 / 4.8	3 / 3.21	1 / 12	2 / 2
Normal	25	—	1 / 4	3 / 22	11 / 78	—	—	—	1 / 4	7 / 8	4 / 29	3 / 36	3 / 12	—	—

TABLE III.

Stature and Weight.

	No.	Weight Superior to the Normal. Per cent.	Normal. Per cent.	Below the Normal. Per cent.	Below the Normal by at least 10 kilogms. Per cent.
SALSOTTO.					
Female poisoners	20	60	15	25	—
Female assassins	130	50.4	14.4	37.6	—
Female infanticides	100	44	25	31	—
TARNOWSKY.					
Professional prostitutes	150	59.40	5.94	29.7	3.96
Normal peasant women	100	45	5	46	4
Normal women of education	50	64	2	32	2
Thieves	100	46	10	36	8
MARRO.					
Female Thieves	19	45	5	25	20
Women of immoral life	8	60	12	24	—
Various women criminals	14	43	—	50	7
Normal	25	60	4	32	4

stature (*see* Table III.), such women are regarded as having a weight equal to the average in whom the number of kilogrammes which represent the weight is equal to the number of centimeters by which their statures surpass the meter.

It is then seen that 60 per cent. of female poisoners, 59.4 per cent. of prostitutes, 50 per cent. of female assassins, and 46 per cent. of female thieves, have a weight above the average, while in only 45 per cent. of Russian peasant women, leading moral lives, and 44 per cent of infanticides is the same the case.

Below the normal, on the other hand, are 46 per cent. of moral peasant women (Russians), 37 per cent. of murderesses, 36 per cent. of thieves, 31 per cent. of infanticides, and 29 per cent. of prostitutes, while Salsotto gives 25 per cent. as the proportion among Italian female poisoners.

5. *Span of arms.*—The average in 44 Modenese (measured by Riccardi) was 1.556 m., while the average stature was 1.52, the consequent relation being as 102.3 to 100 (and in normals as 103 to 100).

Madame Tarnowsky, however, gives the following results among Russian women:—

	150 Prostitutes.	100 Thieves.	50 Murderesses.	100 Moral Poor.
Height	1.53	1.55	1.56	1.56 m.
Span of arms	1.62	1.65	1.63	1.668

the span of the arms being consequently inferior among prostitutes and even criminals when compared to the stature, than among the moral poor, which result must be attributed to the greater development of limbs in women who work; and this we shall find to be the case also among the Bolognese females.

6. *The average height of the body seated.*—Among 30 Bolognese prostitutes this was 82·0, and relatively to the height 53·6 per cent., as against 83·2, or relatively to the height 53·7 per cent. among 30 normal women, also Bolognese; that is to say, there was no remarkable difference.

7. *Limbs. Thorax.*—From the measurements of limbs made by Madame Tarnowsky, it appears that the upper limbs of an illiterate working-woman of moral life measure 0·608, as against 0·597 in thieves, and 0·583 in prostitutes. Even the right arm, which in normal peasant women measures 0·619, falls in thieves to 0·605, and in prostitutes to 0·588. Prostitutes consequently have the shortest arms of all, the reason being in their case, as in that of thieves, that they work less than moral women.

The circumference of the thorax, which is 82·2 in prostitutes, differs but little from that of moral women (in Bologna 82·7, and in Modena 84·7), but relatively to the height (54·0 in prostitutes, as against 53·3 in moral women) the divergence is greater (Riccardi).

8. *The hand.*—The hand, however, according to Madame Tarnowsky, is longer in Russian prostitutes (right, 187; left, 184) than in peasant women and even homicides (right, 185; left, 184), while in thieves it is shorter (right, 178; left, 175).

Fornasari also found that among the prostitutes of Bologna (where it measured from 155 to 198 mm.) the hand was longer than among normals (141 to 184 mm.), while the breadth varied from 65 to 85 among the first-named and from 52 to 84 among normals.

Such differences which were marked in the

figures at both ends gradually disappeared as the median averages were reached; but the net result was that in normal women, even workers, the hands were smaller without exception.

Fornasari measured the length of the middle finger so as to compare it with the breadth of the hand, and from the difference of the two measurements he was able to deduce the large or smaller digital development when compared with the palm.

The length of the middle finger was measured on the back from the point to the head of the third metacarpus, and on the inner side from the point to the fold which separates the finger from the palm.

The difference, in both measurements, between the middle fingers resulted as from about 19 to 20 mm. On the inner side the length of the middle finger varies in prostitutes as from 60 to 85 mm., showing an average of 70 to 74; in normal women the difference is from 53 to 84, but the average is similar. On the outer side the variation in prostitutes is from 75 to 100, with an average of 80-84; in normals from a minimum of 65 there is a rise to the maximum of 99, and the serial average is 85-89.

The second measurement, made on a careful anatomical basis, confirms the result yielded by the first in so far as it shows that the shorter middle fingers belong to normal women, and the longer ones to prostitutes; but that relatively to the serial average, while the first measurement gives a similar length to prostitutes and to normals, the second shows the latter to possess a higher average length.

Comparing now the length of the middle finger (on

the outside) to the breadth of the hand, we obtain the following figures :—

DIFFERENCE BETWEEN FINGERS AND PALMS.

	Prostitutes.	Bolognese Prostitutes.	Normals.
From 1– 9 mm.	13	9	6
,, 10–19	40	15	11
,, 20–25	7	3	3

The difference among the Bolognese is from 1 to 24 in prostitutes, and from 5 to 24 in normal women. Consequently in the former class the digital portion of the hand is less developed than in the latter relatively to the palmary division.

If the length of the hand in relation to the height, taken as 100, be compared, we find :—

	Prostitutes.	Bolognese Prostitutes.	Normals.
< 9·5	2	1	1
9·5	1	1	1
10	4	1	1
10·5	19	8	5
11	21	10	7
11·5	11	5	5
12 and more	1	—	—

These figures would lead to the conclusion that the hand in prostitutes is largest relatively to stature.

9. *Neck, thigh, and leg.*—The measurements for the circumferences of the neck, thigh, and leg were only taken in the case of 14 normal women, it being not too easy to find subjects who will submit to the experiment. Between the least circumference, over the ankle bones, and the largest, round the calf, Fornasari found a difference in Bolognese prostitutes of from 70 to 150, and in normal women of from 100

to 140; the median average for the first-named being 120, and for the last-named 100. Normals consequently have the calves least developed on an average, and prostitutes show the maxima and minima of development. Between the maximum measurement of the calves and that of the thigh the variation was from 120 to 240 in prostitutes of Bologna, and from 120 to 220 in normals; the serial mean being for the first-named 190, and for the second 150.

The thighs of prostitutes are consequently bigger than normal women's in proportion to the calves.

Between the maximum circumference of the leg and the circumference of the neck, the figures in Bolognese prostitutes were from — 55 to + 30, and in normals from — 35 to + 5, the results being as under, the neck < = > calves:—

22	...	4	...	17	... prostitutes.
14	...	—	...	8	... Bolognese prostitutes.
8	...	4	...	2	... normals.

In most cases normal women have the two circumferences equal; their neck, however, is often smaller but rarely larger, and even when larger, only a little; in prostitutes, on the contrary, the neck is often larger or smaller than the maximum circumference of the calves.

10. *Foot.*—The foot in prostitutes is shorter and narrower than in normals.

With respect to length, the prostitutes of Bologna varied as from 200 to 240 mm. (serial average, 230), while the normals differed as from 200 to 235 (serial average, 210 to 220); in breadth, the prostitutes ranged from 64 to 90 mm. (median average, 80 to 84), and the normals from 70 to 96 (with an identical mean).

Between the length of foot and that of hand, prostitutes show a greater difference than normals in the maxima and minima, but the media in the two classes are almost the same. The divergence among prostitutes is from 38 to 73, and among normal women from 20 to 65, while the media are from 50 to 59 for one as for the other.

The foot, therefore, would appear to be shorter proportionately to the hand in prostitutes than in normals.

11. *Cranial capacity.*—Here, as far as measurements can be exact in the case of women with their quantity of hair, Marro found the capacity in 41 criminals to be below that of normal women as 1,477 to 1,508. Among the women he observed, the following series of probable cranial capacities were obtained:—

	41 Criminal Women.	41 Normal Women.
1400–1450	28·8 per cent.	— per cent.
1450–1500	45·6 ,,	44 ,,
1500–1550	16·8 ,,	44 ,,
1550–1597	7·2 ,,	12 ,,

Fornasari's observations on Bolognese women give from 1,400 to 1,559 for prostitutes, and from 1,410 to 1,579 for normal women.

But the cranial capacity can be best demonstrated by the data furnished by Madame Tarnowsky, who studied Russian women all of the same age and locality.

	Prostitutes. No. 150.	Peasant Chaste Women. No. 100.	Educated Chaste Women. No. 50.	Thieves. No. 100.
Horizontal circumference	531·6	537·0	538·0	535·5
Longitudinal curve	316·2	316·2	313·5	317·3
Transversal curve	283·8	285·9	286·9	286·3
Longitudinal diameter	178·2	181·4	183·2	179·4
Transversal diameter	142·5	144·8	145·2	143·9
Probable cranial capacity	1452·3	1465·3	1466·8	1462·4

Thieves consequently would appear to have a probable cranial capacity inferior to that of normals by barely 3 cm., while in prostitutes the inferiority is as 13 cm.

The measurements of the crania confirm this prevalence of small cranial capacities among prostitutes.

12. The *Cranial circumference* among 80 female Piedmontese delinquents corresponded to an average of 530; and the same result was obtained by Marro, who found 535 in the normal woman. By the serial method, criminal women appear as exceeding normal women in their minima, and falling behind them in their maxima.

We find from the figures of Salsotto that 51 per cent. of criminals had cranial capacities between 521 and 540; 22 per cent. had them between 541 and 557; and 27 per cent. between 504 and 520.

With respect to crime, we find the largest cranial circumference in homicides (532), after whom come poisoners (517), then infanticides (501), and finally thieves (494); and these results are almost identical with those obtained by Ziino. The larger circumferences, serially taken, are wanting in thieves and infanticides, while abounding in homicides.

TABLE IV.

CRANIAL MEASUREMENTS.	Tarnowsky.					Salsotto.			Marro.	
	Prostitutes, 150.	Peasants, 100.	Educated, 50.	Thieves, 100.		Poisoners, 20.	Assassins, 130.	Infanticides, 100.	Various Criminals, 42.	Normals, 25.
Antero-posterior Diameter. { From 154–175	13.33	4	—	36		—	—	—	—	48
,, 175–180	29.33	21	20	40		—	—	—	—	48
,, 180–185	40	40	30	16		—	—	—	—	4
,, 185–190	14	24	28	7		—	—	—	—	—
,, 190–195	3.33	11	22	1		—	—	—	—	—
Transverse Diameter. { From 125–135	4.66	1	2	—		—	—	—	—	8
,, 135–145	37.32	26	30	82		—	—	—	—	24
,, 145–155	57.99	71	68	18		—	—	—	—	18
Horizontal Circumference. { From 485–504	1.32	—	—	—		—	—	—	—	—
,, 504–510	1.33	—	—	4		15	4	3	—	20
,, 511–520	8.66	6	2	11		40	19	21	—	—
,, 521–530	26.06	20	12	29		25	36	15	—	44
,, 531–540	33.99	28	34	24		10	25.6	30	—	—
,, 541–550	21.33	24	40	21		10	12.8	21	—	36
,, 551–580	7.28	22	22	11		—	6.4	10	—	—
Longitudinal Curve. { From 280–310	56	37	36.3	38		15	70	10	—	44
,, 311–320	24	29	33	30		45	36	38	—	24
,, 221–330	12	24	21.78	23		25	46	41	—	20
,, 331–340	8	10	4.62	7		15	10	11	—	12

Transverse Curve.	From 250–300 ...	85·46	84	80	86	—	—	—	—	52·8	4
	,, 300–310 ...	10·56	13	12	10	30	30	15	—	16·8	28
	,, 311–320 ...	3·98	3	4	3	50	4	25	—	21·6	36
	,, 321–330 ...	—	—	4	1	5	51	50	—	7·2	32
	,, 331–340 ...	—	—	—	—	15	15	10	—	2·4	—
Index of Cephalon.	Up to 77 ...	23·66	26	24	16	25	21	19	—	12·0	8
	,, 77–80 ...	26	23	38	31	15	41	25	—	38·4	44
	,, 80–85 ...	38·66	40	28	56	25	22	27	—	40·8	28
	,, 85 and over	12	10	10	3	35	16	29	—	4·8	20
Anterior Semi-circumference.	From 292–300 ...	—	—	—	—	25	20·6	25	—	—	—
	,, 301–310 ...	—	—	—	—	35	40	41	—	—	—
	,, 311–328 ...	—	—	—	—	40	39·4	27	—	—	—

FACIAL MEASUREMENTS.

Minimum Frontal Diameter.	From 9·5–10 ...	—	—	—	—	20	20	11	— out of 12	27·2	39
	,, 10·1–10·5 ...	18·48	18	—	3	40	31	29	—	48·4	15
	,, 10·6–11 ...	59·4	74	34	24	40	36	39	—	24·2	29
	,, 11·1–12·0 ...	21·12	8	66	67	—	13	21	—	—	19
	,, 12·1 and over	—	—	—	6	—	—	—	—	—	—
Diameter of Cheek-bones.	From 8·5–11·0 ...	14	19	16	46	—	—	49	—	—	—
	,, 11·1–12·0 ...	68·66	71	64	48	55	43	31	— out of 12	42	29
	,, 12·1–13·0 ...	17·33	10	20	6	45	46	20	—	58	62
	,, 13·1–14·0 ...	—	—	—	—	—	11	—	—	—	9
	,, 14 and over	—	—	—	—	—	—	—	—	—	—
Diameter of Jaws.	From 9·0–10·0 ...	19·33	27	50	75	15	14	23	—	8	14
	,, 10·1–10·5 ...	50·66	56	38	19	35	26·5	31	—	42	14
	,, 10·6–11·0 ...	25·33	13	8	6	45	34	29	— out of 12	25	57
	,, 11·1–11·5 ...	4·66	4	4	—	5	20·5	17	—	17	10
	,, 11·6–12·0 ...	—	—	—	—	—	5	—	—	8	5
Height of Forehead.	From 50–40 ...	—	—	—	—	40	26	25	—	18	14
	,, 41–50 ...	—	—	—	—	30	51	30	— out of 12	54	72
	,, 51–60 ...	—	—	—	—	30	23	45	—	27	14

		Infanticides.		Murderesses (assassins).		Poisoners.
510	...	3 per cent.	...	15 per cent.	...	3·8 per cent.
511–520	...	21 ,,	...	40 ,,	...	19 ,,
521–530	...	15 ,,	...	25 ,,	...	36 ,,
531–540	...	30 ,,	...	10 ,,	...	24 ,,
541–550	...	21 ,,	...	10 ,,	...	12 ,,
551–560	...	10 ,,	...	— ,,	...	6·4 ,,

Andronico, out of 230 prostitutes, found in 87 per cent. of them a circumference between 480 and 500; the writers, in 178 prostitutes, found a mean cranial circumference of 522, which was less than in criminals; and De Albertis found an average of 537.

In 27 prostitutes of Bologna, Fornasari found a minimum of 470 and a maximum of 560; and in 20 moral women a minimum of 490 and a maximum of 534.

Madame Tarnowsky discovered an average circumference of 535 in thieves, 531 in prostitutes, 537 in illiterate peasants, 538 in 50 educated moral women, the result being a smaller cranial circumference in the female criminal. This has indeed been noted by several observers.

Coming now to more detailed results, we have: the least amplitudes (from 485 to 520), above all in prostitutes (11·31 per cent.) and in thieves (15 per cent.), as against 6 per cent. of peasant women and 2 per cent. of educated females (Tarnowsky); the greatest amplitudes (540–580) are rarest above all in prostitutes (28·61 per cent.) and in thieves (12 per cent.), while abounding in peasant women (46·7 per cent.), and especially in educated women (62 per cent.). According to Salsotto, the least circumferences predominate in female poisoners (55 per cent.); while there are fewer of them in infanticides (24 per cent.), in murderesses (23 per cent.), and in thieves (15 per cent.); the widest circumferences among criminals are to be found in thieves (37 per cent.), then in infanticides (31 per cent.), next in murderesses (19·2 per cent.), and in poisoners (10 per cent.). Marro states that the least circumferences (from 485–520) are to be observed in 27·4 per cent. of criminals and in 20 per cent. of normals; the widest (from 541–580) are in 10·4 per cent. of criminals and in 36 per cent. of normals.

13. *Curves. The longtitudinal curve.*—According to Madame Tarnowsky, the lowest figures (280–310) are furnished especially by prostitutes (56 per cent.) and by thieves (38 per cent.), after whom come peasant women of moral lives (37 per cent.), and by educated women (36·3); while Salsotto's figures are: for criminals, thieves (38 per cent.); poisoners (15 per cent.); assassins and infanticides (20 per cent.). The highest figures (321–340), as given by Tarnowsky, are 34 per cent. in peasants, 30 per cent. in thieves, 26·3 per cent. in educated women, and 20 per cent. in prostitutes. Salsotto calculates them as follows: 56 per cent. in murderesses, 52 per cent. in infanticides, 40 per cent. in poisoners, and 30 per cent. in thieves. Marro says that the least longitudinal curves (280–310) are in 57·6 per cent. of criminals, and in 14 per cent. of normals; the greatest (331–340) are in 7·2 per cent. of criminals and in 12 per cent. of normals.

Transverse curves.—Here the data contributed by

Madame Tarnowsky are widely different from those given by Salsotto; and the reason of the divergence is ethnical.

Among Italian female criminals Salsotto does not find one with a transverse curve measuring from 200 to 300 mm.; while Tarnowsky, in Russia, finds 86 per cent. among thieves, 85·46 among prostitutes, 84 per cent. among peasant women, 80 per cent. among educated women.

Between the limit of 321–340 Madame Tarnowsky finds only 4 per cent. of educated women, and 1 per cent. of thieves, while Salsotto gives 66 per cent. among assassins, 60 per cent. among infanticides, and 20 per cent. among poisoners.

Marro noted a great preponderance (5 per cent.) among criminals of the least curves (280–310), and a scarcity (7·2 per cent.) of the large ones (331–340). In normal subjects the first are present in 4 per cent. only, the second in 32 per cent. Grimaldi, among the prostitutes observed by him, noted a great prevalence of the longitudinal over the transverse curve.

The anterior circumference was found by Salsotto in the following order: from 292–300, 52 times (22 per cent.); 301–310, 98 times (41 per cent.); 310–328, 87 times (37 per cent.); 292–300, in 25 per cent. of infanticides and poisoners, and in 20·6 per cent. of murderesses (assassins); 301–310 in 48 per cent. of infanticides, in 40 per cent. of assassins, and in 35 per cent. of poisoners; 311–325 in 40 per cent. of poisoners, in 39·4 per cent. of assassins, and in 27 per cent. of infanticides, with a prevalence of higher numbers among murderesses as compared to infanti-

ANTHROPOMETRY OF FEMALE CRIMINALS.

cides. De Albertis found a low, anterior, semi-curve (282) in prostitutes.

14. This small development repeats itself in the cranial diameters furnished by Madame Tarnowsky, which are important because obtained from women of the same country. The results are as follows:

Medium antero-posterior diameter	among educated women		183
,,	,,	in illiterate peasants ..	181
,,	,,	in thieves	153
,,	,,	in prostitutes	178
,,	,,	in homicides...	177
Maximum transverse diameter	in educated women		145·0
,,	,,	in illiterate peasants	144·9
,,	,,	in homicides	144·2
,,	,,	in thieves	143·9
,,	,,	in prostitutes	143·1

Antero-posterior diameter.—According to Madame Tarnowsky and to Marro, the smaller diameters prevail among prostitutes, and above all among female thieves, with a corresponding scarcity of the larger diameters. For instance, we have 165–180 for 42·66 per cent. of prostitutes and 82 per cent. of thieves, as against 25 per cent. of moral peasant women and 20 per cent. of educated women; and, on the other hand, from 183–195 are to be found only in 17·33 per cent. of prostitutes, in 8 per cent. of thieves, as against 35 per cent. of moral peasant women and 50 per cent. of the educated.

Marro's figures are: from 154–175 among 70 per cent. of criminal women and 41 per cent. of normals; with 175–185 for 28·8 per cent. of criminals and 52 per cent. of normals.

Transverse diameter.—The inferiority of prostitutes and still more of thieves to normals is, according to

Madame Tarnowsky, especially apparent in the lesser frequency of the long diameters, as 145–155; the percentage of these figures among prostitutes and thieves being respectively 57·99 and 18, as against 71 and 68 per cent. among peasants and educated women; while Marro states that the superiority of normal women is revealed by the greater frequency among them of the large diameters, such as 145–155, which are found in 50·4 per cent. of criminals and 78 per cent. normals.

Minimum frontal diameter.—In Russia, Madame Tarnowsky found no woman, whether normal, criminal, or prostitute, whose frontal diameter was between 95 and 105; Salsotto, on the other hand, found this measurement in 60 per cent. of poisoners, in 51 per cent. of murderesses (assassins), and in only 40 per cent. of infanticides. Madame Tarnowsky found a minimum frontal diameter of 121 and upwards in 66 per cent. of cultivated women, in 21·17 per cent. of prostitutes, in 8 per cent. of peasant women, and in 6 per cent. of thieves, but never once in any Italian female criminal. Salsotto observed a diameter of 10·6 to 12 in 60 per cent. of infanticides, in 49 per cent. of murderesses, and in 40 per cent. of poisoners.

According to Marro, the maxima from 12 centimeters upwards are found in 19 per cent. of normals, and are wanting in criminals.

The medium smallest frontal diameter among the 30 prostitutes of Modena observed by Riccardi was 106·2, or lower than that of moral women, which was 108·2.

Frontal height.—The minima here, or 30–40, are found in 25 per cent. of infanticides, in 26 per cent. of murderesses, and in 40 per cent. of poisoners; the maxima, or 51–67, are among 45 per cent. of infanticides, 30 per cent. of assassins, and 23 per cent. of poisoners.

In the Bolognese prostitutes the average height is given at 40–70, and in moral women of the same town, at 40–60. In prostitutes the breadth is 100–129, in moral women 95–124.

The proportion between the height of the forehead and that of the face among Bolognese women is as follows: Prostitutes, 32–64; moral, 34–52.

The cephalic index is too ethnical in character for us to attach much value to the results obtained by various observers: we have already noted a marked inclination, amounting to 10 per cent., to the brachycephalic form among Piedmontese female criminals; but Marro found hardly any difference between criminals and normals (the last-named showing 86, and the first 85), except that the lower indexes as far as 77 were found in 2·6 per cent. of criminals and in no normals, while the highest, from 85 upwards, existed in 54 per cent. of criminals and in 20 per cent. of normals.

Both Grimaldi and De Albertis noted a marked number of brachycephali among prostitutes.

Madame Tarnowsky, who is most to be relied upon for ethnical comparisons, gives the media of the cephalic index as almost identical in prostitutes, in thieves, and in moral women, the chief difference being the greater proportion of brachycephali among the first of these three classes.

The figures were as under:—

Cephalic index of	prostitute	...	...	...	...	80·0
,,	,,	thief	...	...	...	...	80·2
,,	,,	peasant	...	...	...	...	79·9
,,	,,	educated	...	...	...	...	79·1

Bizygomatic diameter.—Madame Tarnowsky gives this diameter as between 8·5 and 11·0 in 46 per cent. of thieves, 19 per cent. of peasants, 16 per cent. of educated, and 14 per cent. of prostitutes, all in Russia. In the educated the average is 112; in peasant women it is 111; and rises in prostitutes to 113, and in thieves to 114.

Among the Bolognese prostitutes the bizygomatic diameter was 85–129, with a mean of 113; in moral women the breadth was 101–104, with an average of 102.

But the great development of the facial osseous structure has been already amply demonstrated in our references to heavy jaws and projecting cheek-bones. In Italy, all the criminals examined by Salsotto had wide cheek-bones. He gives the diameter as between 13·1 and 14·0 for 45 per cent. of poisoners, 70 per cent. of infanticides, and 11 per cent. of murderesses; while in Russia Madame Tarnowsky found no women with an equally wide diameter.

In Bologna, prostitutes had a diameter of 104–139 as against 90–133 among women of moral lives (Fornasari).

Bimandibular diameter, &c.—In moral women of Bologna this varies as from 95–99; among prostitutes, as 100–104. The minimum, or 90–100, was observed by Madame Tarnowsky in 75 per cent. of thieves, 50 per cent of educated women, 27 per cent. of peasants, and 19·33 per cent. of prostitutes; in Italy, where comparisons with moral women are wanting, the minima found by Salsotto are in 23 per cent. of infanticides, 15 per cent. of poisoners, and 14 per cent. of murderesses.

The maximum (11·1 to 12·0 in Russia) was observed by Madame Tarnowsky in 4·66 per cent. of prostitutes, and in 4 per cent. both of peasant women and the educated; and by Salsotto in 25 per cent. of murderesses, in 17 per cent. of infanticides, and in 5 per cent. of poisoners.

Marro's figures as regards the diameters of cheek-bones and jaws and the height of the forehead refer to so small a number of subjects that no certain conclusions can be drawn from them; moreover Marro's normals being from the rural classes and his criminals from the population of towns, his respective data cannot be compared; for even among normal peasant women the figures indicate a large diameter of the cheek-bones.

Nevertheless, it may be mentioned that the diameter of the jaws exceeded 11 centimeters in 25 per cent. of criminals as against 15 per cent. of normals.

The bigonial diameter is—

In Russian normals	... ...	99·5
,, prostitutes	... ...	97·8
,, thieves	... ...	99·4
,, homicides	... ...	101·6

The gonio-symphitic diameter is—

In Russian normals	... ...	93·9
,, prostitutes	... ...	94·2
,, thieves	... ...	95·5
,, homicides	... ...	96·6

the highest number being evidently among criminals and prostitutes.

The facial angle is—

In Russian normals	... ...	72°·02
,, prostitutes	... ...	71°·01
,, thieves	... ...	71°·07
,, homicides	... ...	72°·01

15. *Hair.*—The hair of criminals and prostitutes is darker than among normals.

The following comparative table is by Madame Tarnowsky:—

	Russians.		
	100 Moral Women.	100 Thieves.	100 Prostitutes.
Dark hair	42	62	52
Fair hair	58	35	47
Red hair	2.6	3	0·5

Prostitutes appear to have a smaller proportion of dark hair than thieves, because the fair-haired specimens of their class are the most sought after. Marro already, even in his scanty figures, had noted a predominance of fair and red-haired women among the unchaste, and this observation accords with our own. His results were:—

	Criminals.	Normals.
Fair-haired	26 per cent.	12 per cent.
Dark-haired	26 ,,	20 ,,
Red-haired	48 ,,	0 ,,
Chestnut-haired	41 ,,	68 ,,

An unusual quantity of hair is also frequent among criminal women.

Riccardi in a total of 33 prostitutes found 6 with an exaggerated amount of hair, 9 with a moderate quantity, and 4 with wavy hair. Fornasari among 60 found 48 with very abundant hair.

Archæology, indeed, has furnished us with an example of thick, fair hair in Messalina, and records also the abundant tresses of Faustina.

Madame Tarnowsky, on the contrary, found only 13 per cent. of criminals with very thick hair.

Among the women most noticeable for their quantity of hair were Heberzeni, Trossarello, and Madame la Motte. Of the last-named, Samson, the executioner, observed, "The most remarkable thing about her was her abundance of hair."

16. *Iris.*—The intensity of the pigments is still better proved by the dark colour of the eye, which is most frequent in prostitutes and thieves.

The following results are given by Madame Tarnowsky:—

	150 Normals.	Russians. 100 Thieves.	100 Prostitutes.
Dark iris	30 per cent.	39 per cent.	52 per cent.
Blue or grey iris	70 ,,	61 ,,	66 ,,

She remarked that the grey or green irises were strewn in the proportion of 30 per cent. with orange yellow spots.

17. *Wrinkles.*—Taking into account only the deeper wrinkles, I concluded, after examining 158 normals (working-women and peasantry) and 70

criminals, that among the latter class wrinkles are

	14 to 24 years.		25 to 49 years.		50 years & over.	
	Norm. 54. p. c.	Crim. 20. p. c.	Norm. 72. p. c.	Crim. 41. p. c.	Norm. 32. p. c.	Crim. 9. p. c.
Deep frontal, horizontal wrinkles	9·2	25	41·7	53·6	90·6	88·8
Deep fronto-vertical wrinkles	1·8	—	6·9	7·3	40·6	71
Crow's-feet	5	12.5	20	33	78	88·8
Wrinkles under the eyelids	1·8	—	15	14·6	46·6	44·4
Naso-labial wrinkles ...	25·9	25	69·5	63·3	96·7	100
Zygomatic wrinkles ...	—	—	5·5	12·2	28·1	22·2
Goniomental wrinkles...	—	25	36·1	31·7	53·1	44
Labial wrinkles	—	—	6·9	12·2	28·1	44

not more common than among the former. Nevertheless, certain wrinkles, such as the fronto-vertical, the wrinkles on the cheek-bones, crow's-feet, and labial wrinkles are more frequent and deeply marked in criminal women of mature age.

In this connection we may recall the proverbial wrinkles of witches, and the instance of the vile old woman, the so-called *Vecchia dell' Aceto* of Palermo, who poisoned so many persons simply for love of lucre. When already of mature age, the idea of these murders occurred to her on hearing that a man, by means of a certain arseniated vinegar, removed vermin from the heads of children, and she at once saw how with a similar liquid she could kill adults with impunity and at a small cost. The bust (from a photograph politely presented by Comm. Prof. Salinas, Director of the Museum of Palermo) which we possess of this criminal, so full of virile angularities, and above all so deeply wrinkled, with its Satanic leer, suffices of itself to prove that the

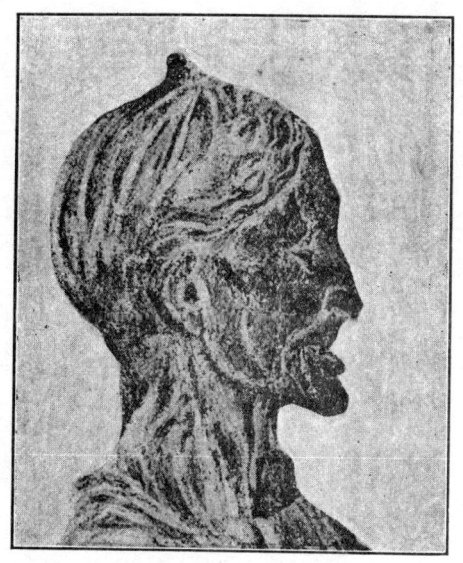

OLD WOMAN OF PALERMO.

To face page 72.]

woman in question was born to do evil, and that, if one occasion to commit it had failed, she would have found others.

This characteristic is wanting among prostitutes.

18. *White hairs.*—Not only is both senile and precocious greyness much more frequent in female than in male criminals, but it is even more common among the former than among normal women, who from our figures appear, contrary to assertions in treatises on the subject, to turn white sooner than men of the criminal class. Nor do these results

	20 to 29 years. p. c.	30 to 34 years. p. c.	35 to 40 years. p. c.	40 to 49 years. p. c.	50 to 59 years. p. c.	60 years. p. c.
200 Normal women of operative and peasant classes	8·1	31	57	84	90	100
80 Criminal women	15	50	74	100	100	100

contradict the theory that greyness is in direct relation to psychical activity, for the female criminal, who is almost always a criminaloid, is less than the male to the emotions of an agitated life; while among normals, on the other hand, the woman grows grey later than the man, because she leads a much more tranquil life, and is much less sensitive and active than he.

19. *Baldness.*—Women do not turn bald more frequently than men, in spite of certain modes of coiffure which more or less spoil the hair, and in spite also of certain special physiological circumstances, such as pregnancy and childbirth, which tend to cause loss of hair. Still, in female criminals baldness is less common than among the normal class.

We find, for instance, the following percentages of baldness in women :—

	20 to 29 years. p. c.	30 to 34 years. p. c.	35 to 40 years. p. c.	40 to 49 years. p. c.	50 to 59 years. p. c.	60 × years. p. c.
200 Normal women (operatives and peasants)...	7	3	18	26	37	45
80 Criminals	4	0	25	10	25	25

20. *Summary.*—It must be confessed that these accumulated figures do not amount to much, but this result is only natural. For if external differentiations between criminal and normal subjects in general are few, they are still fewer in the female than in the male. We saw already from the cranium that stability of type is much greater in the woman, and differentiation much less, even when the skull is anomalous.

The following are our most important conclusions.

Stature, stretch of arms and length of limbs are less in all female criminals than in normals: and, in proportion to the stature, the average weight of prostitutes and murderesses is greater than in moral women.

Prostitutes have the longer hands and bigger calves; while their feet are smaller. Their fingers, however, are less developed than their palms.

Female thieves, and above all prostitutes, are inferior to moral women in cranial capacity and circumference, and their cranial diameters are less; but, on the other hand, their facial diameters are larger, especially in the jaw.

Criminals have the darker hair and eyes, and this

holds good also to a certain extent of prostitutes, in whom fair and red hair now surpasses and now approximates to the normal.

Greyness, rarer in the normal woman (than in man), is more than twice as frequent in the criminal woman, and *vice versâ*, in the latter baldness is *less* common both in youth and maturity ; and the same is true of wrinkles, these being markedly more frequent only in criminals of ripe years.

Little of all this can be positively affirmed of prostitutes, who are painted and made up when not (as is usual) very young; but so far as it is possible to judge, they are as little subject to precocious greyness and baldness as are congenital male criminals.

CHAPTER V

FACIAL AND CEPHALIC ANOMALIES OF FEMALE CRIMINALS.

FOR the sake of brevity we append a table of the principal anomalies in the cephali and faces of female criminals and prostitutes, as observed by us and others. (*See* Table V.)

The prevailing characteristics are thus shown to be:—

Cranial asymmetry.—Present in 26 per cent. of criminals and in 32 per cent. of prostitutes, with special prevalence among female assassins (46 per cent.) and poisoners (50 per cent.). (*See* Plate I., Fig. 18.)

Platycephali are common in 15 per cent. of poisoners and in 2 per cent. of thieves. The average among criminals of all classes is 8 per cent., while among prostitutes the proportion falls to 1·6 per cent. only, which is about the figure of normals. Platycephali, however, are not specifically characteristic. (*See* Plate I., Fig. 14.)

Oxycephali. — The percentages of this peculiarity are:—Among criminals, 13·5 ; among prostitutes,

PHYSIOGNOMY OF RUSSIAN FEMALE OFFENDERS

PLATE I.

To face page 76.]

PHYSIOGNOMY OF RUSSIAN FEMALE OFFENDERS.

PLATE I.

PHYSIOGNOMY OF RUSSIAN FEMALE OFFENDERS.

PLATE I.

PHYSIOGNOMY OF RUSSIAN FEMALE OFFENDERS.

PLATE 1

26·9 ; and among criminals, murderesses stand highest, showing 22 per cent.

Receding foreheads are in the proportion of 11 per cent. in criminals, 12 per cent. in prostitutes, and only 8 per cent. in normals.

Among Russian women the figures were: 14 per cent. for homicides, 10 per cent. for thieves, 16 per cent. for prostitutes, and 2 per cent. for normal women.

Over-jutting brows were found by us in 15 per cent. of cases, by Salsotto in 6 per cent., and among normals in 8 per cent. by the writers; while Madame Tarnowsky observed the feature in 6 per cent. of homicides, in 12 per cent. of thieves, in 10 per cent. of prostitutes, and in 4 per cent. of normals. (*See* Plate I., 2, 14, 17, 20 *bis*; Plate II., 18, 24.)

Cranial anomalies.—Present in 35·5 per cent. of criminals and in 45 per cent. of prostitutes.

Frontal anomalies.—Present in 20 per cent. of female delinquents, in 22 per cent. of prostitutes, and in 6 per cent. of normals. (*See* Plate I., 2, 17, and Plate II., 17.)

Asymmetry of the face.—Present in 7·7 per cent. of delinquents and in 1·8 per cent. of prostitutes.

Enormous lower jaw.—Found in 15 per cent. of delinquents, in 26 per cent. of prostitutes, in 9 per cent. of normals. (*See* especially Plate I., 2, 3, 4, 7, 19, 20; Plate II., 1, 15, 17, 23.)

Projecting cheek-bones.—Found among 19·9 per cent. of criminals, especially murderesses (30 per cent.), among 40 per cent. of prostitutes, and 14 per cent. of normals. (*See* Plate I., 3, 7, 9, 15, 20; Plate II., 2, 3, 4, 6, 7, 8, 16, 17, 23.)

TABLE V.

Physiognomical Anomalies in Criminal Women (from 964 Observations on the Living Subject and 150 on Crania) and on Prostitutes (349 Observations on the Living).

	Normal Woman – Marro	Normal Woman – Lombroso	Crania of normals – Lombroso	Crania of Criminals – Romberg	Crania of Criminals – Lombroso	Photographs – Lombroso	Photographs – Marro	Lombroso and Pasina: Female criminals in general	Lombroso and Pasina: Thieves	Lombroso and Pasina: Infanticides	Lombroso and Pasina: Murderesses	Lombroso and Pasina: Poisoners	Female criminals in general	Thieves	Assassins	Aggressors	Poisoners	Unnatural offences	Swindlers	Incendiaries	Infanticides	Female Criminals observed by Zitino	Criminal Crania studied by Varaglia and Silva	Thieves observed by Lombroso and Ottolenghi	Thieves observed by Tarnowsky	Thieves observed by Marro	Grimaldi	De Albertis	Andronico	Tarnowsky	Lombroso and Ottolenghi	Aver. Female Criminals	Aver. Prostitutes	Normals observed by Roncoroni
Number of observations	25	100	30	25	66	83		122	20	20	61	19	409	90	130	20	20	25	20	4	100	188	60	120	100	100	26	28	230	150	115	26		50
Cranial asymmetry			17	21				40	45	22	46		30	22	46	25	59	12	15		20		12·6	8·44	23	47	23			40·9	4	6·5	32	
?rocephali			0·1						36				8·5	1·1	5·3		10	16			13			2		5	26·9				1·61	13·5		
?cephali		0		1·15									13·5	7·7	5·3	5	15	15·7			17											26·9		
?cephali													6	1·04	22	5	15	4		75	12	7·9									3·22			
?drocephali					6									5·5	15									1·14										
microcephali													1											4										
?rocephali		2											6											18·4			20				24·11	4	26·9	
Exaggerated Brachycephali																																		

nial anomalies ...	—	4	18	—	—	—	40	45	36	—	46	—	70	37·3	93·6	35	90	67·7	20	75	62	—	—	11·7	—	—	
eding forehead ...	—	—	—	5	6·8	—	2	42	10	4·5	1	16	7·5	5·5	5·3	10	5	—	10	—	8	—	—	—	33·98	23	27	73	—			41·3	12	—	35	15	—	33	11	35	35	45
jecting frontal knobs	4	10	19	—	—	15	10	—	—	—	—	5·5	3·8	—	5	—	—	—	—	—	—	—	—	—						10			12	11	12	
ormous frontal sinuses	—	8	19	29	—	15	—	5·8	—	—	—	6·6	10·7	—	5	—	—	—	—	—	—	—	—	—				3·8					9·9			10	
jecting orbital angle of																																				
orehead. ...	16	6	—	7	—	17	—	—	—	—	3·5	19·8	10	15	—	—	—	—	—	10·9	—	65	3·8	—							20	22
ntal anomalies ...	20	8	35	5·4	2·8	13	15	9	8·2	15·3	12·1	8	25	20	—	—	4	—	10	—	—	—	1	15	1	15	1·74			27	33	68·8			40	17	19	9·2	77
ial asymmetry ...	—	—	—	45	—	—	—	—	—	—	5	—	—	—	—	4	—	—	—	—	—	—	12	15·2	42	52	—	19	99	9·9	9·2	99	1·8
at development of lower																																				
aw ...	12	6·3	10	36	—	15	9·8	4·5	9·8	—	4·6	10·5	5	—	—	—	—	—	15	11·35	77	—	—						26·2	15	26
jecting cheek-bones...	8	6·9	—	12	—	15	14·7	9	1·4	—	4·6	—	—	—	—	—	—	—	—	—	—	—	—						40	17	19·9	40
jecting ears ...	4	—	—	3	—	—	—	—	—	—	17	8·8	5	—	—	—	—	—	12·5	46	—	—						12	9·2	99
omalies of the ear	16	35	—	6	—	8	10	10	3·3	5·5	3·2	5	5	5	—	—	—	—	—	33	—	—						52	8·5	
abismus ...	—	—	—	8	—	—	3	—	—	—	2	10	10	—	4	—	—	—	—	23·7	—						6	7	13
eolar prognathism	4	4	—	22	—	—	9·8	—	—	7·5	5·5	10	15	—	7	—	—	—	—	—	—							17·5	11·8
ile physiognomy	4	—	—	—	—	—	4·5	—	3·3	1	—	5·6	10·7	—	4	—	—	—	—	—	4	5	—	—						11·8	4
ocious physiognomy	2	10	—	—	—	—	14·7	—	—	—	3·3	—	—	—	—	—	—	—	—	—	—	—	—								
otic physiognomy	—	2	—	—	—	—	—	—	—	1·5	—	—	—	—	—	—	—	—	—	—	—	—	—								
ngolian physiognomy	—	4	—	—	—	—	4·1	—	—	—	—	—	—	—	—	—	—	—	24	—	—			16				10	13	7
malous nose ...	4	—	—	14	—	15	15	18·3	—	5	—	9·6	10	—	5	—	—	—	—	—	—					7			41	16	28
n lip	2	—	—	—	—	—	15	10	9	—	—	14	15	—	—	—	—	—	—	—	—									
riness	—	7	—	—	—	—	13	36	10	5	—	—	—	—	—	—	—	—	—	—	—							9	
cocious wrinkles	11	11	—	—	—	—	—	—	—	2·3	—	—	—	—	—	—	—	—	—	—	—									
tooing	—	—	—	—	—	—	—	—	—	—	—	—	—	—	—	—	—	—	—	34	—	—				40·92				
at occipital protuberance																																				
gnathism and facial																																				
symmetry	—	—	—	—	—	—	—	—	—	—	—	—	—	—	—	—	—	—	—	59	—	—	—	—						41·24

Anomalous ears.—Gradenigo gives a complete table of the ears in 245 criminals as compared to 14,000 normal women :—

	Normal.	Criminal.
Regular external ear (ala)	65 per cent.	54 per cent.
Sessile ear	12 ,,	20 ,,
Scaphoid fossa prolonged to lobe	8·2 ,,	21·2 ,,
Projecting ears	3·1 ,,	5·3 ,,
Prominent anti-helix	11·5 ,,	14·2 ,,
Darwin's tubercle	3 ,,	2·9 ,,

From which the conclusion is that among criminals the anomalies are more than twice as frequent, with the exception only of Darwin's tubercle, which is, however, abnormal in Fig. 10, Plate I.

Projecting ears. — Proportion, among criminals observed by us 9·2 per cent., among prostitutes 9·9 per cent., normals 6 per cent. As regards delinquents the peculiarity is most frequent in swindlers (17 per cent.), in wounders (10·5 per cent.), and in poisoners (15 per cent.). (*See* Plate I., 1, 2, 2 *bis*, 8, 13, 14, 17 ; Plate II., 8, 12, 22, 23.)

Strabismus.—The percentage among delinquents is 8·5, among prostitutes 5, and normals 4 ; while as regards criminals the greater frequency is in thieves (16 per cent.) and in poisoners (10 per cent.).

Alveolar prognathism.—Proportion among delinquents 7 per cent., assassins standing highest (12 per cent.), and among prostitutes 13 per cent.

Virile physiognomy.—This feature shows a percentage of 11·8 in delinquents, 4 in prostitutes. (*See* Plate I., 6, 6 *bis*, 20, 20 *bis*, and note how, especially in profile, the peculiarity gives a hard, cruel look to faces which on a front view are sometimes hand-

FACIAL ANOMALIES OF FEMALE CRIMINALS. 81

some; for instance, 2, 3, 8, 11, 12, 16, 19. For prostitutes, *see* Plate II., 21, 24.)

A crooked nose was found by us in 25 per cent. of criminals, in 8 per cent. of prostitutes (Plate I., 1, 2 *bis*, 5, 12).

A flat nose was noted in 40 per cent. of normals, in 12 per cent. of homicides, in 20 per cent. of thieves, and in 12 per cent. of prostitutes. (*See* Plate I., 10, 19; Plate II., 8, 12, 13, 18.)

Mongolian physiognomy.—Found in 13 per cent. of criminals and in 7 per cent. of prostitutes.

Asymmetry of the face is wanting in prostitutes. The proportion among thieves was 10 per cent. only, and in homicides 6 per cent.

Anomalous teeth.—Observed in 16 per cent. of delinquents, in 28 per cent. of prostitutes, in 8 per cent. of normals. In Russia the figures were 40 per cent. in homicides, 58 per cent. in thieves, 78 per cent. in prostitutes, and 2 per cent. in normals.

CHAPTER VI.

FURTHER ANOMALIES.

THE list of characteristics of degeneration is not yet complete.

1. *Moles.*—Hairy moles form a feature that has been but little studied, but must be added to those which mark degeneration in the female subject. It is a kind of indirect supplement of the beard, by which the female approximates to the male. We have noted it among normals in 14 per cent., among criminals in 6 per cent., among prostitutes in 41 per cent.

Gurrieri found it, however, only in 8 per cent. of the latter. Zola mentions the moles of Nana and those of the profligate Countess, her worthy rival.

2. *Hairiness.*—Among 234 prostitutes one of the present writers, like Ardù, found a virile quantity of hair in 15 per cent., as against 5–6 per cent. in normals and 5 per cent. in criminals.

On the other hand, down which is present in 6 per cent. of prostitutes in Russia and in 2 per cent. of homicides is wanting in thieves and in normals in that country. In Italy it was found in 11 per cent.

of normals, in 36 per cent. of homicides, and in 13 per cent. of thieves and infanticides.

In No. 7 of Plate I. it is seen to form almost a beard.

3. Madame Tarnowsky observed yet another series of anomalies, which the writers did not find in their subjects, and which seem to be characteristic of Russian women. This is a cleft palate, which she found among 8 per cent. of normals and 14 per cent. of homicides, among 18 per cent. of thieves and 12 per cent. of prostitutes. She remarked asymmetry of the eyebrows (of which there is a striking example in No. 18, Plate I.) among 4 per cent. of normals, 40 per cent. of homicides, 20 per cent. of thieves, and 44 per cent. of prostitutes.

4. *Masseter muscles.*—Madame Tarnowsky found another peculiar feature in 6 per cent. of homicides and in 4 per cent. of thieves (while it was wanting in both prostitutes and normals). This was an unusual development of the masseter muscles, which was doubtless to be connected with the exaggerated size of the jaws.

Yet another, still more singular and atavistic, peculiarity which she noted in two criminals, was hypertrophy of the muscles of the neck, such as may be seen in large quadrupeds. (*See* Plate I., 8.)

5. *Prehensile foot.*—From observations made by Ottolenghi and Carrara it seems that the prehensile foot in normal women is almost three times as frequent as in normal men, being as 11 to 28. In female criminals it is only a little rarer than in

normals (24). In prostitutes the proportion (42) is almost double that observed among normals.

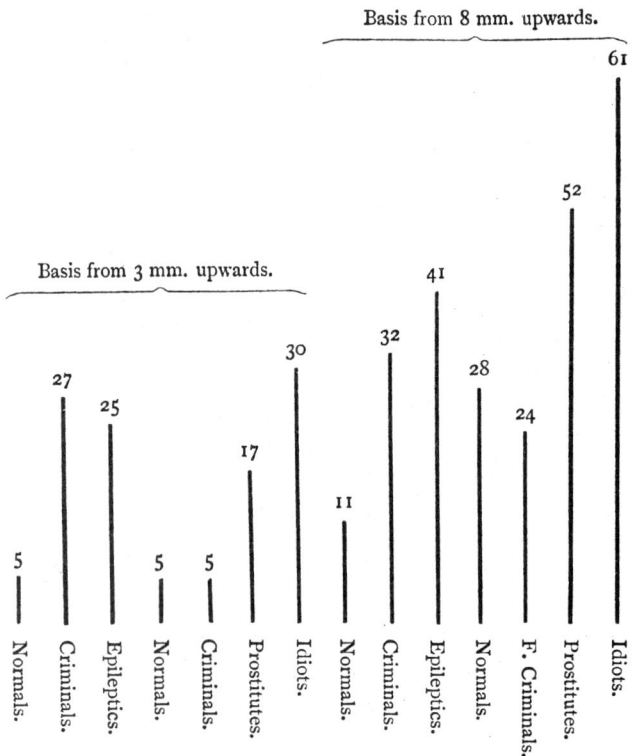

In one out of 60 prostitutes Gurrieri found that the second and third toe coalesced as far as the small phalange.

6. *The larynx of prostitutes offers several anomalies.* —Professor Masini in 50 prostitutes [1] found 15

[1] "Arch. di psich.," xiv., fasc i.–ii.

with deep voices, and vocal chords that were large in proportion to the size of the laryngeal opening. Twenty-seven had still more masculine voices, with high bursts of sound followed by low, deep tones.

On external observation the larynxes of these women were of normal movement in all. Chiefly remarkable was the exaggerated size of the wings of the thyroid, and a very flat thyroid angle. To this external conformation the glottis corresponded in width; the vocal chords were thick and close together; the vocal tubercle was marked, and the bases of the arytenoid cartilages very wide.

In each case the larynx resembled a man, thus showing once again the virility of face and cranium characteristic of the prostitute class.

7. *Summary.*—Almost all anomalies occur more frequently in prostitutes than in female offenders, and both classes have a larger number of the characteristics of degeneration than normal women.

Only the asymmetrical face, strabismus, virile and Mongolian types of physiognomy are more common among criminals than among prostitutes; while outstanding ears are only a little less frequent in the former than in the latter class.

Prostitutes are almost quite free from wrinkles, hypertrophy of the masseters, platycephali, crooked noses and asymmetrical faces; what they have more frequently are moles, hairiness, prehensile feet, the virile larynx, large jaws and cheek-bones, and above all anomalous teeth. That is to say they show fewer of the anomalies which produce ugliness, but are marked by more of the signs of degeneration.

If we compare infanticides who, from the very nature of their offence, depart least from the type of normals, with other delinquents, we find percentages such as are recorded in Table VI. (*see* following page). They are least subject to asymmetry, to strabismus, to virility of face, to anomalous teeth and cheek-bones, but have, more frequently than others, peculiarities of the ears and hydrocephalic heads. Female poisoners, thieves, and assassins are most remarkable for cranial asymmetry and strabismus; while the female assassin has most often a virile and Mongolian type of face.

Female homicides and poisoners offer most examples of cranial depressions and diasthema of the teeth; and incendiaries are most characterised by flat and deformed noses.

Homicides, poisoners, and incendiaries have the more prominent cheek-bones, and infanticides resemble them in showing the largest number of asymmetrical faces and exaggerated jaws; but on the whole the type of murderesses (whether assassins or poisoners) is more degenerate than that of infanticides.

TABLE VI.

	100 Infanticides observed by Salsotto.	Infanticides (photographs obtained by Tarnowsky).	20 Poisoners observed by Salsotto	Poisoners (photographs obtained by Tarnowsky).	130 murderesses (assassins) observed by Salsotto.	Homicides (photographs obtained by Tarnowsky).	20 Aggressors observed by Salsotto.	25 Unnatural Criminals (Salsotto).	20 Swindlers (Salsotto).	90 Thieves (Salsotto).	Incendiaries (photographs obtained by Tarnowsky).
	p.c.	p.c.	p.c.	p.c.	p.c.	p.c.	p.c.	p.c.	p.c.	p.c.	p.c.
Less numerous among Infanticides.											
Cranial asymmetry	20	—	50	—	46·1	—	25	127	15	22	—
Eurignathism	9	—	10	—	12	—	15	16	—	4·4	12·5
Strabism	7·5	0·0	15	4·5	8·8	7·4	—	—	20	16·5	12·5
Thin lips	7	0·0	5	4·5	15·2	—	5	4	5	—	—
Virile physiognomy	2	—	5	—	10·7	—	10	—	—	—	—
Mongolian physiognomy	4	0·0	5	—	8	18·5	—	—	—	—	37·5
Cranial depressions	—	—	—	—	—	—	—	—	—	—	25
Goître	3	0·0	15	22·72	4·6	44·4	—	—	—	—	37·5
Diasthema of teeth	—	0·0	—	18·18	22·2	40·7	—	—	—	—	12·5
Sessile ear	—	22·2	—	40·9	—	14·8	—	—	—	—	37·5
Flattened nose	—	22·2	—	36·3	—	22·2	—	—	—	—	12·8
Crooked nose	—	0	—	13·6	—	14·8	—	—	—	—	—
Prognathous jaw	—	11·11	—	9·09	—	8·1	—	—	—	—	12·5
Narrow palate	—	11·11	—	9·09	—	22·2	—	—	—	—	—
Prominent occipital bump	—	0·0	—	9·09	—	—	—	—	—	—	—
Prominent cheek-bones	—	11·11	—	13·63	—	—	—	—	—	—	—
Equally numerous, or with only small and uncertain diversity.											
Oxicephalic	17	—	15	—	22·3	—	—	16	—	—	—
Platycephalic	13	11·11	15	—	5·3	—	10	4	5	17	13·63
Platycephalic ears	10	55	15	54	4·6	7·4	—	—	—	—	37·5
Facial asymmetry	4	22·2	25	4·5	8	37	—	—	—	—	—
Receding forehead	—	11·11	—	13·6	—	14·8	5	15	5	—	12·5
Enormous jaw	—	—	—	—	—	7·4	—	—	—	—	—
More numerous among Infanticides.											
Hydrocephalic	12	11·11	—	—	1·5	37	—	—	—	5·5	—
Deformed ears	—	33·3	—	25	—	25·9	—	—	—	—	9·09

CHAPTER VII.

*PHOTOGRAPHS OF CRIMINALS AND PROSTI-
TUTES.*

ANYBODY wishing to observe with his own eyes the anomalies we have detailed will derive assistance from Plates I., II., III., which contain photographs of French and Russian prostitutes and delinquents.

If asked why we have chosen these examples from distant countries, we can but reply that, beyond not finding in any other European land a co-operation so intelligent as that afforded by Madame Tarnowsky, we are also hampered by juridical considerations.

Among the most ridiculous of the prohibitions obtaining in Italy, or rather in the Italian bureaucracy, which is certainly not the first in Europe, is the absolute impossibility of measuring, studying, or photographing the worst criminals once they have been condemned.

So long as there is a presumption of innocence, so long as these persons are only suspected or accused, one can discredit them in every way, and hold them up to publicity by recording their answers to their judges.

But once it is admitted beyond question that

they are reprobates, once the prison doors have closed for good upon them—oh, then they become sacred; and woe to him who touches, woe to him who studies them!

Consumptive patients, pregnant women, may be manipulated, even to their hurt, by thousands of students for the good of science; but criminals—Heaven forefend!

When one of the writers wished to publish photographs of male criminals in his "Uomo Delinquente," he was driven to the German prison "album"; and the difficulties thrown in his way by the Italian authorities were doubled in the case of female offenders and prostitutes, whose sense of shame it was considered necessary to respect in every way.

In Russian prisons Madame Tarnowsky was afforded every facility, and after making a complete study of the body and mind of the delinquents, she forwarded us their photographs.

1. *Female criminals.*—We will first take 5 homicides, of whom the two first have the true type of their class. (*See* Plate I.)

The first, aged 40, killed her husband with reiterated blows of a hatchet, while he was skimming the milk, then threw his body into a recess under the stairs, and during the night fled with the family money and her own trinkets. She was arrested a week later and confessed her crime. This woman was remarkable for the asymmetry of her face; her nose was hollowed out, her ears projecting, her brows more fully developed than is usual in a woman, her jaw enormous with a lemurian appendix.

No. 2, aged 60. Was constantly ill-treated by her husband, whom she finally joined with her son in strangling, hanging him afterwards so as to favour the idea of suicide.

Here again we have asymmetry of the face, breadth of jaw, enormous frontal sinuses, numerous wrinkles, a hollowed-out nose, a very thin upper lip, with deep-set eyes wide apart, and wild in expression.

No. 3, aged 21. Was married against her will, ill-treated by her husband, whom she killed, after a night altercation, with a hatchet while he slept.

In her we find only a demi-type. Her ears stand out, she has big jaws and cheek-bones, and very black hair, besides other anomalies which do not show in the photograph, such as gigantic canine teeth and dwarf incisors.

No. 4, aged 44. Strangled her husband by agreement with her lover, and threw him into a ditch. She denied her crime. Hollowed-out nose, black hair, deep-set eyes, big jaw. Demi-type.

No. 5, aged 50. A peasant. She killed her brother at supper, so as to inherit from him. She denied her guilt persistently. Was condemned, together with her hired accomplices, to twenty years' penal servitude. She had black hair, grey eyes, diasthema of the teeth, a cleft palate, precocious and profound wrinkles, thin lips, and a crooked face. Demi-type.

Passing now to poisoners, we find the following to be the most remarkable out of twenty-three:—

No. 6, aged 36. Of a rich family, with an epileptic mother, and a father addicted to alcohol. She poisoned her husband with arsenic after sixteen years of married life. Nose hollowed out and club-shaped, large jaws and ears, squint eyes, weak reflex action of left patella. She confessed nothing. Character resolute and devout. Type.

No. 7, aged 34. Also poisoned her husband with arsenic; also denied her guilt. An enormous under jaw. On close examination displayed gigantic incisors, and down so long as to resemble a beard. Demi-type.

No. 8, aged 64. Poisoned her son's wife and the mother of the same. Deep wrinkles, ears much higher than the level of the brows. A singularity is the size of the neck-muscles, exaggerated as in oxen. Thin lips, and a cleft palate. Demi-type.

No. 9, a peasant, aged 47. Poisoned her daughter-in-law because of inability to work. Fluent in speech, never confessed the crime. Asymmetrical face, oblique eyes (a feature, however, which might be ethnological), huge, unequal jaws, small ears, nose club-shaped and hollowed out. On a near view she displayed big canine teeth, and a great parieto-occipital depression. Her children like her grandfather were epileptic. Type.

No. 10, aged 20. Attempted to poison her husband, an old man, who treated her ill. Darwin's lobule was enormously developed in her ear, as may be seen even from the photograph. Hydrocephalic forehead, nose hollowed out and club-shaped, large, unequal jaws, eyes and hair black. Type.

No. 11, aged 35. Poisoned her daughter-in-law, for an unknown reason, with some medicine. Fair hair, asymmetrical face, overlapping teeth. Guilt confessed.

Now we come to the incendiaries, of whom there are 10, four of a striking type.

No. 12. Set fire to the village palisades to revenge herself on some malignant gossips. A large nose, thin lips, lowering expression, with incisors replaced by molars. Type.

No. 13, aged 63. Sets fire to a neighbour's house because of a quarrel about money. Denied the offence. Defective teeth, big, feline eyes, very large ears, asymmetry of eyebrows. Demi-type.

No. 14, aged 25. Set fire, in concert with her husband, to a neighbour's house out of revenge. She accused her husband and denied her own complicity. Many wrinkles, projecting parietal bones, big ears and jaws, low forehead. Demi-type.

No. 15, aged 41. A peasant. Set fire to nine houses out of revenge; pretended to have done it while drunk. Very ferocious countenance, asymmetrical, with enormous ears and jaws. Sullen, very black eyes, fair hair, diasthema of the incisors, narrow arch of palate. Type.

No. 16, aged 45. Convicted more than once as a receiver, who had twice hidden convicts in her house. Crooked face and teeth, hollowed-out nose, large, prognathous face, enormous superciliary arches.

Out of 9 infanticides, 3 presented the salient type.

No. 17, aged 60. Killed a newborn babe to save her daughter's reputation. Cut the infant into pieces and hid it. Confessed nothing. A strong character. Many wrinkles, enormous cheek-bones, ears, and frontal sinuses. Right side of face higher than the left. Forehead receding as in savages. Canine teeth gigantic and badly placed. Sunken eyes, brownish-green in colour.

No. 18, aged 60. Assisted her daughter to drown the latter's newborn child; then afterwards accused the daughter, in consequence of a quarrel about a lover whom the two women shared.

Physiognomy relatively good, in spite of the subject's licentious tendencies which age could not eradicate. Nothing anomalous beyond the hollowed-out nose and very wrinkled skin. The face, however, though it does not appear so in the photograph, was really asymmetrical, and the woman had the cleft palate and fleshy lips which betray a luxurious disposition.

No. 19, aged 19, the domestic servant of a priest, had a child, of which the father was a stable-boy. Driven out of every house, she killed her child by beating it on the frozen ground. Crooked face, a hollowed-out nose, big ears and jaws, incisors overlapping.

Finally comes a female brigand—No. 20, aged 25. Was the companion in arms of a band of brigands, one of whom was her lover. A hollowed-out nose, large jaws and ears, a virile physiognomy; and in her also there is congenital division of the palate.

Many may find that after all these faces are not horrible, and I agree, so far, that they appear infinitely less repulsive when compared with corresponding classes among the men whose portraits were reproduced by us from the "Atlas de L'Homme Criminel." Among some of the females there is even a ray of beauty, as in Nos. 19 and 20; but when this beauty exists it is much more virile than feminine.

To understand this at once, let the reader look at the lower profile in Nos. 20 *bis*, 6 and 6 *bis*, and then even the most inexperienced will see how hard, cruel, and masculine are these lines, which yet are not wanting in grace.

It is useful also to remark the physiognomical resemblance among the most different criminals. Nos. 6, 10, 9, and 3 look like members of the same family. And let anybody compare these with the few French thieves reproduced by Macé[1] (Plate III.), and he will see how little race can do; for the French women seem Russians, and the Russians French. No. 2, for instance, in Plate III., in her jaws and long face, resembles No. 7 in Plate I., who is a Russian; Nos. 4 and 8 are like the sisters of Nos. 2 and 9, Russians, having the same oblique eyes, big, hollowed-out noses, and precocious wrinkles; while No. 9, Plate III., resembles No. 20, Plate I. All have the same repulsive, virile air, the same big, sensual lips, &c.

The French women, however, are infinitely more typical and uglier, and here I would remark that the more refined a nation is, the further do its criminals differ from the average. It is, for instance, well known in Russia that among Tartar criminals the depraved type is less striking than in the Russians, especially those who are natives of Moscow and St. Petersburg (Kennan's "Siberia," ii.).

The photographs (*see* Plate III.) chosen haphazard from the note-books of Macé (a police official who was certainly unbiased and quite ignorant of criminal anthropology) only confirm our conclusions; for there

[1] "Mon Musée Criminel," Paris, 1890, p. 148.

are but three out of all the examples, namely, Nos. 1, 3, and 7, who show either a small number of abnormal features (such as big ears and lower jaws, very black hair, strong brows, and coarse full lips), or else show them to a limited degree.

Among the rest of the specimens eight or nine anomalies are present, and the type is often complete.

Note, in No. 2, the immense jaws, thick lips, crooked face, the oblique, squinting, cruel eyes; in No. 6 the marked strabismus, the sessile ear, the asymmetrical face; in Nos. 4 and 5 a repetition of these peculiarities; and in No. 8 the flat, crooked nose, low forehead, and slanting eyes. In every instance the jaws are huge. The types are singularly virile. Nos. 2, 4, 5, 8, and 9 are striking examples, having the bodies of women, but all the air of brutal men: whom they resemble sometimes, even in their dress.

Nos. 12 and 13 are German women, whose vertical wrinkles and thin lips seem to me to mark them out as thieves.

A typical assassin is No. 14, also a German, with her still, glassy eyes, big jaw, and masculine aspect.

Characteristic again is No. 10 (Plate III.), a certain Z., first a prostitute, then a thief, finally a murderess, who killed her guest and calumniated her benefactor, but was absolved on her trial. For, although handsome at first sight, she presents, nevertheless, all the features which I consider typically criminal: immensely thick, black hair, a receding forehead, overjutting brows, and an exaggerated frontal angle, such as one notes in savages and monkeys; while the jaws and lip—indeed her whole face is essentially virile.

The same may be said of the Italian female brigand (No. 11), who betrays the type not so much in her oblique glance and heavy jaw, as in her long face and masculine physiognomy, so that if she had dressed as a man she could have been taken for one, like Gabrielle Bompard.

The last-named, whose photograph is given, exhibits, as Brouardel, Ballet and Motet correctly remarked,[1] all the characteristics, generally rare in women, of the born criminal. Her stature was 1 metre 46; her hips and breasts rudimentary, and she consequently looked so masculine that she was able, when dressed as a man, to accompany Eyraud everywhere without being recognised. She had thick hair, abnormal and precocious wrinkles, a livid pallor, a short, hollowed-out nose, a heavy jaw. Above all, she had an asymmetrical face, and Mongolian eurignathism.

Still more typically homicidal and lascivious, in my opinion, is the female criminal Berland.[2] Here we have sunken eyes, a receding forehead, a small head, sessile ears, numerous deep, precocious wrinkles, thick, crooked lips, a flat, crooked nose, which curved outwards, a receding chin, and a virile physiognomy (Figs. 7, 8).

Talmeyr (*Sur le Banc*) has painted a veritable band of assassins and thieves, of which the leader was

[1] "Archives d'Anthropologie Criminelle," Lyons, 1891.
[2] I owe these two portraits to the kindness of Prince Roland Bonaparte, who possesses one of the finest anthropological collections in Europe, and who had the likenesses done specially for me.

[face page 96.]   GABRIELLE BOMPARD

a working woman, who was always drunk, had corrupted her own son, led the most profligate life, and little by little had turned all the men she had to do with, her son not excepted, into a gang of murderers.

Another woman, Thomas by name (Figs. 9, 10), was profligate and drunken, besides habitually practising abortion as a profession. She always fell into a dipso-epileptic state after accomplishing her crime. She resembled Nos. 4 and 8, Plate III., and was remarkable for facial asymmetry, sessile, protruding ears, a crooked nose, thin, crooked lips, and many wrinkles.

These two photographs give a very good idea of the criminal type in women, which evidently is less brutal than the corresponding type in the male offender.

Very often, too, in women, the type is disguised by youth with its absence of wrinkles and the plumpness which conceals the size of the jaw and cheek-bones, thus softening the masculine and savage features.

Then when the hair is black and plentiful (as in No. 10, Plate III.), and the eyes are bright, a not unpleasing appearance is presented. In short, let a female delinquent be young and we can overlook her degenerate type, and even regard her as beautiful; the sexual instinct misleading us here as it does in making us attribute to women more of sensitiveness and passion than they really possess. And in the same way, when she is being tried on a criminal charge, we are inclined to excuse, as noble impulses of passion, acts which arise from the most cynical calculations.

For this reason many will hardly agree with us in finding the criminal type in No. 10, Plate V., nor yet in Messalina, who, all flattered though she was by contemporary writers, yet offers many of the features of the criminal and born prostitute—having a low forehead, very thick, wavy hair, and a heavy jaw.

Magnan (*see* "Actes du 2ᵉ Congrès d'Anthropologie Criminelle," Paris, 1889) mentions the following examples, as showing the absence of the type peculiar to born criminals.

Margherita, the first of the two, must be admitted not to show, on a casual view, the usual characteristics of degeneration; but when one learns that she is only 12 years of age, one can but feel surprise at her unusual precocity, for her physiognomy is that of a woman of twenty. She has very strong jaws and cheek-bones, sessile ears, hypertrophy of the middle incisors, atrophy of the lateral teeth, and dulness of the sense of touch. She is, in short, the complete type, not of a born criminal, but of a prostitute, and yet Magnan mentions her as completely non-typical!

We learn that her fits of anger were violent; that she broke everything, threatened her mother, stole, and incited her brother to steal. She used to bite her little brother without any motive, and putting a pin between her teeth would invite him to kiss her. Her memory was good. What chiefly distinguished her were sexual disorders, and especially an invincible tendency to onanism. "I would be glad not to do it," she said to her mother, "but I cannot help myself."

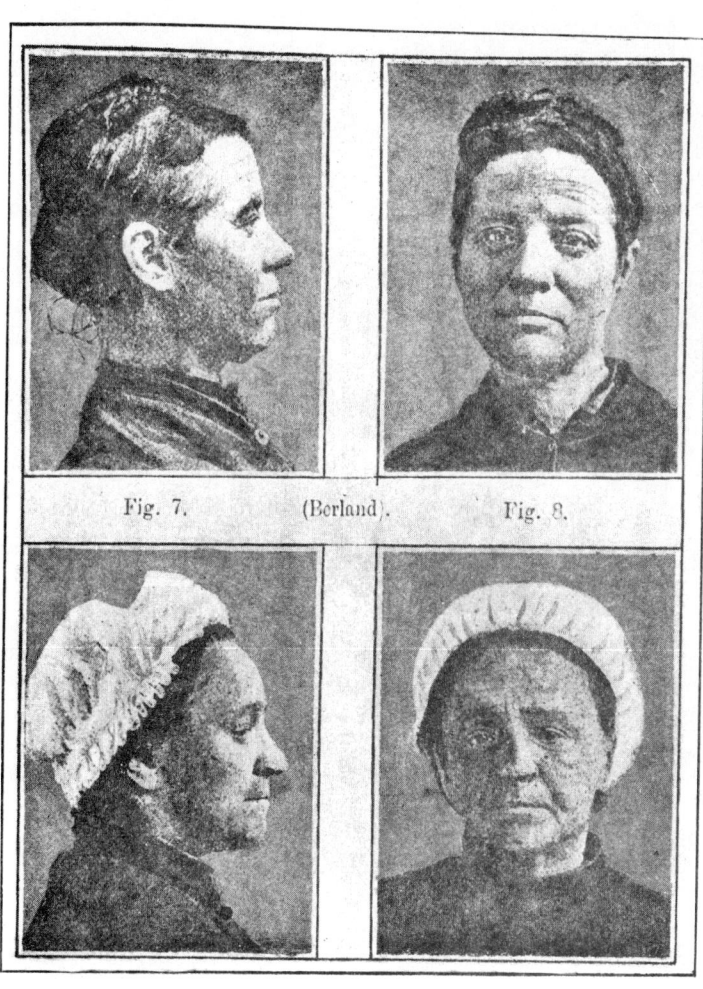

Fig. 7. (Borland). Fig. 8.

Fig. 9. (Thomas.) Fig. 10.

MESSALINA.

To face page 98.]

All medical remedies were useless. At 11 years of age she underwent chloridectomy, and the bandages were hardly removed when the old practices recommenced.

Let us take the next example, that of a born thief.

Louise C. (Magnan writes of her), aged 9, was the daughter of a mad father, always in a condition of sexual excitement. She was of weak intelligence; her instincts had always been bad, her conduct turbulent, and her mind incapable of concentration.

At three she was a thief, and laid hands on her mother's money, on articles in shops, on everything, in short, that came in her way. At five she was arrested and conveyed to the police-office, after a determined resistance. Her habits were vagabond and unruly. She shrieked, tore off her stockings, threw her dolls into the gutter, lifted up her skirts in the street.

Magnan asserts that she has no morbid peculiarity of face; but on looking at her photograph (Fig. 13), one perceives that, although only nine years old, she offers the exact type of the born criminal. Her physiognomy is Mongolian, her jaws and cheek-bones are immense; the frontal sinuses strong, the nose flat, with a prognathous under-jaw, asymmetry of face, and above all, precocity and virility of expression. She looks like a grown woman—nay, a man.

Precocity and virility of aspect is the double characteristic of the criminal-woman, and serves more than any other feature to destroy and mask her type.

2. *Prostitutes.* — With the aid of Madame Tar-

nowsky we have examined 100 prostitutes, all from Moscow, and all aged from 18 to 20 years. We do not undertake to say that among them there are no Germans and no Jewesses; but the greater number are Russians from Moscow. (*See* Plate II.)

Contrarily to criminals, these women are relatively, if not generally, beautiful; still among them there is not wanting the type which we are accustomed to regard as the criminal one; but it is only found in 10 per cent. of the examples, being especially marked in Nos. 18, 23, 16, 2, 3, 10. In 15 per cent. we have only a half-type; and in all the examples there are the characteristics of madness as well as of criminality. Observe Nos. 17, 18, 19, 22, 23, where the wild eyes and perturbed countenance, together with facial asymmetry, recall women seen in asylums for the insane, especially the maniacal cases.

The faces of these women are singularly monotonous as compared to those of criminals. Nos. 1, 2, 3, 4, 6, 8, 12, and 14, seem all to have the same face, the same jaws, cheek-bones, and hair.

Some of the photographs are quite pretty. No. 25 might be called a Russian Helen, and No. 20 is very handsome in spite of her hard expression. The first fifteen might pass in the streets for beauties; and indeed our more fashionable *cocottes* have exactly the same type. Ninon de Lenclos and Marion were justly celebrated for their beauty.

This absence of ill-favouredness and want of typical criminal characteristics will militate with many against our contention that prostitutes are after all equivalents of criminals, and possess the same qualities

To face page 100.] MARGHERITA. LOUISE.

PHYSIOGNOMY OF FALLEN WOMEN, RUSSIAN

PLATE II

PHYSIOGNOMY OF FALLEN WOMEN, RUSSIAN.

PLATE II.

PHYSIOGNOMY OF FALLEN WOMEN, RUSSIAN.

PLATE II.

PHYSIOGNOMY OF FALLEN WOMEN, RUSSIAN

in an exaggerated form. But in addition to the fact that true female criminals are much less ugly than their male companions, we have in prostitutes women of great youth, in whom the *beauté du diable*, with its freshness, plumpness, and absence of wrinkles, disguises and conceals the betraying anomalies.

Moreover, most people do not find ugliness in the black, thick hair (Nos. 1 to 8, 21 and 22), outstanding nose (Nos. 1, 2, 9, 11, 12, 16, 17, 18, 21, 23, 24), strong jaw (Nos. 1 to 15, 17, 21, 23), hard, spent glance, which we have pronounced to be characteristics of degeneration, and which distinguish all these examples except Nos. 16, 21, and 22, with their wild air, and Nos. 5 and 28 with their beautiful eyes. And yet another thing to be remembered is, that the profession of these women necessitates a comparative absence of peculiarities which, when existing, excite disgust and repulsion, and require as much as possible to be artificially concealed. Most certainly the art of making up, imposed by their trade on all these unfortunates, disguises or hides many characteristic features which criminals exhibit openly. And it may happen, therefore, that we are only permitted to see abundant hair, black eyes, and absence of wrinkles, where acquaintance with reality would reveal the exact opposite.

Again, if external anomalies be rare in prostitutes, internal ones, such as overlapping teeth, a divided palate, &c., are more common among them than among female criminals; and male offenders offer a corresponding phenomenon in the superior personal attractiveness of swindlers and forgers to homicides or assassins, who naturally do not require beauty as an aid to the accomplishment of their special crimes.

Where delicacy of mien and a benevolent expression are useful, however, we find them—a truly Darwinian trait. But even the handsomest female offenders have invariably strong jaws and cheek-bones, and a masculine aspect. These peculiarities are shared by *cocottes*, among all of whom there is a family resemblance so marked as to merge the differences between Russian prostitutes and the unfortunates who flaunt in fine equipages, or wander in rags through the streets of Italian towns. And when youth vanishes, the jaws, the cheek-bones, hidden by adipose tissue, emerge, salient angles stand out, and the face grows virile, uglier than a man's; wrinkles deepen into the likeness of scars, and the countenance, once attractive, exhibits the full degenerate type which early grace had concealed.

PHYSIOGNOMY OF FRENCH, GERMAN AND RUSSIAN FEMALE OFFENDERS.

PLATE III.

PHYSIOGNOMY OF FRENCH, GERMAN AND RUSSIAN FEMALE OFFENDERS.

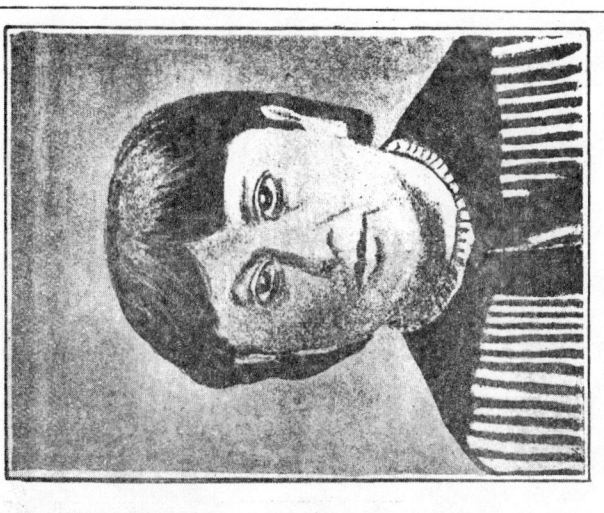

PLATE III.

[To face page 102.]

PHYSIOGNOMY OF FRENCH, GERMAN AND RUSSIAN FEMALE OFFENDERS.

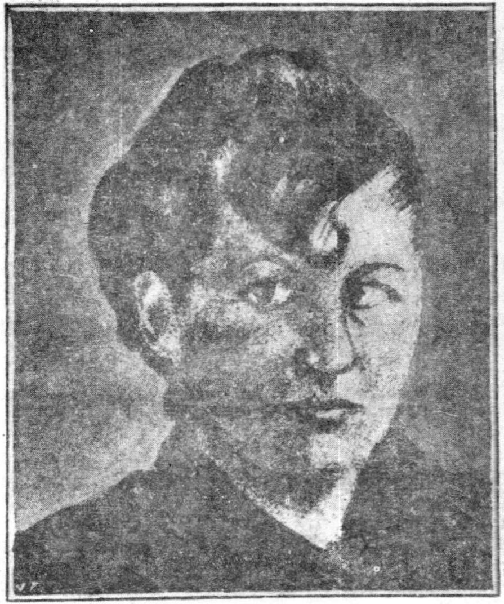

N. 6.

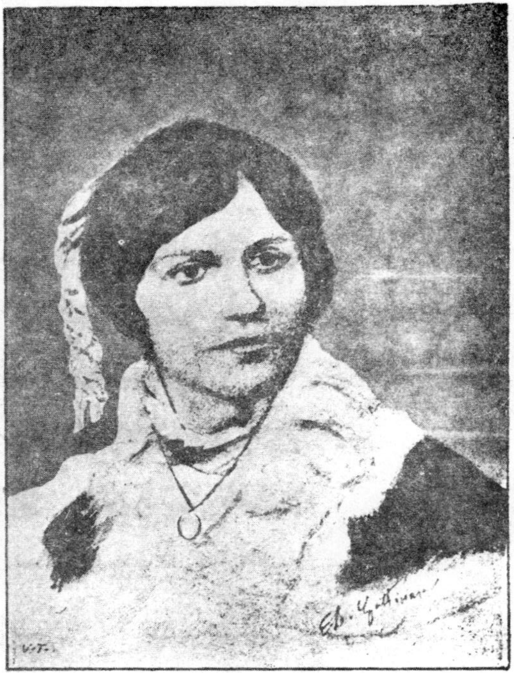

PLATE III.

To face page 102.]

PHYSIOGNOMY OF FRENCH, GERMAN AND RUSSIAN FEMALE OFFENDERS.

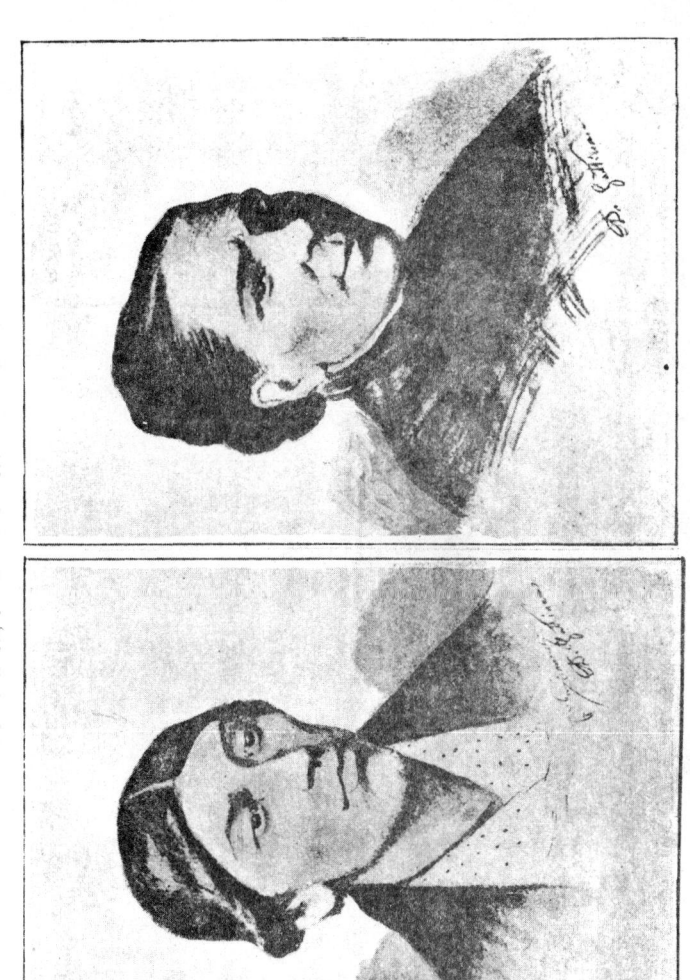

PLATE III.

[To face page 102.

PHYSIOGNOMY OF FRENCH, GERMAN AND RUSSIAN FEMALE OFFENDERS.

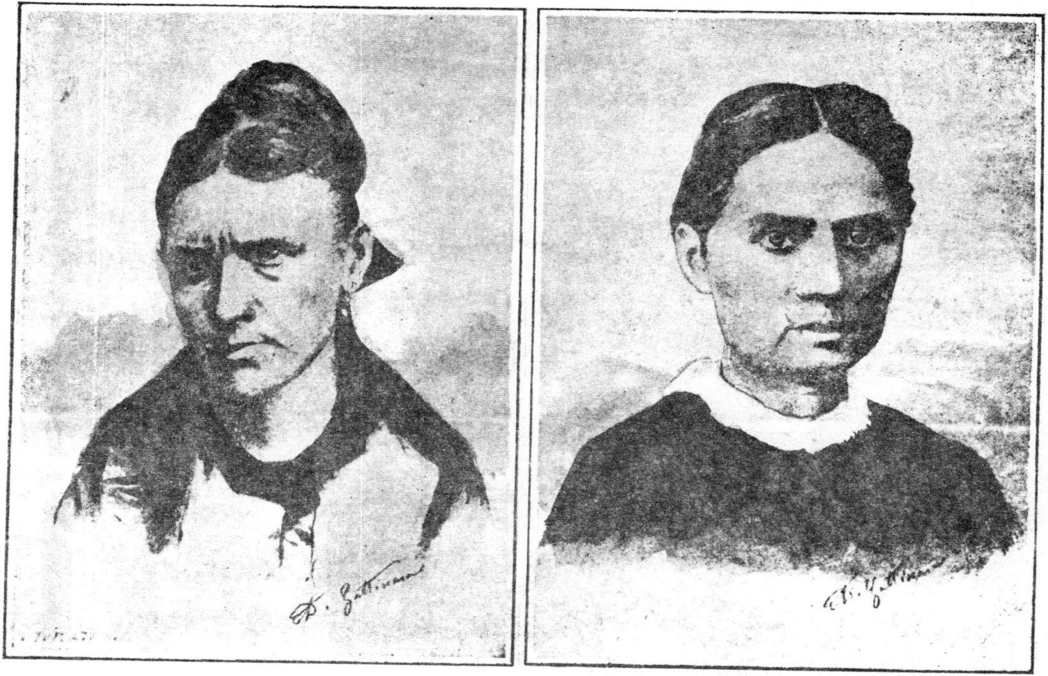

PLATE III.

To face page 102.

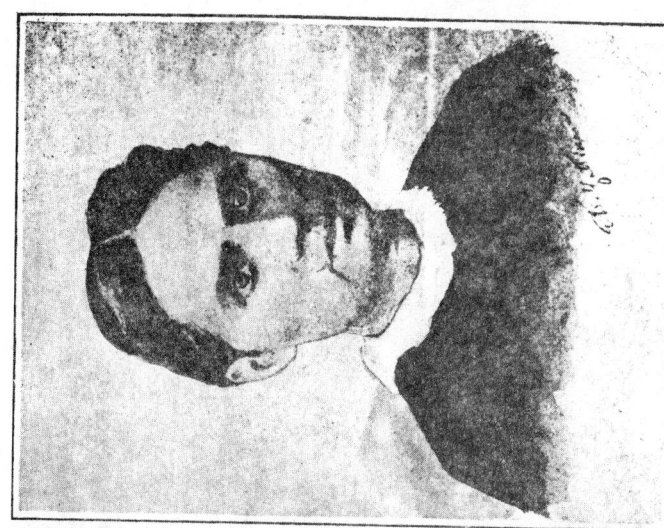

CHAPTER VIII.

THE CRIMINAL TYPE IN WOMEN AND ITS ATAVISTIC ORIGIN.

1. *Quota of the type.*—More instructive than a mere analytical enumeration of the characteristics of degeneration is a synthesis of the different features peculiar to the female criminal type.

We call a *complete type* one wherein exist four or more of the characteristics of degeneration; a half-type that which contains at least three of these; and no type a countenance possessing only one or two anomalies or none.

Out of the female delinquents examined 52 were Piedmontese in the prison of Turin, and 234 in the Female House of Correction were natives of different Italian provinces, especially from the South. In these, consequently, we set aside all special characteristics belonging to the ethnological type of the different regions, such as the brachycephali of the Piedmontese, the dolichocephali of the Sardinians, the oxycephali.

We studied also from the point of view of type the 150 prostitutes whom we had previously examined for their several features; as well as another 100 from Moscow whose photographs Madame Tarnowsky sent us.

And we classified under the same heads the various data furnished by Marro, by Grimaldi, and by Madame Tarnowsky, so as to compare the results obtained by all three.

One glance at Table VII. suffices to show the reader how little these various returns differ. The subjects we examined in the House of Correction resemble those we saw in prison; nor do our results differ much from the averages of the other observers, allowance being made for the personal equation or individual divergences in the mode of regarding the same peculiarity.

The results of the examination may be thus summarised:—

1. The rarity of a criminal type in the female as compared with the male delinquent. In our homogeneous group (286) the proportion is 14 per cent., rising, when all other observations are taken into account, to 18 per cent., a figure lower almost by one-half than the average in the male born criminal, namely, 31 per cent.

In normal women this same type is only present in 2 per cent.

All observers agree as to the rarity of the criminal type. Marro records the absence of the type in 58·7 per cent., Madame Tarnowsky in 55 per cent., we found it wanting in 55·9 per cent. of the cases in the House of Correction, and in 55·8 of those in prison; so that altogether the criminal type results as wanting in 57·5 per cent. of delinquents.

TABLE VII.

Type of Degeneration in the Female Criminal and Prostitute.

	No.	0 type	0 character-istic	1 character-istics	2 character-istics	⅓ type, 3 character-istics	Complete type	4 character-istics	5 character-istics	6 character-istics	7 character-istics	8 character-istics
Soldiers	71	89	37·2	—	51·8	—	11·8	11·8	—	—	—	—
Normal males	200	84	32	—	52	—	16	16	—	—	—	—
Normal females	600	—	—	—	—	—	1·89	—	—	—	—	—
Criminal males	353	64·8	8·2	—	56·6	—	35·2	32·6	—	2·3	0·3	—
Great criminals (men)	346	59·1	11·9	—	47·2	—	40·9	33·9	—	6·7	0·3	—
Male criminals (photographs)	228	61	16	17	28	16	24	14	7·5	1·3	1·3	—
Female criminals (German photos.)	83	15	—	—	—	—	28	—	—	—	—	—
Female criminals (Italian)	122	16	—	—	—	—	26	—	—	—	—	—
F. crims. observed by Marro	41	58·7	4·8	32	21	22	19	7·3	9·7	4	2·4	—
" " Tarnowsky	150	55	3	18	34	21	24	10	10	—	—	—
Females in penal establishments (?)	234	55·9	—	—	—	29	14·9	—	—	—	—	—
Murderesses	106	55·7	—	—	—	31·1	13·2	—	—	—	—	—
Thieves	38	55·2	—	—	—	28·9	16	—	—	—	—	—
Infanticides	45	64·4	—	—	—	26·6	8·7	—	—	—	—	—
Swindlers	18	61·1	—	—	—	27·8	11·1	—	—	—	—	—
Corrupt	16	50	—	—	—	31	18·7	—	—	—	—	—
Poisoners	12	33	—	—	—	25	41·6	—	—	—	—	—
Females in prison (thieves)	52	55·8	—	—	—	28·9	15·3	—	—	—	—	—
Average 286 (Lombroso, Ottolenghi)	—	57	19·6	26·8	16	29·3	14	7·1	—	—	—	—
Female criminals photographed	56	62·4	—	—	15	19·6	17·8	26	—	—	—	—
Prostitutes (Grimaldi)	26	38	—	10	22·66	27	31	20	10·7	7·6	—	—
" (Tarnowsky)	100	32·9	—	—	—	23·33	43	—	7·6	4	2·66	0·66
" (Lombroso, Ottolenghi)	100	30	—	—	—	32	38	—	9·33	—	—	—
Average of female criminals	533	57·5	—	—	—	25·7	18·7	—	—	—	—	—
" prostitutes	226	33·6	—	—	—	27·5	37·1	—	—	—	—	—
Female lunatics (Roncoroni)	40	59	2·5	12·5	45	17·5	22·5	15	7·5	—	—	—

The demi-type is present in almost constant proportions, Marro finding it in 22 per cent., Madame Tarnowsky in 21 per cent., we in 29 per cent. in the House of Correction, and in 28·9 in the prison. Average: 25·20 per cent.

2. Prostitutes differ notably from female criminals in that they offer so much more frequently a special and peculiar type. Grimaldi's figures are 31 per cent. (of anomalies), Madame Tarnowsky's 43 per cent., our own 38 per cent.; making a mean of 37·1 per cent. These results harmonise with the conclusions to which we had already arrived in our study of particular features, and our survey of the various types of born prostitutes as distinguished from ordinary female offenders.

3. In the differentiation of female criminals, according to their offences, our last observations on the 286 criminals (made first without knowing the nature of their crimes and classified afterwards) give the prevalence of the criminal type among thieves as 15·3 and 16 per cent.; among assassins as 13·2 per cent., and as rising to 18·7 per cent. in those accused of corruption, among whom were included old prostitutes.

The least frequency was among swindlers, 11 per cent., and infanticides, 8·7 per cent., such women being indeed among the more representative of occasional criminals.

In a yet more complete table Madame Tarnowsky shows how the percentages among homicides prevail over those among thieves, and how the averages among prostitutes are higher than any others, besides giving us the various proportions of the anomalies.[1]

0 Anomalies	Normals 150. 32 per cent.	Homicides 100. 10 per cent.	Thieves 100. 40 per cent.	Prostitutes 100. — per cent.
1 ,,	35 ,,	—	6 ,,	4 ,,
2 ,,	26 ,,	14 ,,	18 ,,	12 ,,
3 ,,	4 ,,	38 ,,	22 ,,	22 ,,
4 ,,	2 ,,	16 ,,	14 ,,	30 ,,
5 ,,	—	16 ,,	20 ,,	16 ,,
6 ,,	—	4 ,,	10 ,,	12 ,,
7 ,,	—	2 ,,	6 ,,	22 ,,

Here we see the crescendo of the peculiarities as we rise from moral women, who are most free from anomalies, to prostitutes, who are free from none, and we note how homicides present the highest number of multiple anomalies.

All the same, it is incontestable that female offenders seem almost normal when compared to the male criminal, with his wealth of anomalous features.

2. *Social and atavistic reasons for the rarity of the type.*—The remarkable rarity of anomalies (already revealed by their crania) is not a new phenomenon in the female, nor is it in contradiction to the undoubted fact that atavistically she is nearer to her origin than the male, and ought consequently to abound more in anomalies.

We saw, indeed, that the crania of male criminals exhibited 78 per cent. of anomalies, as against 27 per cent. in female delinquents and 51 per cent. in prostitutes; but we also saw that the monstrosities in which women abound are forms of disease, consequent on disorder of the ovule. But when a departure from the norm is to be found only in

[1] "Arch. di psich.," xiv. i., 1893.

the physiognomy, that is to say, in that portion of the frame where the degenerative stamp, the type declares itself, then even in cases of idiotcy, of madness, and, what is more important for our purpose, of epilepsy, the characteristic face is far less marked and less frequent in the woman. In her, anomalies are extraordinarily rare when compared with man; and this phenomenon, with a few exceptions among lower animals, holds good throughout the whole zoological scale.

For this reason, as Viazzi well observes (Anomalo, 1893), the *common* characters of a genus are more evident in the forms of the female. Most naturalists are agreed [1] that for the type of a species also one must look to the female rather than to the male; and this remark may be applied with equal justice to the moral sphere.

Helen Zimmern, in her "Philosophy of Fashion," observed that women show their individuality better than men in the details of their dress, but that the principal lines of every fashion of attire in every age are due to the active, creative element in man. And in truth, beginning with the primitive Greek chiton, sleeveless and flowing, confined by a belt, from which all feminine and masculine habiliments have successively sprung throughout the course of European civilisation, how many have been the varieties of male attire from age to age, among different nations, while the female dress in its general lines is substantially always the same (Viazzi).

Compilers of public statutes have also noted the

[1] Morelli, "Lezioni di Antropologia" (in course of publication), p. 220.

conservative tendency of women in all questions of social order; a conservatism of which the primary cause is to be sought in the immobility of the ovule compared with the zoosperm.

To this add that the female, on whom falls the larger share of the duty of bringing up the family, necessarily leads a more sedentary life, and is less exposed than the male to the varying conditions of time and space in her environment. More especially is this the case among the greater number of vertebrates, and still more of savages, where the struggle for life, both for parents and progeny, devolves primarily upon the male, and is the incessant cause of variations and peculiar adaptations in functions and organs (Viazzi).

Now, once we admit that the primitive type of a species is more clearly represented in the female, we must proceed to argue thence that the typical forms of our race, being better organised and fixed in the woman through the action of time and long heredity, joined to fewer ancestral variations, are less subject to transformation and deformation by the influences which determine special and retrogressive variations in the male.

Another very potent factor has been sexual selection. Man not only refused to *marry* a deformed female, but ate her, while, on the other hand, preserving for his enjoyment the handsome woman who gratified his peculiar instincts. In those days he was the stronger, and choice rested with him.

It is almost superfluous to record once again the instance of the aboriginal Australian, who, in reply to an inquiry as to the absence of old women in his country, said, "We eat them all!" and on being remonstrated with for such treatment of his wives, answered, "For one whom we lose, a thousand remain."

It is quite certain that the ladies whom they lost were neither the loveliest nor the most attractive. The only anomalies which prevail are such as form no obstacle to sexual selection, either because the male finds them convenient for other reasons, or has no objection to them, or attaches no importance to them. Such is the cushion of the Hottentot women, which is useful for the transport of children; and when this and other anomalies prevail among the women of any tribe, they assume a stable and perpetual character in virtue of the tenacity peculiar to the feminine organism.

Yet another reason for the comparative rarity of the criminal type in women is that congenitally they are less inclined to crime than men. Atavism must be held to account for this fact, savage females, and still more, civilised females, being by nature less ferocious than males. It is the *occasional* offender whom we meet with most frequently among women; and as occasional criminals have no special physiognomy, they can offer no examples of the type. And woman's inability in this respect is all the greater that even when a *born* offender she is, in the majority of cases, an adulteress, a calumniator, a swindler, or a mere accomplice—offences, every one of them, which require an attractive appearance, and prohibit the development of repulsive facial characteristics.

The primitive woman was rarely a murderess; but she was always a prostitute, and such she remained until semi-civilised epochs. Atavism, again, then explains why prostitutes should show a greater number of retrogressive characteristics than are to be observed in the female criminal.

Various as are these solutions of a singular problem, we may, I think, seek yet another. In female animals, in aboriginal women, and in the women of our time, the cerebral cortex, particularly in the psychical centres, is less active than in the male. The irritation consequent on a degenerative process is therefore neither so constant nor so lasting, and leads more easily to motor and hysterical epilepsy, or to sexual anomalies, than to crime. For a similar reason genius is more common in men than in women; and the lower animals remain insensible to narcotics, which intoxicate the human species, and are not subject to delirium or mania when attacked by fever.

We have now got to the reason why criminality increases among women with the march of civilisation. The female criminal is a kind of occasional delinquent, presenting few characteristics of degeneration, little dulness, &c., but tending to multiply in proportion to her opportunities for evil-doing; while the prostitute has a greater atavistic resemblance to her primitive ancestress, the woman of pleasure, and, as we shall see, has consequently a greater dulness of touch and taste, a greater propensity for tattooing, and so on.

In short, the female criminal is of less typical aspect than the male because she is less essentially criminal; because in all forms of degeneration she deviates to a less degree; because, being organically conservative, she keeps the characteristics of her type even in her aberrations from it; and finally because beauty, being for her a supreme necessity, her grace of form resists even the assaults of degeneracy.

But it cannot be denied that when depravity in woman is profound, then the law by which the type bears the brand of criminality asserts itself in spite of all restraint, at any rate as far as civilised races are concerned (*see* Plate III.); and this is particularly true of the prostitute, whose type approximates so much more to that of her primitive ancestress.

3. *Atavism.*—Atavism helps to explain the rarity of the criminal type in woman. The very precocity of prostitutes—the precocity which increases their apparent beauty—is primarily attributable to atavism. Due also to it is the virility underlying the female criminal type; for what we look for most in the female is femininity, and when we find the opposite in her we conclude as a rule that there must be some anomaly. And in order to understand the significance and the atavistic origin of this anomaly, we have only to remember that virility was one of the special features of the savage women. In proof I have but to refer the reader to the Plates opposite, taken from Ploss's work ("Das Weib," 3rd ed., 1890), where we have the portraits of Red Indian and Negro beauties, whom it is difficult to recognise for women, so huge are their jaws and cheek-bones, so hard and coarse their features. And the same is often the case in their crania and brains.

The criminal being only a reversion to the primitive

NEGRO WOMAN. RED INDIAN WOMAN

type of his species, the female criminal necessarily offers the two most salient characteristics of primordial woman, namely, precocity and a minor degree of differentiation from the male—this lesser differentiation manifesting itself in the stature, cranium, brain, and in the muscular strength which she possesses to a degree so far in advance of the modern female. Examples of this masculine strength may still be found among women in country districts of Italy, and especially in the islands; and the reader should now be able to understand why I detect the criminal type in that Z.... (Plate III., No. 10), whose likeness would strike many as being very beautiful.

The excessive obesity of prostitutes, to which we have already drawn attention, is perhaps of atavistic origin.

"The fatness of many prostitutes," observes Parent Duchatelet, "strikes those who look at them *en masse* when many are together in one place. Persons living among these women and observing them every day have certified that this obesity only begins at about the age of 25 to 30 years. It is rarely noticeable in young girls or beginners. To what," he continues, "are we to attribute this peculiarity? The most simple explanation seems to lie in the great number of hot baths which such women are accustomed to take throughout the year, and, above all, to their inactive lives and abundant nourishment."

But the lower orders of prostitutes, who are the fattest, do not take baths; and if their lives in the daytime are inactive, they are not so at night, when their wakeful hours are frequent and diversified by dances and orgies. And if we must admit that, as a rule, they grow fat only after the age of 20 years, yet we have but to look at the likenesses furnished by Magnan to observe that the tendency shows itself sometimes in the very young.

Many attribute this obesity to the mercurial preparations of which these women make so large a use. But it is well known that workers in quicksilver mines and makers of looking-glasses, so far from being fat, are noted for their thinness. Moreover, prostitutes who do not use mercury incline to be fat, and mercurial treatment does not produce fleshiness in those who undergo it.

Hottentot, African, and Abyssinian women when rich and idle grow enormously fat, and the reason of the phenomenon is atavistic.

Maternal and sexual functions produce the cushion of the Hottentot woman, who by increasing in adipose and connective tissue reverts to a peculiarity of primitive women—or is, in other words, an example of atavism. Indeed, in Oceania and in Africa the standard of beauty consists in weight, to increase which, various artifices are resorted to, such as imbibing enormous draughts of milk and beer in a progressive ratio, until at last the venal women of those societies are simple monsters of obesity.

In conclusion, I would remark that in prisons and asylums for the insane, the female lunatics are far more often exaggeratedly fat than the men. In Imola there is a girl of 12 years with hypertrophy of the breasts and buttocks (the former weighing two kilogrammes), so that she is fatter than a Hottentot woman, and has to wear special stays.

CHAPTER IX.

TATTOOING.

1. *Criminals.*—Among male criminals the practice of tattooing is so common as to become a special characteristic; but in female delinquents it is so rare as to be practically non-existent.

Out of 1,175 sentenced women observed by me, by Gamba, and Salsotto, only 13, or 2·15 per cent., were tattooed.

Among female lunatics the percentage is larger; at any rate in Ancona, where Riva found 10 tattooed out of 147—that is to say, 6·8 per cent. All were tattooed on the arm, and almost all the signs were either religious symbols, such as seals or crosses, or else they were dates. There were no images.

One had on the arm a cross surmounting a globe, with which she had been tattooed by a mountebank. Another had, also on the arm, self-inflicted, four initials, being those of her mother and two lovers. This woman was a Venetian, an adulteress, condemned for wounding her paramour, and was affected with syphilis. Yet another Venetian woman had four initials on her arm.

A female homicide, aggressor and thief, aged 24,

who suffered from epilepsy, who had been first a model, then a prostitute, and had killed her lover, a painter, out of jealousy and because he would not pay her, bore on her forearm, in large letters, beginning with a W, the name of the man she had killed, and underneath the date of the abandonment which he had thus expiated; while on her *other* forearm was the contradictory declaration, "*J'aime Jean.*"

2. *Prostitutes.*—Among prostitutes, especially those of the lowest class, the case is very different. The proportion of tattooed among them is higher, even setting aside the tattooing of the face with moles, which doubles and even trebles the number of examples.

Segre found 1 in 300 in Milan, De Albertis 28 in 300 at Genoa; I found 7 in 1,561 at Turin—in all, 36 in 2,161, or 2·5 per cent. The principal characteristics of the practice are almost negative. There are few religious symbols (only one in thirty-three cases), but frequent allusions to love mostly illicit, for the instances only include two allusions to parents, while twenty-four out of thirty-three referred to lovers. The small degree of constancy in these attachments is betrayed by the multiplicity of references to lovers, of whom in two cases two were indicated, and in two more, three. The marks consisted :—

In 31	...	Names and initials.
In 6	...	Transfixed hearts.
In 3	...	Men's heads.
In 2	...	Mottoes.
In 3	...	Own names.

De Albertis found on the arm of a prostitute, 84 years old, a Genoese, the figure of a zouave between two initials, C. D. One had "W., my love," and two transpierced hearts on the right forearm. One had caused herself to be tattooed on the breast by an expert practitioner with the figure of her lover, and underneath, the letters "E. I. M. B." (*Evvia il mio Bruno*). This was an allusion to her first lover whom she had known when only fourteen, by whom she had had a child and then been abandoned at the end of two years. She was, nevertheless, a woman of some education.

In Paris also, as a rule, prostitutes are tattooed only with the initials or names of their lovers, followed by the declaration, "*Pour la vie,*" flanked sometimes by two flowers or two hearts. The marks are almost always on the shoulders or breast. Only twice was any obscene allusion found.

La Rosny was covered all over with the names and initials of her lovers and the dates of her new attachments.

As to the places chosen for tattooing they are as follows:—

Covered parts	27
Uncovered (face)	1
Right arm	7
Left arm	4
Forearm	19
Thighs	7
Breasts	3

The age at which the tattooing begins is almost always early.

In 1 case	7 years.
,, 3 ,,	15 to 17 ,,
,, 9 ,,	18 to 24 ,,
,, 3 ,,	25 to 28 ,,
,, 2 ,,	38 to 44 ,,

Parent Duchatelet noticed that the tattooing is most frequent in the more degraded girls, who are accustomed to mark themselves with the names of their lovers, effacing always the old with the new, so that in one case there had been 15 names. Old unfortunates prefer to tattoo themselves with the names of women.

De Albertis observed that among prostitutes those who are tattooed are the most depraved.

Out of 28, 15 had been in prison, 10 of them several times, and one 24 times. Nine were covered with scars, 28 were wanting in moral sense, and 20 even in a sense of religion; 25 out of 28 had dulness of touch, and 1 was absolutely wanting in it. All had been precociously depraved, one at 9, another at 10 years—8 between 12 and 14 years. Seven of the number had tattooed themselves, one at the age of 9 out of imitation. Fourteen out of twenty-eight showed anxiety to exhibit the marks.

Very accurate researches made by Bergh in Denmark yielded similar results to the above.[1]

Among the unfortunates of Copenhagen the fashion came in when a young man, formerly a sailor, who possessed an aptitude for drawing, and especially for tattooing, began to take advantage of the well-known frivolity of this class of women.

Within the last five years Bergh found 80 women tattooed out of a total of 801, and 49 of the number, or more than half, had been tattooed by the sailor in question. The others had been tattooed by their

---

[1] "Archivio di psichiatria," xii.

female friends in the houses of correction, or in the police stations, and some by the procurers.

Thirty-four were tattooed with letters, 10 with names, 22 with letters and figures, 11 with names and figures, and 8 with figures alone. The greater part of these tattooings were in red and black.

In 73 out of 80 cases eternal love was proclaimed by an E affixed to the names of the lovers. Twenty-three of the same women had written their own names, either partially or entirely; and in 5 cases there was the date and the year of their loves.

Twenty-six had tattooed themselves with the names of 2 lovers, 3 with the names of 3, 4 with 4, and 2 with 5 or 6. The lovers of Parisian prostitutes have never been equalled in number. Five had erased the name of one lover by replacing it (in the same spot) with that of another, and adding the image of a funereal cross. This was observed also in some cases in France.[1] Two bore the name of a female friend beside that of the lover. Four were tattooed only with their own names, one with the name of a brother, another with that of a boy, and thirty-five with different figures.

For the rest there was no great variety, the same marks being generally repeated. Naturally there are often symbolical figures, the same as in France and Italy. Fifteen women had a kind of knot formed by two leaves turning in different directions; 7 showed a rose surrounded with leaves; 6 a heart with two hands clasped across it, with two letters and an arrow in the middle.

[1] Laccasagne, *Les tatouages*, Figs. 15, 35, 36.

Five women bore the half-length likeness of a young man; four showed two clasped hands; nine a heart, that well-worn symbol of love; three a kind of ribbon; two a branch with leaves, and two a leaf only. Eight had a bracelet, or a funereal cross, or a rosary, a ring, a star, a ship with sails, or a flag with cannon. Two women were tattooed in nine places, one in eleven, and another in fifteen. All these marks were on the upper part of the body; rarely on the legs or chest; and eight were on the joints of the fingers.

Three women were marked with a ring on the thumb, on the index and on the middle finger of the left hand. Three had marks on the left knee, one on the right knee, and three on both knees. One showed a design on the sternum, and another on a spot lower down, between the breasts.

In Copenhagen, as in Paris and Genoa, the tattooed prostitutes were the lowest of their class; but none of the designs which they exhibited were obscene. Generally they bore allusions to the love of men.

The tattooings are usually always in the same places and of the same colour; and sometimes they are superimposed, an effort being made to cover the name of an old lover with that of the new one. The chief difference seems to be, that while in Copenhagen only male names are found, on Parisian prostitutes there are often female ones.

Tattooing among the lower class of prostitutes is frequent, but rare among the upper sort, and almost unknown in the ranks of the clandestine.

Out of 1,502 women, almost all young, who between

1886 and 1890 were admitted to the division in the Vestne Hospital of Copenhagen reserved for clandestine prostitutes, only 31 were tattooed, 15 of them when very young, by the sailor already mentioned, and the remainder by their female friends or their lovers.

3. *Conclusions. Atavism.*—On the whole, therefore, even the peculiarity of tattooing is found to a far smaller degree among criminal women than among men. In females of this class the proportion is as two per thousand, while in young men, especially the military, the proportion rises to 32 and 40 per cent., with a minimum of 14 per cent.

In prostitutes, on the other hand, the average is 2.5 per cent., and has been trebled of late through the recent practice of tattooing the face with moles.

In Denmark, setting moles aside, the proportion is 10 per cent. Still more remarkable is the fact that even among the tattooed female criminals the majority were prostitutes also; and it was the most vicious and the most degraded of the unfortunates themselves who were tattooed, and tattooed more especially on the covered portions of their bodies, such as thighs and breasts. Finally, prostitutes alone, especially in Denmark and France, showed a multiplicity of tattooings, the number amounting to 9, 11, or even 15.

The predominating meaning of all these designs is love; but it is a love which proves the inconstancy of the unfortunate class, since in 26 cases out of 73 the letter E, which constituted a declaration of eternal affection, was followed by the names of 2, 4, 5, and even 6 lovers; while 5 women were tattooed with a funereal cross above the name, or had effaced an old name with a new one.

We have here, then, yet a further proof that phenomena of atavism are more frequent among prostitutes than among ordinary female criminals, while in both classes they are rarer than in the male.

Other differences between the tattooings on women and those on men are a much greater want of variety; an absence of epigrams, obscene signs, and cries of vengeance, and the presence of ordinary symbols and initials only. Here we have another effect of the smaller ability and fancy, the lower degree of differentiation in the female intellect; for even the female criminal is monotonous and uniform compared with her male companion, just as woman is in general inferior to man.

Once again, then, we must seek an explanation of the type in atavism, and this becomes doubly significant when we learn that even the savage woman is tattooed less frequently and more simply than the aboriginal man.

In the Natchez tribe warriors alone are tattooed. In Polynesia and the Marquesas Islands the men are so thickly tattooed as to look clothed, the marks forming a complete record of their age, rank, honours, the enemies they have overcome, and even the property which they possess. But the women limit themselves at most to some delicate designs on feet or hands or arms, choosing the images of gloves and shoes in preference to the plants, serpents, sharks, &c., with which the men adorn themselves.

At Nouka Hiva it is a privilege of the more aristocratic woman to be tattooed with fantastic designs, plebeian females being restricted to simple ones.

Among the Arabs especially prostitutes are tattooed on the hands, forearms, arms, and upper neck, with garlands, arabesques, or circular lines, and the men are also tattooed on the face.

This custom is dying out among the women of Japan, has ceased among those of Burmah, and in New Zealand is reduced to two or three lines on the lips and chin.

The same may be said of the women of Toba, in India, where the marks signify puberty only, or are perhaps intended for adornment, but have no religious, political, or commercial significance.

So that here again is less tendency to differentiation.

The desire to beautify herself, which is so great in the modern woman, was not present in the primordial female, who was a mere beast of burden or of generation; therefore even such a simple and primitive adornment as tattooing, which required time and some trouble, and was accompanied with religious rites, and had besides to be durable, because serving as a register of descent and legal claims, was practised only by and for men. Among women for a long time its place was taken by blue and red painting of the hair, nails, and even teeth, which was resorted to probably only at the epoch of puberty. The fine ladies of Bagdad dyed their lips, legs, and chest blue, outlining the curves of the breasts with blue flowers.

In Burmah the nails of feet and hands are coloured red ;[1] while in Sackatu indigo is used to dye the hair, teeth, feet, and hands. By all which we see that even simplicity of tattooing is a sign of atavism in the criminal prostitute.

[1] C. Variot, "Les tatouages et les peintures de la pean" (*Revue Scientifique*, iii.).

CHAPTER X.

VITALITY AND OTHER CHARACTERISTICS OF FEMALE CRIMINALS.

WOMEN are not only longer-lived than men, but have greater powers of resistance to misfortune and deep grief. This is a well-known law, which in the case of the female criminal seems almost exaggerated, so remarkable is her longevity and the toughness with which she endures the hardships, even the prolonged hardships of prison life. It is a well-known fact that the number of aged female criminals surpasses the male contingent. "Witch" is a synonymous term for old woman in the language of the people; and there are some proverbs which point to similar conclusions.

We shall see later that if the proportion of precocious criminals is slightly greater among women (Roncoroni, "Senola Positiva," ii.), the number of old female offenders is relatively much larger. I know of some denizens of female prisons who have reached the age of 90, having lived within those walls since they were 29, without any grave injury to health. As to comparative official statistics, I append a list of prison returns, which, because of their nature, are subject to fewer manipulations and fewer errors than judicial lists.

Between 1870 and 1879, the inhabitants of prisons and convict establishments in Italy who were over sixty years of age, showed a percentage of 4·3 among the women, and 3·2 among the men.

The results for lesser ages were as follows:—

	Women.			Men.	
Years—50 to 60 :	10·8	per cent.	...	8·1	per cent.
,, 40 to 50 :	22·8	,,	...	19·4	,,
,, 30 to 40 :	32·6	,,	...	33·0	,,
,, 20 to 30 :	27·6	,,	...	33·2	,,
,, under 20	2·5	,,	...	2·7	,,

These figures show how many more female offenders reach advanced age than males, and prove also how the women stand punishment better. For among male criminals the number condemned to the galleys for life, or for periods longer than 10 years, is far greater than among women, as may be seen by these returns:—

Condemned to			
10-15 years.	15-20 years.	20 and more years.	Life.
p. c.	p. c.	p. c.	p. c.
Men, 13·5	Men, 14·4	Men, 7·5	Men, 13·2
Women, 9	Women, 8·9	Women, 2·8	Women, 10·3

It is not possible to know the average length of life of prostitutes, owing to scarcity of numbers and the nomad habits of the class.

Parent Duchatelet failed to settle the question in spite of the facilities afforded him by the accurate bureaucratical system of his country. But he succeeded in showing that many of the class, when forced by years and infirmities to abandon their trade, remain members of society as workwomen, wives or concubines of rag-pickers, sweepers, &c., or become attached to brothels, convents, refuges for mendicants, hospitals, and prisons. Out of 1,680, for instance, 972 took up a means of livelihood (108 keepers of brothels, 17 actresses), 247 founded establishments, such as shops, reading-rooms, and so on, 461 became domestics (in inns, hotels, &c.). Out of 3,401 in ten years (1817–27), 177 became chronically affected with the following complaints:—

    70 had different affections.
    32 ,, epilepsy.
    28 ,, paralysis.
    18 ,, old age.
    15 ,, blindness.
    10 ,, syphilis.
     5 ,, deafness.

428 died—that is, 1·2 per cent. in the year, while among Frenchwomen, aged from 15 to 50, the mortality in 1880–85 was 1·0 per cent., these figures proving therefore that the mortality among prostitutes is not above the average. Indeed, when it is remembered that the census among normals was taken at a time in which average length of life rose from 31 to 40 years (for Parisian women, indeed, to 43),[1] and when due allowance has been made for the special maladies to which prostitutes are subject, such as uterine and bronchial phthisis, syphilis, alcoholism, &c., it becomes clear that the average mortality of these unfortunates is lower than that of other classes.

"Many medical men," adds Parent, "pretend that they die of phthisis, or syphilis, in early youth, but

[1] Levasseur, "La population Française," 1890.

many others assert that they have iron constitutions, that their profession does not exhaust them, and that they can resist anything." That the latter must be the correct view is confirmed by many special observations.

There was Marion de Lorme, who lived to be 135 (from 1588 to 1723), so that when the Parisians wished to instance something which resisted the assaults of time, they mentioned her and the towers of Notre Dame. She buried four husbands, and was over 80 before losing her freshness of mind or body. Ninon de Lenclos at 80 still had glossy black hair as in youth, white teeth, bright eyes, full form, and is reported to have excited a violent passion in the Abbé de Châteauneuf, a youth of twenty.

Among the Greek courtesans many were celebrated even in old age: such as Plangone, Pinope, Gnatone, Phryne, Theano.

In Lucian's Dialogues Tryphon, when speaking of Filematium, says, "Have you noticed her wrinkles? her age? the hair which is turning white at her temples?"

Historians maintain that Thaïs died at 70, without ever having abandoned her profession. Plutarch, indeed, relates that her death was owing to her having pursued a young Thessalian, with whom she was in love, into the Temple of Venus, where the women of the country killed her out of anger at her audacity, and, stranger still, out of jealousy of her charms.

Even Phryne, when quite old, had lost nothing of her beauty, and she exacted large sums to the day of her death—describing the practice with much wit as "selling the dregs of her wine dear."

Plato loved Archeanassa when decrepit. "Archeanassa is mine—she conceals a conquering love in her wrinkles." Others say that the epigram which counts the wrinkles wherein little Loves nestle, refers to Asclepias.

Even the famous Lamia, the mistress of Demetrius Poliorcetis, reached extreme old age. The Chloe of Martial earned sufficient to restore to her lovers in old age the gold she had received in her youth—and of which she had availed herself to take seven husbands, to whom she erected seven tombs—sepultures of little honour.

Martial also alludes jokingly to Vetustilla, who lived under three hundred consuls; and Ligella, whose age equalled that of the mother of Ceres.

In short, if statistics are silent, and must so remain on this subject, history and tradition are there to show that the women who most frequently survive accidents and incidental and professional maladies are not the women of purest life.

Voice.—Parent Duchatelet remarked that many prostitutes have a coarse voice like carmen, especially after they have passed the age of 25 years, and when, also, they belong to the lowest class. Many attributed the peculiarity to habits of drinking wine and shrieking; he put it down to the effect of weather, of exposure, and of alcohol. This may be true, but the result of Signor Masini's investigations has been to show me that the voice of these women is masculine because they have a masculine larynx.

Handwriting.—The handwriting also, in the very few prostitutes who have any education, is somewhat masculine, and the same is true of born criminals. Examples are: Trossarello, Ninon de Lenclos, Catherine de Medicis, &c., &c., but the examples are not numerous enough to afford positive data.

Muscular force.—There is no proof of extraordinary muscular force. In 100 infanticides of normal stature the dynamometer showed a force of 30 kilogrammes on the right side and 30 on the left. In 20 poisoners the results were 24 kilogrammes on the right and 26 on the left side. In 130 assassins, 30 kilogrammes on the right side and 31 on the left; so that we have a noticeable left-handedness in poisoners and murderesses. And, indeed, left-handedness has been observed in 23 per cent. of murderesses, in 43 per cent. of poisoners, in 13 per cent. of infanticides, and I found the same peculiarity in 11 per cent. of prostitutes; while among normals the proportion is from 9 to 12 per cent. And the number of left-handed prostitutes would appear to be very great if one were to trust the dynamometer, which, however, is not always possible.

Gurrieri, with the help of this instrument, found 33 per cent. of left-handed prostitutes; Ricard found 10 per cent. left-handed, and from 8 to 5 per cent. ambidexter.

As to manual ability, only 5 per cent. of the left-handed showed it, and the proportion was the same for the ambidextrous.

More important, perhaps, is the singular agility

and force displayed by a few very extraordinary criminals.

One of the writers has recorded the story of the woman Perino, of Oneglia, who jumped from trees on to the roofs of houses into which she penetrated for purposes of robbery, and from which she escaped in the same way, evading detection for years.

We know of a prostitute-model (epileptic and tattooed) who killed her lover, a painter, and who, especially when hurt in her vanity, was subject to such fits of violence that five gaolers could not restrain her. She had embroidered a pair of epaulettes on a red shirt, and was accustomed to say, "This is my uniform." "I am a chieftainess of brigands." She was, in fact, the leader of all the worst characters in Turin, and the terror of the surrounding neighbourhood.

The celebrated Bonhours, a prostitute and murderess who wore masculine garments, and was as strong as a man, killed several men by blows from a hammer.

The celebrated Bell-Star, who led a band of assassins, on one occasion rode in a race in North America, dressed as a man, and carried off several prizes.

Zola, with great justness, in his "Bête Humanie" endowed the murderous virago Flora with such strength of arm that she was able to run a train off the line so as to kill her lover and her rival.

It is a familiar remark in farmhouses that the most active and the readiest servant-girls are the least honest; while as for prostitutes, their agility is proved by the numbers among them who are dancers and tight-rope performers; and there is no *cocotte* who does not fence.

Philenis, Martial's prostitute heroine, half a woman and half a man, played balls and threw in the air the big blocks of lead used by athletes. She wrestled with the athletes, and like them was beaten with a whip.

Reflex actions.—The reflex actions of the tendons as observed by Madame Tarnowsky furnished the following comparisons:—

		Prostitutes.	Thieves.	Homicides.	Normals.
Normal	in	16 per cent.	56 per cent.	60 per cent.	80 per cent.
Excessive	,,	10 ,,	6 ,,	4 ,,	2 ,,
Weak	,,	30 ,,	26 ,,	26 ,,	18 ,,
Wanting	,,	14 ,,	12 ,,	10 ,,	—
Anomalous	,,	54 ,,	46 ,,	40 ,,	20 ,,

The figures given by Gurrieri are still more remarkable. They are:—

Slow	in 78 per cent. of prostitutes.
Wanting	,, 16 ,, ,,
Excessive	,, 7 ,, ,,
Normal	,, 16 ,, ,,
Anomalous	,, 54 ,, ,,

Salsotto obtained the following:—

		Poisoners.	Murderesses.	Infanticides.
Slow	in	58 per cent.	30 per cent.	10 per cent.
Wanting	,,	10 ,,	3·6 ,,	1·0 ,,
Excessive	,,	5 ,,	10 ,,	16 ,,
Normal	,,	35 ,,	54 ,,	73 ,,
Anomalous	,,	65 ,,	46 ,,	27 ,,

We found them excessive in 25 per cent. of criminals, slight in 16 per cent., normal in 54 per cent., and wanting in 5 per cent.

It will be seen consequently that even in reflex

VITALITY OF FEMALE CRIMINALS. 133

actions the majority of anomalous cases is to be found among prostitutes. In them, indeed, tardy and abolished action may be explained by alcoholism, or by syphilis, which so easily attacks the anterior roots; but it must be said that in the larger number of the cases observed there was no proof of any syphilitic process.

Out of 100 prostitutes we found 20 with exaggerated reflex action, and 21 in whom it was slight or wanting. After prostitutes, the abnormal figures are furnished by poisoners and murderesses, in whom the action, when anomalous, is tardy. The least abnormal are infanticides.

The reflexes of the pupils were tardy in 10 per cent. of criminals and in 16 per cent. of prostitutes, and normal in 78 per cent. of the latter.

Reddening with nitrate of amyl was wanting in 90 per cent. of thieves.

		Murderesses.	Poisoners.	Infanticides.
It was	Rapid in	35 per cent.	40 per cent.	70 per cent.
	Slow ,,	65 ,,	55 ,,	30 ,,
	Wanting or slight ,,	81 ,,	80 ,,	82 ,,

thus proving once again the functional abnormality of murderesses.

Fifty per cent. of assassins and 25 per cent. of poisoners blushed at the mention of their crime; 45 per cent. of them received any allusion to it in absolute silence.

CHAPTER XI.

ACUTENESS OF SENSE AND VISUAL AREA OF FEMALE CRIMINALS.

1. *Touch.*— In our first inquiries into the sense of touch we found a greater dulness among criminal than among normal women.

Our results were as follows :—

	Criminal and Prostitute.	Normal.
Fine touch	1·7 per cent.	16·0 per cent.
Dull touch	46·2 ,,	25·0 ,,
Medium touch	51·6 ,,	56·0 ,,

These figures differ somewhat from those obtained by Marro, who in 40 female delinquents found an average of 1·96 on the right side, and 1·94 on the left, as against 25 normals whose average was 1·94 on the right side and 1·99 on the left, thus giving only four criminals in whom the touch was dull. But he adds that the normal women whom he examined were peasants and continually handling carbolic acid. Among 36 female thieves I found in the index finger an average sense of touch of 3·75 (right hand), 3·73 (left), and 1·97 in the tongue; and among 35 infanticides 3·76 (right), 3·46 (left), and 2·75 in tongue.

The average among 101 delinquents was 3·46 (right hand), 3·67 (left hand), and 2·06 in tongue. The dulness is thus greater than among male criminals, in whom we have 2·94 (right hand), 2·89 (left), 1·9 in tongue.

Salsotto, however, found in 20 female poisoners, who certainly belonged to the highest class, a much smaller average, namely, 1·9 (right hand), 1·8 (left), also 13 per cent. of left-handed subjects. Among 100 infanticides his results were 2·0 (right hand) and 3·0 (left hand), with left-handedness in 17 per cent. In 130 murderesses he found 2·2 (right hand), and 2·2 (left), with 45 per cent. of left-handed subjects. So that, according to him, the sense of touch would be normal in poisoners, rather duller in infanticides and murderesses, while among the latter there would be a great prevalence of left-handedness.

Madame Tarnowsky, comparing 50 homicides,

	Arms. Inside surface.		Hands. Palm.		Fingers. Inside phalanx.	
	R.	L.	R.	L.	R.	L.
Murderesses	mm. 23	22	14	14	4	4
Thieves	,, 16	15	12	12	4	4
Prostitutes	,, 13	12	9	9	3	3
Normals	,, 14	14	9	9	3	3

("Archivio di psichiatria e scienze penali," 1893, xiv., fasc. i.-ii.)

50 thieves, and 50 Russian prostitutes, with 50 normal peasant women, found the dulness in the arms and hands of thieves and homicides to be almost double that observed in normals; but the difference was very much less in the phalanx of the index finger, and this was one respect in which prostitutes showed no difference. And the normals were peasant women in whom the sense of touch was much deadened by manual labour.

2. *Prostitutes.*—I, also, in studying prostitutes, found the results, as to difference of touch in the

hand, slight and often contradictory, so that in 15 young prostitutes the average touch was relatively very fine, being 1·90 (right hand), 1·45 (left), 1·48 (tongue); while in 68 of middle-age it was dull: 3·04 (right), 3·02 (left), 2·11 in tongue, and very marked tactile left-handedness.

De Albertis among 28 prostitutes of the lowest class found a tactile sensitiveness of 3·6 (r.) and 4 (l.), with a maximum of 1·0 and a minimum of 18.

Gurrieri, from observations made on 60 prostitutes as compared with 50 normals or quasi-normals, concludes that the fleshy part of the finger in both hands is more sensitive in normals. For instance, at a distance of 2 to 2·5 mm. 60 per cent. of normals feel the two points in the right hand, and 70 per cent. in the left, while only 57 per cent. of prostitutes feel them in the right, and 64 per cent. in the left hand. The left hand is the most sensitive both in normals and in prostitutes. Prostitutes are slightly more sensitive in the tip of the tongue: 80 per cent. of them as against 78 per cent. of normals feeling the experiment at from 0·5 to 1·5, although 18 per cent. of normals were sensitive at from 2 to 2·5, and only 10 per cent. of prostitutes.

But here we must take into consideration three factors which have not been mentioned hitherto: these are culture, age, and degenerative characteristics. In young girls, even those who show signs of degeneration, the sense of touch is very fine.[1] In 12

---

[1] Touch, general sensitiveness, sensitiveness to pain and degenerate type in normal, criminal, and lunatic females ("Archivio di psichiatria," 1891).

girls aged from 6 to 15 years there appeared an average of 1·56 (right) and 2·57 (left); and the average obtuseness in educated women is less (2) than in women of the people (2·6), and is also very much less frequent (being only 16 per cent.) in normal women who have no signs of degeneration. The average is higher (28 per cent.) in those who have some degenerative characteristics, and is very high (75 per cent.) in those women, even when normal, who have many of these characteristics.

Consequently all divergences may arise from having compared criminals with normal peasant women (as did Marro and Madame Tarnowsky) or with old women, or with normal women who had many signs of degeneration.

For when studying the sense of touch with reference to the type we found the following results in 56 female criminals:—

	Very fine touch.	Medium (1·5 to 2·5).	Dull (3 and over
19 with 0 type,	5 per cent.	42 per cent.	52 per cent.
21 ,, ½ type	—	61 ,,	39 ,,
16 ,, type	—	50 ,,	50 ,,

These figures show how the greatest dulness and the greatest sensitiveness are found in those who do not present the type, while in the ½ type the maximum sensitiveness of touch is middling, with minimum deadness: in the complete type the sensitiveness and the deadness are equal.

3. *General sensitiveness and sensitiveness to pain.*— With the help of Dubois Reymond's sleigh we studied the general sensitiveness, and found an average of 58·2 mm. for men of moral lives, 59·1

for the corresponding class of women, 57·6 (right) and 58·6 (left) for female thieves, 59·0 (right) and 56·5 (left) for prostitutes, with only a slight difference, therefore, between the different classes.

As regards sensitiveness to pain, observed with the Lombroso algometer, the average among normal men was 42 mm., among normal women 45, in female thieves 21·4 (right) and 20·5 (left); in prostitutes 19·0 (right) and 21 (left), thus showing the greatest dulness and tactile left-handedness in the latter. In 28 per cent. of prostitutes we found complete insensibility to pain.

Gurrieri studied general sensitiveness and sensitiveness to pain in various parts of the body, and found that 10 per cent. of normals, and only 7 per cent. of prostitutes felt the current, in the palm of the hand, when the points were at a distance of 130 mm. At a distance of 40 mm. and more 16 per cent. of normals and 39 per cent. of prostitutes was the proportion found, thus showing (what Madame Tarnowsky has since confirmed) that prostitutes are more sensitive in the palm than normal women.

The results as to all other parts were as follows:—

	General sensitiveness.				Sensitiveness to pain.			
	Fine.		Dull.		Fine.		Dull.	
	Norm. p. c.	Prost. p. c.	Norm. p. c.	Prost. p. c.	Norm. p. c.	Prost. p. c.	Norm. p. c.	Prost. p. c.
Throat	82	50	10	9	18	38	8	3
Forehead & hand	4	4	20	49	6	5	20	16
Tongue	14	3	28	55	4	13	—	2
Clitoris	8	5	24	32	33	5	8	16

Consequently the normal woman is much more sensitive than the prostitute, whose greatest deadness is in the clitoris, and whose least is in the palm of the hand. And that is natural. For the hand of the female operative, and still more of the peasant, grows insensible through thickening of the skin consequent on hard work, and in Russian women especially the deadness is extraordinary (10 mm.). But in the case of the prostitute abstention from hard work and idleness refine her sense, not indeed from central or cortical causes, but from the accident of her profession, and for converse reasons the deadness of the clitoris in her case is explicable. The insensibility to pain of the prostitute which corresponds to that of the born criminal (male) is shown by the facility with which these women allow themselves to be injured. Most of them are covered with wounds (out of 392 prostitutes observed by Parent, 90 were treated for this cause). They also bear grave syphilitic lesions with indifference, and endure with equal fortitude external cauterisation and surgical operations.

Professor Tizzoni lately related to me the case of a prostitute whose leg he had to amputate and who refused the administration of ether, only begging as a favour that she might be so placed as to be able to watch the operation of which she followed all the stages, as though a stranger to them, without uttering a cry. Such women are true *filles de marbre*.

Gurrieri has noted a very important fact, namely, that the greatest sensitiveness to pain among prostitutes is found in those who have had children. In them the lingual sensibility is 99 mm. as against 76 for the others. Similarly the sensibility of the clitoris in the child-bearing is 102 and 97 in the rest. But the same peculiarity does not appear to hold good always for the breasts, tongue, and hand.

4. *Magnetic sensibility.*—Salsotto found magnetic sensibility in 12 per cent. of murderesses (130) and in 6 per cent. of poisoners and infanticides.

5. *Taste.*—Fifty per cent. of normals and 15 per cent. of criminals observed by us showed great delicacy of gustation. They detected 1 in 500,000 of strychnine. Among 10 per cent. of normals, 20 per cent. of criminals, and 30 per cent. of prostitutes, there was, on the contrary, a marked deadness (1 in 100 of strychnine).

Madame Tarnowsky, whose methods, however, were less exact, found that 2 per cent. of homicides and thieves and 4 per cent. of prostitutes could not distinguish any one of the four solutions, bitter, sweet, and salt, used in experimenting on their sense of taste; the salt solution especially being the one in which they made most mistakes. This is a phenomenon which has never been observed in normals.

6. *Sense of smell.*—The olfactory sense, tested by Dr. Ottolenghi with essences of cloves, resulted as 3 times duller in criminals (6 per cent.) than in normals (2 per cent.).

Among born prostitutes there were 19 per cent. without sense of smell. As an average result we obtained the 5th degree of the osomometer—1 in 2,500 of essence of cloves.

According to Madame Tarnowsky, the olfactory sense was normal in 82 per cent. of moral women, in 66 per cent. of prostitutes and homicides, and in 77 per cent. of thieves; it was below the normal in

18 per cent. of moral women, in 24 per cent. of prostitutes and homicides, and in 20 per cent. of thieves; it was wanting in 10 per cent. of homicides and prostitutes and in 8 per cent. of thieves.

7. *Hearing.*—This sense, according to Madame Tarnowsky, was normal in 86 per cent. of moral women, in 74 per cent. of prostitutes, in 68 per cent. of thieves, in 54 per cent. of homicides; it was weakened in 14 per cent. of normals, in 24 per cent. of prostitutes, in 30 per cent. of thieves, and in 40 per cent. of homicides. It was wanting in 2 per cent. of prostitutes and thieves and in 6 per cent. of homicides.

8. *Field of vision.*—Ottolenghi in my wards studied the field of vision of typical female criminals, of occasional criminals, and of born prostitutes.

Only 3 in 15 of the born criminals had a normal field of vision. In 12 of them it was more or less limited, in 9 there were deep peripheric recesses, forming that more or less broken peripheric line which he noticed in the male born delinquent and in epileptic subjects (Ottolenghi, "Anomalie del campo visivo nei psicopatici," &c. Bocca, 1890).

I give as a first example the field of a certain F. M., aged 15 years, a typical criminal, the daughter of a thief, who sent her out to steal on pretence of asking alms. She practised her profession only too well, and almost always succeeded in carrying off something wherever she was received. She had the face of an old woman, marked cheek and frontal bones, small, very unsteady eyes, and wrinkles on her forehead. Her tactile dulness was remarkable (3 mm.); she had almost complete analgesia (5 mm. of pain when tested with Dubois Reymond's sleigh); was subject every now and again to attacks almost of mania, perhaps epileptic in character, during which she was sleepless and sang continually. She was extremely voluble, and possessed very acute senses.

Her field of vision (Laudolt method) when tranquil showed diminution, especially on the left side, asymmetry, profound peripheral scotomata.

When the subject was excited the field of vision grew much larger, but became in no wise more regular.

Her other senses varied in the same way—her touch was much more delicate : 0·5 (right), 0·5 (left); her sensitiveness to pain more marked (30 on the right, 30 on the left); her smell became most acute, responding to the first solution of the osomometer; but she was wanting in the power of tasting anything bitter, and could not detect strychnine, even in the strongest solution (1 : 100).

In Plate. IV. are other examples of remarkable fields of vision in female criminals.

No. 3 is the completely typical visual area of a thief, Nov. F., aged 40, who had been several times convicted. Her field of vision is limited, with an irregular periphery in both eyes, especially the right one.

No. 4 belongs to another thief, also relapsed, aged 25, who had but few typical peculiarities. Her field of vision is normal in size, but on the right side is a peripheral scotomata in the internal inferior quadrant.

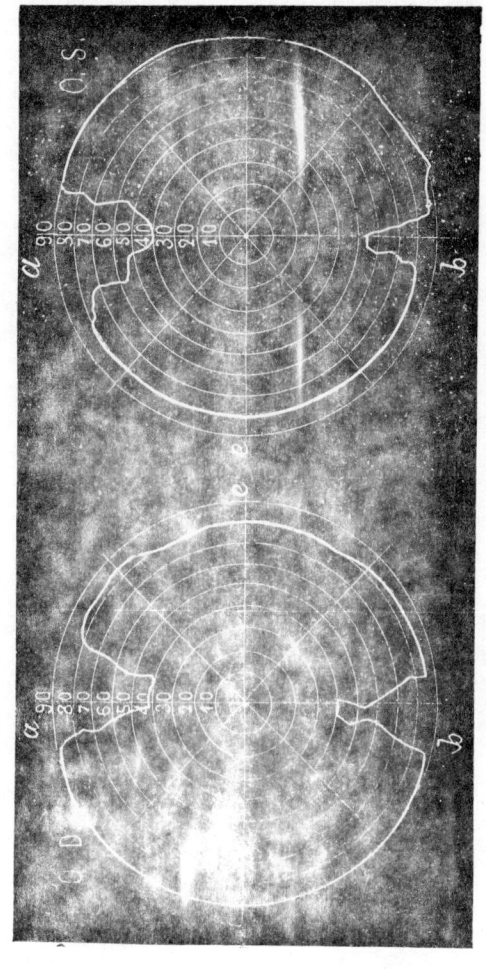

FIELD OF VISION OF F. M. DURING AN EPILEPTIC ATTACK.

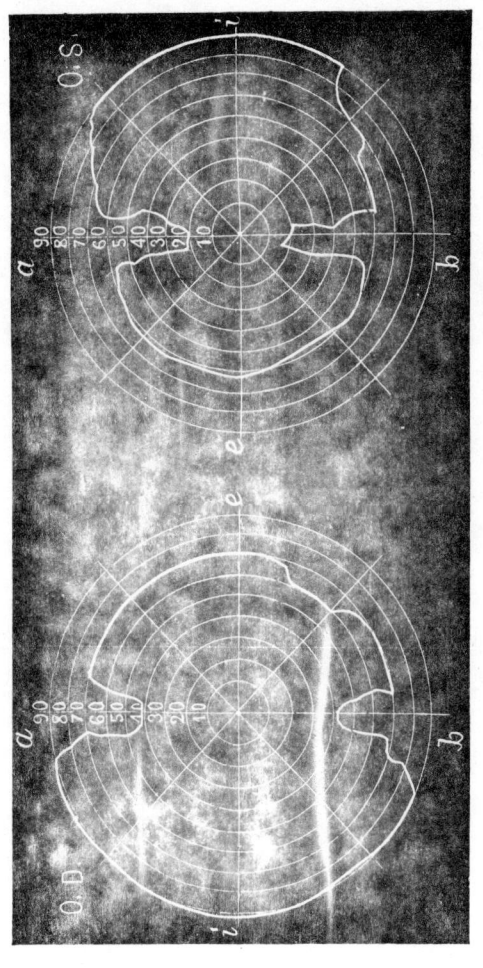

Field of Vision of F. M. in a Tranquil State.

Field No. 5 belongs to a clever swindler, and is normal on the left side, but rather limited on the right under side. (In this connection we may mention that male swindlers have all a normal field of vision.)

A very abnormal visual field, typical of crime, is No. 6. This woman, aged 39, killed her husband (with the help of her lover) under circumstances of the utmost premeditation and indifference.

The field is very small, and irregular throughout the whole periphery, especially on the left—but there was neuro-retinitis of syphilitic origin.

Another typical case of anomaly in the field of vision is in the born criminal, M. C., who at 9 years of age attempted to poison, and at 12 really did poison, a companion, while at 14 she was condemned for corruption of minors and for theft.

Her field of vision, No. 1, is regular, but limited on the left, anomalous on the right, owing to peripheral scotomata, and with an irregular periphery.

Br. M., aged 43, criminal, thief, and prostitute, has a field of vision showing a deep scotomata in the internal inferior quadrant of the left eye, while the right eye is normal. (*See* No. 2.)

Among 15 occasional criminals, only 4 had anomalous fields of vision. No. 7 is quite regular. It belongs to a girl of 16 years who tried stupidly to poison her old and brutal husband by putting sulphate of copper into his food.

No. 8 is a large field and quite regular, in spite of the hysterical nature of the subject, a Frenchwoman who was brought to Italy by her *souteneur*, and was tried with him for passing false money.

In 8 out of 11 prostitutes the field was found to be very limited, and with a broken, irregular perimetrical line, forming four true peripheral scotomata.

Typical in its irregular periphery is the field of vision of No. 9, belonging to a woman of 28, entirely wanting in moral sense—rachitic, with huge jaws and frontal sinuses, whose mother died in prison, whither she had been sent for prostituting herself and her daughters.

Yet another field abnormal in its periphery and peripheral scotomata is No. 10. The subject, aged 18, was a typical prostitute, and an accomplice in theft. The field is limited above, especially on the right, has an irregular periphery with a broken line, and two peripheral scotomata, one large and corresponding to the lower external sector on the right, the other smaller, and corresponding to the upper external sector on the left. The visual faculty was good, but there was deadness of touch in this subject (3 mm. on right and 4 on left).

In regard to sensitiveness of the retina, born prostitutes approximate to the male born criminal, more than does the true female criminal.

In making the above recorded observations it was found that there was a relation, in the case both of criminals and prostitutes, between general sensibility (especially sensitiveness to pain) and sensibility of the retina, and a similar relation between this and the characteristics of anatomical degeneration.

Madame Tarnowsky, in a too rapid survey, concluded that the visual field in homicides is smaller than in other criminals, and especially than in normal

FIELD OF VISION OF FEMALE OFFENDERS.

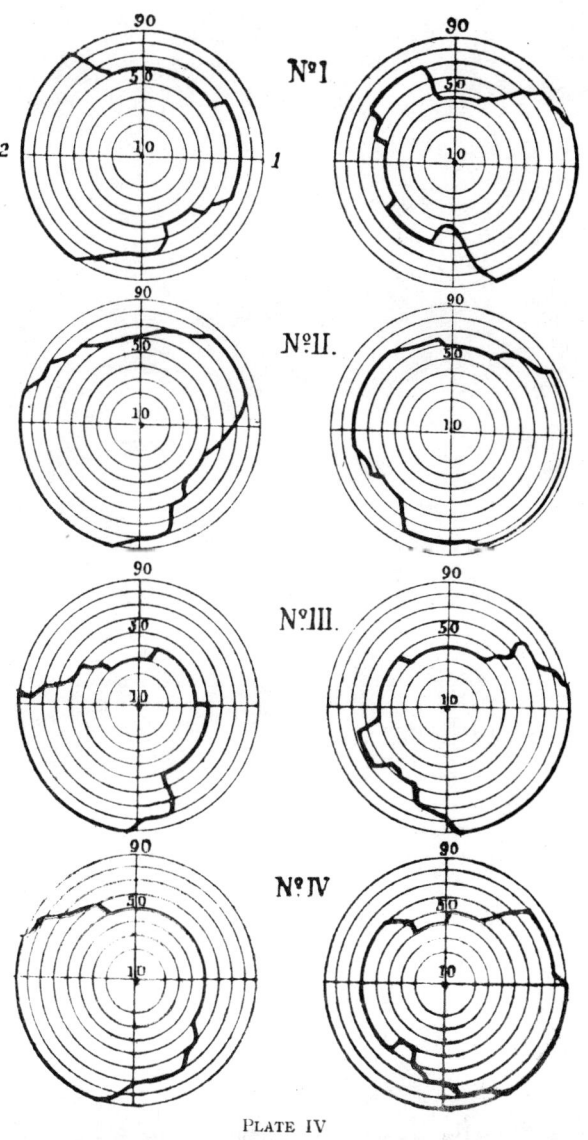

PLATE IV

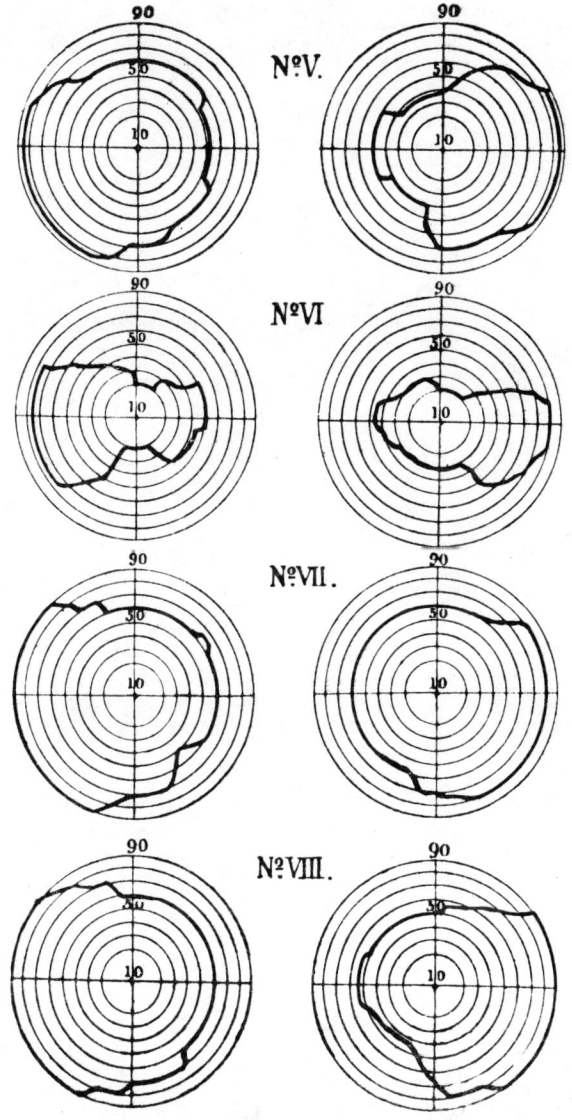

PLATE IV

women.[1] De Sanctis also [2] measured the visual area of 28 prostitutes in a Lock hospital, all of whom were not typical; in 17 he found the field normal, in 4 it was limited concentrically, in 3 it was limited asymmetrically in several sectors, and in 3 again there was an irregular periphery with a very exaggerated curve.

Rarisotti examined the visual area of 10 prostitutes, and in only 3 of the number found concentric limitation with scotomata and peripheral depressions.

On the whole, therefore, congenital female criminals, and still oftener prostitutes, present scotomata and peripheral depressions, but both classes exhibit these phenomena less frequently and less markedly than congenital male criminals.

The absence of the special characteristics of hysterical subjects, especially the most frequent, such as hemiopia and variability, in the women of whom we treat, even when slightly inclined to hysteria, proves that the moral and functional anomalies of criminals, &c., are not due to hysteria.

This plea so often advanced when women are on their trial for offences consequently falls to the ground; and the fact really is that hysteria is more common among normal women.

9. *Sharpness of vision.*—There was no remarkable difference in the above respect between 10 normals and 20 prostitutes and 20 congenital female criminals

Of the 20 prostitutes 20 per cent. had less than

---

[1] "Archivio di psichiatria," xiv., fasc. i.-ii.
[2] "Osservazioni perioptometriche nei degenerati" (*Riv. Med.*, 1892).

normal sight, 40 per cent. had sight above the average, and 40 per cent. were normal.

Of the 20 criminals 15 per cent. had less than normal sight, 50 per cent. were above the average, and 35 per cent. were equal to the average.

Twenty per cent. of prostitutes and 30 per cent. of criminals showed myopia of 15″ to 20″.

The chromatic sense was normal in 30 criminals and 50 prostitutes; but in 4 among the latter class the perception of colour was feeble.

10. *Summary.* — On the whole, dulness of sense (except in touch) and visual anomalies are greater among prostitutes than among female criminals, but less in both classes than among male congenital criminals.

The reflexes of prostitutes are slower than in the male criminal, perhaps because of the direct action of syphilis upon the nervous centres.

CHAPTER XII.

THE BORN CRIMINAL.

The analogy between the anthropology and psychology of the female criminal is perfect.

Just as in the mass of female criminals possessing few or unimportant characteristics of degeneration, we find a group in whom these features are almost more marked and more numerous than in males, so while the majority of female delinquents are led into crime either by the suggestion of a third person or by irresistible temptation, and are not entirely deficient in the moral sense, there is yet to be found among them a small proportion whose criminal propensities are more intense and more perverse than those of their male prototypes.

"No possible punishments," wrote Corrado Celto, an author of the fifteenth century, "can deter women from heaping up crime upon crime. Their perversity of mind is more fertile in new crimes than the imagination of a judge in new punishments."

"Feminine criminality," writes Rykère, "is more cynical, more depraved, and more terrible than the criminality of the male."

"Rarely is a woman wicked, but when she is she surpasses the man" (Italian Proverb).

"The violence of the ocean waves or of devouring flames is terrible. Terrible is poverty, but woman is more terrible than all else" (Euripides).

"The perversity of woman is so great," says Caro, "as to be incredible even to its victims."

Cruelty.—Another terrible point of superiority in the female born criminal over the male lies in the refined, diabolical cruelty with which she accomplishes her crime.

To kill her enemy does not satisfy her, she needs to see him suffer and know the full taste of death. In the band of assassins known as "La Taille," the women were worse than the men in torturing captives, especially female captives.

The woman Tiburzio, after having killed a companion who was pregnant, bit her ferociously, tearing away pieces of flesh, which she threw to the dog.

Chevalier killed another woman in the same condition by driving a pair of scissors through her ear into her brain.

P . . . did not care to wound the lovers on whom she was revenging herself, a wound being in her view too small a thing. She preferred to blind them by throwing into their eyes a powder made of fine glass which she had crushed with her teeth.

Da . . ., asked why she had not stabbed her lover instead of throwing vitriol at him, answered in the words of the Roman Tyrant, "*Because I wished him to feel the bitterness of death!*"

Sophie Gautier killed, by slow torture, seven children who had been given into her care.

History has recorded the mingled immense cruelty

and lust of women who have enjoyed royal or popular power. We know of instances among Romans, Greeks, and Russians from Agrippina, Fulvia, Messalina, down to Elizabeth of Russia, Théroigne de Méricourt, and the female cannibals of Paris and Palermo.

And the same may be said of Asia. Amestris, to revenge herself on a rival, begged Xerxes to hand over to her the rival's mother, whose breasts, ears, lips, and tongue she cut off and threw to the dogs, after which she sent the mutilated woman home.

Parysatis, the mother of Artaxerxes, caused the mother and sister of a rival to be buried alive, while the rival herself she ordered to be cut to pieces. And for ten whole days she had a soldier tortured for boasting that he had killed Cyrus.

Ta-ki, the mistress of the Emperor Cheon-Sin (1147), not only succeeded in separating him from his ministers and subjects, and plunging him into vicious excesses, but when a rival appeared on the scene she had her killed, and sent the body, cut in pieces, to the murdered woman's father whom she also caused to be assassinated.

Among other barbarities, Ta-ki used to order pregnant women to be torn limb from limb.

But the culminating examples of such barbarity are offered by mothers in whom maternal affection, the most intense of human sentiments, is transformed into hatred.

Hoegli beat her daughter, and plunged her head into water to suffocate her cries. One day she kicked her downstairs, thus bringing on a deformation of the spine. Another time she broke the child's shoulder with a blow from a shovel; and when by all this ill-treatment she had reduced her to be a monster of ugliness, she turned her into ridicule, calling her "a camel," &c. When the little one was ill, to make her cease crying she threw pailfuls of icy water over her head, covered her face with filthy sheets, and forced her to keep awake by counting "two and two make four" for hours at a time.

Stakembourg, a woman of bad life, on finding herself at 42 abandoned by her lovers, took to persecuting her daughter. "I do not like girls," she used to say. She hung her daughter from the ceiling by the armpits, knocked her on the head with a brick, and burnt her with a hot iron whenever she came near her. One day, after having beaten her black with a shovel, she said, laughing, "Now you are a little negress."

Rulfi starved her little girl, and, in order that she might suffer more, made her sit fasting at the table during meals. She engaged a master to beat and reprove her when she did not know her lesson, which, seeing the child's starving state, happened very often. She tied and gagged her, and then made her little brothers stab her with pins, so that she might suffer not only pain but humiliation.

In short, we may assert that if female born criminals are fewer in number than the males, they are often much more ferocious.

What is the explanation? We have seen that the normal woman is naturally less sensitive to pain than a man, and compassion is the offspring of sensitiveness. If the one be wanting, so will the other be.

We also saw that women have many traits in common with children; that their moral sense is deficient; that they are revengeful, jealous, inclined to vengeances of a refined cruelty.

In ordinary cases these defects are neutralised by piety, maternity, want of passion, sexual coldness, by weakness and an undeveloped intelligence. But when a morbid activity of the psychical centres intensifies the bad qualities of women, and induces them to seek relief in evil deeds; when piety and maternal sentiments are wanting, and in their place are strong passions and intensely erotic tendencies, much muscular strength and a superior intelligence for the conception and execution of evil, it is clear that the innocuous semi-criminal present in the normal woman must be transformed into a born criminal more terrible than any man.

What terrific criminals would children be if they had strong passions, muscular strength, and sufficient intelligence; and if, moreover, their evil tendencies were exasperated by a morbid psychical activity! And women are big children; their evil tendencies are more numerous and more varied than men's, but generally remain latent. When they are awakened and excited they produce results proportionately greater.

Moreover, the born female criminal is, so to speak, doubly exceptional, as a woman and as a criminal. For criminals are an exception among civilised people, and women are an exception among criminals, the natural form of retrogression in women being prostitution and not crime. The primitive woman was impure rather than criminal.

As a double exception, the criminal woman is consequently a monster. Her normal sister is kept in the paths of virtue by many causes, such as maternity, piety, weakness, and when these counter influences fail, and a woman commits a crime, we may conclude that her wickedness must have been enormous before it could triumph over so many obstacles.

Affections ana passions. Maternity.—A strong proof of degeneration in many born criminals is the want of maternal affection.

Lyons, the celebrated American thief and swindler, although very rich, abandoned her children when she fled from America, leaving them dependent on public charity.

Bertrand deserted her child in its infancy without troubling herself either to nourish or to clothe it.

Madame Brinvilliers tried to poison her daughter of sixteen, of whose beauty she was jealous. Gaaikema also poisoned her daughter in order to inherit her fortune of 20,000 francs.

Often women criminals make their own children accomplices of their bad deeds; while, on the other hand, many prostitutes desire a pure life for their daughters.

Leger, assisted by her son, killed and robbed a neighbour. D'Alessio, with the aid of her daughter, killed her husband; and Meille urged her son to murder his father.

All these instances prove that for such women the child is almost a stranger, whom, instead of loving and protecting, they make the instruments of their passions, thus exposing them to dangers which they have not the courage to face themselves.

One of the writers saw in prison a woman called Marenco, a thief of idiotic aspect, who, having by a rare concession been allowed to nurse her baby in the cell where she was confined alone, and with nothing to do, allowed the infant almost to die of hunger under the plea that "to nurse it bored her"; and finally the child had to be weaned.

This want of maternal feeling becomes comprehensible when we reflect on the one hand upon the union of masculine qualities which prevent the female criminal from being more than half a woman, and on the other, upon that love of dissipation in her which is necessarily antagonistic to the constant sacrifices demanded of a mother. Her maternal sense is weak because psychologically and anthropologically she belongs more to the male than to the female sex. Her exaggerated sexuality so opposed to maternity would alone suffice to make her a bad mother.

Sensuality has multiple and imperious needs which absorb the mental activity of a woman, and, by rendering her selfish, destroy the spirit of self-abnegation inseparable from the maternal function.

In the ordinary run of mothers the sexual instinct is in abeyance: a normal woman will refuse herself to her lover rather than injure her child; but the female criminal is different. *She* will prostitute her daughter to preserve her paramour.

Finally the organic anomaly, the moral insanity (of epileptoid form) which forms the substratum of born female criminals, tends to introvert their natural sentiments and extinguishes maternity in a mother just as it extinguishes religion in the nuns, whom it transforms into blasphemers.

A parallel case in men is military insubordination, such as in Misdea leads at times to murderous attacks upon superior officers.

The beneficent influence of maternity upon women is made clear in the case of criminals on whom the child-bearing function acts for a time—at least, as a moral antidote.

Thomas, a woman vicious from her infancy, had but six months of goodness in her whole life. During that period the child she had borne seemed to have transformed her nature, but when it died she relapsed into the gutter.

Never, then, is maternity the motive power of crime in a woman. That lofty affection is foreign to the degenerate nature of criminals, and the excesses to which it contributes are suicide or madness.

Vengeance.—Vengeance plays a principal part in the offences committed by women.

The inclination to acts of revenge which we noted even in the normal woman is carried in the criminal to an extreme. The psychic centres being in an excited condition, the smallest stimulus provokes a reaction out of all proportion to its cause.

Jegado poisoned her employers because they had reproved her, her fellow-servants because they had done her some small ill-turn.

Closset tried to poison her employers in return for a scolding, and stabbed her master when he dismissed her.

Rousoux, when her mistress (a farmer) forbade her to take some cherries out of a basket, warned her that she would have cause to repent the prohibition, and a few days later set fire to the farm.

The same offence, under almost similar circumstances, was committed in June, 1890, by Bekendorf. M. tried to kill a friend who had spoken ill of her. "*I nurse vengeance in my heart,*" said Trossarello, "*and I advise my friends to do the same.*"

Pitcherel poisoned her neighbour out of revenge for his having refused his consent to his son's marriage. When condemned to death and urged to imitate our Lord by forgiveness, she replied, "God did what He liked, but as for me, I shall never forgive."

As a general thing the female born criminal is far less rapid in her vengeance than the man.

Revenge in her case follows after days, months, or even years, the explanation being her weakness and the relative timidity of nature which restrains where reason alone is powerless.

"In her," wrote one of the authors, referring to Trossarello, "vengeance is not sudden, it is not a species of reflex action, as the doctors say, and as it is in most men; but it occupies her mind for months and years; it is a pleasure which she secretly gloats over, and which, even when she has realised it in action, leaves her satiated but not content."

Most often the hatreds and the vengeances of women are of complicated origin. The personal susceptibility which we noted both in the child and the normal woman rises in criminals to a pitch of morbid intensity. They conceive mortal hates with extraordinary facility. Every small check in the struggle for life produces hatred of somebody in them, and frequently the hatred ends in crime.

A disappointment turns to hate for the person who has caused it, even involuntarily: an unsatisfied desire breeds resentment towards the person representing the obstacle, even though he may only have exercised a personal right. Defeat results in a detestation of the conqueror, which is most violent in cases where the defeated one's own incapacity has been the cause of his overthrow.

All these are but slower forms of the same passion which causes children to administer a shower of blows on any object against which they have knocked their heads; and they prove an inferior psychical development, common not only to children, but, according to Romanes and Guyau, also to the lower animals.

The woman Morin conceived a violent hatred against a lawyer whom she had employed in an affair by which he, through his superior cunning, had profited, while she had lost; and she attempted to murder him.

Rondest killed her old mother after having, partly through persuasion and partly through force, obtained from her all she had to give. The old woman would not have needed even to be supported much longer, but her daughter through the irritation of unsatisfied desire had come so to hate her that she preferred to risk her head even when there was no longer anything to be gained, rather than leave this hatred ungratified.

Lévaillant tried to kill her mother-in-law (although she could not succeed to her fortune) because she did not give her enough money to make a fine figure in society: and Plancher murdered her brother-in-law because he was rich and respected while she and her husband were poor.

Naturally these sentiments of hatred are most ferocious when excited by an offence to the feelings which are strongest in women and represent their worst passions. If sexuality comes to complicate jealousy and vengeance these manifest themselves under a more terrible aspect than usual. M. . . ., for instance, poisoned a friend, a member of the *demi-monde*, because of her beauty and social success.

Sometimes the hatred which fills these women has no cause whatever, and springs from blind and innate perversity.

Many adulteresses, many poisoners commit perfectly uncalled-for crimes.

Imperious and violent, they dominate the weak husbands, who, out of fear of the consequences of any attempt at control, leave them free to go their own way, and thus generate towards themselves a hatred in inverse proportion to the indulgence they have exhibited.

The elderly husband of Madame Fraikin shut his

eyes to her profligacy; he was ill and had but a few months to live; yet she had not the patience to await his death, but murdered him. Madame Simon's case is identical. Madame Moulins had been married against her will to a rough but excellent man, who treated her as a sister, tolerated her adultery with the man she loved before marriage, and even went so far as to acknowledge her son as his own. Nevertheless she hated him every day more intensely. "*He must die!*" she exclaimed continually; and she caused him to be murdered.

During twenty years Enjalbert's husband never addressed a reproach to her on the subject of her dissolute life; but at last he mildly complained, and roused such a hatred towards himself in her that she murdered him.

Jegado constantly poisoned people without any object.

Stakembourg conceived a hatred of her daughter as soon as with advancing years she found that she could exercise her own trade as a prostitute with less profit than formerly. The child became the object on which she visited her wrath.

These women have the same passion for evil for its own sake which characterises equally the male born criminal and epileptic and hysterical subjects. Their hatreds are automatic, springing from no external cause, such as an insult or an offence, but from a morbid irritation of the psychical centres, which finds relief for itself in evil action. Continually under the influence of this irritation, the women we are describing must visit their anger upon some victim, and the unhappy being with whom they are brought most frequently into contact becomes, for the merest trifle, the slightest defect or contradiction, the object of their hatred, and the sufferer by their wickedness.

Love.—Intense as are the erotic tendencies of the female born criminal, love is yet very rarely a cause of their crimes.

Love, like hatred, is in their case only another form of insatiable egotism. In their love there is no altruism, no spirit of self-sacrifice: only the satisfaction of their own desires. Their passion of love is extraordinarily impulsive and casual. When they conceive a passion for a man they are impelled to gratify it instantly, even at the cost of a crime.

Possessed by one idea, hypnotised, one may say, they can think of nothing except how to appease their passion : they are unconscious of peril and rush into crime to get that which, with a little patience, they might obtain without risk.

Ardilouze had but to wait a few months before attaining her majority and being free to marry her lover without her father's consent. Nevertheless, rather than wait, she murdered her father. The letters addressed by Avéline and Béridot to their lovers betray a desperate impatience.

Their love often derives its very intensity from the obstacles which it encounters.

Buscemi fell in love first of all with a lame and humpbacked barber; next with a swindler, who was also a married man. The more opposition she encountered from her parents the stronger grew her passion. It finally led her into crime and then evaporated.

Such a love is less a lofty and generous sentiment than the violent resistance (similar to that which we see in children) of wounded vanity to anything which impedes the gratification of its own caprices.

Until the desire of these women is gratified it seems as if the world must come to an end; but once their object is obtained they cease to care for it. The man they adored yesterday is forgotten to-day, and soon replaced by another. Béridot, when her parents opposed her marriage, fled from the house with her lover, whom two years later she caused to be murdered by his successor.

If arrested and tried, these criminals are plunged by the fear of punishment into a new obsession.

Self-salvation then becomes their one idea, their sole desire; and like Queyron, Béridot, Buscemi, Saracemi, and Bompard, they are willing to betray the very accomplice for whom they so blindly compromised themselves a few months previously.

Indeed, hatred and love being only two forms of their insatiable egotism, their love shows a morbid tendency to polarise itself (so to say) into violent hatred at the first act of infidelity, the first offence, or even at the birth of a new passion.

Béridot, to begin with, idolised the husband whom she learnt to hate as soon as a new lover had replaced him in her affections.

Cabit, a prostitute, madly in love with her *souteneur* Léroux, to whom she gave almost all her money, killed him when he deserted her in favour of another woman.

The Countess de Challant caused her old lovers to be killed by the new ones.

Dumaire was disinterestedly in love with a young man for whose studies she paid, but killed him the day he left her to take a wife; and before the judge she declared that she would have murdered him twice, a hundred times over, rather than see him belong to another.

Weiss worshipped her husband, and for his sake remained shut up a year and a half in the house, as if in prison; nevertheless, she forgot him at once, and tried to poison him when another man inspired her with a passion still more violent.

Lévaillant hated, abused, and insulted the husband whom she had previously been crazy to marry, when he, by his extravagance and folly, had no longer money enough to enable her to shine in society.

This is like the affection of children—intense—but incapable of disinterested sacrifices or noble resignation.

It results in a tyranny such as is more often found in the love of a man than of a woman. P. . . ., anxious to prevent her lover from going near other women, sent round a circular to all the ladies of the town warning them that he belonged to her, and that they should suffer if they attempted to invite him. Often when she heard that he was dining in some house, she would go there and make a scandalous scene before everybody. But a few months later, when she had replaced him with a new lover, she addressed a second circular to the ladies, saying that they were welcome to him, just as she might have done had he been an animal or a chattel in her possession.

Greed and avarice.—To a less degree than vengeance, greed is a moving cause of crime in women, in whom it shows itself sometimes under a different form than in men.

Among dissolute criminals, indeed, who need much money for their orgies and their pleasures, and are too lazy to work for it, there is a great resemblance to the male criminal, who also desires to have large sums of money to waste. Women of the sort we are considering will attempt or instigate the crime which promises to bring in a rich harvest of valuables. Thus Bompard, attracted by the prospect of a rich booty, urged Eyraud to assassinate the porter; and Lavoitte persuaded her lover to kill and rob a rich old woman.

Other instances are Bonhours, Brinvilliers, Rob.

Messalina caused the richer citizens of Rome to be killed, that she might have their villas and their wealth; and Fulvia suggested murderous crimes partly out of vengeance and partly out of greed.

Crimes inspired by avarice (the opposite of prodigal greed) are frequent among female criminals, although rare among males.

Gaaikema, who was extremely parsimonious, poisoned her daughter in order to inherit 22,000 florins.

C. . . . killed her son because to keep him was too expensive

Another woman—a lady of high birth, out of whose reach her relatives had removed one victim for fear of scandal—began to ill-treat her third child simply because he was an additional expense. "Of him," she said, "we had really no need."

Corre and Rykère have already noticed how much more frequently than men, women — especially peasant-women—are guilty of the murder of old or invalid parents who, being unable to work, represent only an additional burden on the family. For this cause Lébon, aided by her husband, burned her mother alive.

Madame Lafarge, at Gers, in 1886, murdered her husband, a useless old man; and what is more significant, murdered him with the assistance of her daughter-in-law.

Similar are the instances of Faure and Chevalier.

The Russian woman whose portrait we give in Plate I. (No. 9) killed her daughter-in-law as being too weak to work.

Domestic avarice, being characteristic of women in general, leads, where it exists in an exaggerated degree (and all passions are easily exaggerated in women), to crime. For a woman an unnecessary expense in the household is as terrible as the loss of a large sum or the danger of commercial ruin is to a man; for the house is her possession, her kingdom, so to speak, and she attaches to it the same importance as a man attaches to *his* usual field of activity, whether that be the professorial chair, the seat in Parliament, or the country over which he reigns as a sovereign.

Hence the ferocious hatreds and the crimes to which avarice gives rise in the female sex.

Dress.—Yet another frequent cause of crime in a woman is love of dress and ornaments. Dubosc, who had helped to murder a widow, on being asked why she had done it, answered, "To obtain beautiful hair."

M. B. began her career by stealing 1,000 francs, which she spent almost entirely in objects of personal adornment.

M. and S. were accused of shoplifting, and elected to wear in prison the very articles they were charged with stealing, thus choosing to furnish clear proofs of their guilt rather than give themselves a chance of acquittal by renouncing for one day the pleasure of being well-dressed.

Madame Lafarge stole her friend's diamonds, and ran grave risks in order to keep possession of them.

Madame D. stabbed a creditor of her husband's who had threatened to seize a rich necklace in payment of the sum owing to him.

V. gave as a reason for killing her lover that he had pledged her jewels. This was true, but he had done it with her consent—a consideration which did not avail to shield her victim from the effects of the hatred she had conceived for him.

Madame Tarnowsky says that many Russian women steal not from need—as they are employed in remunerative work—but simply in order to buy articles of luxury to dress and adorn themselves.

And according to Rykère and Guillot the money which women obtain by the crimes they commit, either as accessories or principals, almost always goes in the purchase of personal ornaments.

In the psychology of the normal woman dress and personal adornment enter as factors of immense importance. A woman who is ill-dressed looks upon herself as disgraced. A similar feeling is visible in children and in savages, dress appearing among the last-named to be the earliest form of property, and we need not wonder consequently that it should be a frequent source of crime.

A woman steals or murders to be well-dressed as a commercial man will swindle in order to make a brave show on settling day.

Religious feeling (*religiosity*) is anything but rare or weak in these born criminals.

The wife of Parency, while her husband was murdering an old man, addressed prayers to God that all might go well.

G., when setting fire to her lover's house, cried aloud, "May God and the Holy Virgin do the rest."

The Marchioness of Brinvilliers was so fervent a Catholic that one of the principal documents against her at her trial was a narrative of her principal crimes, which she had written out for the confessional.

Avéline burned tapers in church "for the accomplishment of our projects," she wrote to her lover, meaning for the success of the crime about to be committed; and in another letter she said, "He (her husband) was ill yesterday. I thought God was beginning His work."

Pompilia Zambeccari had vowed to give a candle to the Madonna if she succeeded in poisoning her husband.

The woman Mercier belonged to a family of five

sisters and a brother, who were all subject to religious mania. She herself had visions wherein Jesus Christ appeared to her, and frequent auditive hallucinations during which she had fancied communications with God. Only the religious delirium was less intense in her case than in that of her brother and sisters—a fact which partly explained why she alone was a criminal, and why, in the intervals of her madness, she possessed so clear and lofty an intelligence.

Maria Forlini, who had strangled and torn to pieces a child in order to revenge herself on its parents, on being condemned to death, turned to one of her counsel and said, "Death is nothing. One must think of the salvation of one's soul. The rest is of no importance."

V. B., before murdering her husband, threw herself on her knees to pray to the Virgin for strength to accomplish the deed.

In 1670 the Parisian female poisoners of high rank alternated the administration of lethal powders with Satanic masses for the death of their husbands or the fidelity of their lovers. A priest read the ritual over the body of a pregnant woman (of bad life), after which the fœtus was strangled, and its blood and ashes served for the concoction of philtres. Voisin alone killed 2,500 of these little victims.

Trossarello imagined God to be the accomplice of her crimes, and declared that the death of her victim Gariglio was decreed in heaven as a punishment for having abandoned her. In fact, she added, his associate was also to die.

Contradictions.—The born criminal is not wanting in a paradoxical and intermittent goodness which makes a strange contrast to her habitual depravity.

Madame Lafarge was extremely kind to her servants. In her own neighbourhood she was called the Providence of the poor and the sick, whom she visited and assisted.

Jegado was extremely affectionate to her fellow-servants, but poisoned them the moment they offended her. D'Alessio caused her husband to be assassinated, but only a few years previously she had nursed him devotedly through a dangerous illness.

F. . . ., who murdered her husband with the assistance of her lover, supported a child whom she had taken from the orphanage.

Dumaire, who had enriched herself by prostitution, was generous with her money. She supported almost all her relatives, who were very poor; and she paid for the studies of the lover whom she finally killed when he deserted her.

Thomas relieved the wants of the poor, and often wept at the recital of their miseries. She bought presents and clothes for children.

P. T., one of the most ferocious female criminals who ever came under our notice, was very kind in succouring her companions, and showed a passionate love for children.

Trossarello sat up whole nights long by the bedsides of poverty-stricken patients.

All this altruism, however, is intermittent and of short duration.

Criminal women are kind to the unhappy simply

because the latter are in worse case than themselves. And this is a source of instinctive satisfaction to natures in whom the good fortune of others inspires only hatred. Moreover the exercise of charity enables them to feel that the party benefited is at their feet; that is to say, their love of power is gratified by good methods for once.

Their kindness, in short, is of an inferior sort, springing from what may be described as a composite selfishness.

This intermittent goodness explains the facility with which such women listen to sentimental suggestions, and the behaviour of the most ferocious among them in the presence of the scaffold, which to ordinary observers seems so heroically Christian and resigned as to appear a miracle worked by God for the redemption of a lost soul.

Madame Brinvilliers, as her confessor Pirot relates, died the death of a true Christian. She wrote letters to the families she had injured begging them to forgive her. She was full of kind consideration for her gaolers, to whom she left the few objects still in her possession. She addressed a letter to her husband in which she urged him to bring up her children in virtue and the fear of God.

The woman Tiquet listened devoutly to the sermons of her confessor. When her accomplice was decapitated she lamented that he should have suffered so severely for a crime to which she was the truly guilty party; and she kissed the executioner so that he might feel that she did not hate him.

Jegado, after an interview with a priest, declared

that she died happy and perfectly prepared for another life. Guillaume admitted that for her crime she deserved death. Balaguer showed herself pious. She left the few things she could dispose of to the wife of her lawyer, and during her last days succeeded so well in winning the affection of her prison companions that they all wept when she left them to mount the scaffold. She assured the executioner that she forgave him.

In all this there is some truth of feeling if little depth. The criminal receives a sentimental suggestion from her spiritual adviser, whose influence she falls under all the more easily because of her peculiar position. Alone, removed from evil, able to speak only with the priest, she is naturally moved by his appeals to the milder feelings in which she is not totally wanting, and her conscience reasserts itself in the absence of all stimulus to evil. This effect is produced the more easily that the female criminal is usually very accessible to religious impressions.

Add to this the instinctive yearning for sympathy and protection, even moral protection, which possesses women in general, and is likely to make itself strongly felt when they are rejected by the world and on the brink of the tomb. The priest is the only person with whom they have intercourse: they wish to captivate him, and with their feminine facility for assimilating the ideas and feelings of others they assume all the Christian virtues for a few days, even that virtue which is most foreign to their nature, namely forgiveness.

Sentimentalism.—If strong, true feelings are wanting

to these women, its place is supplied by a mawkish sentimentality, especially in their letters.

Avéline wrote to her lover: " I am jealous of nature which enrages us with her beauty. Do you not find, dear, that this beautiful weather is made for lovers and speaks to them of love?" Again: " How I wish we had accomplished the deed (her husband's murder) which will make us free and happy! I must see the end of it, for there is Paradise. At the turn of the road are roses."

Trossarello wrote to her lover letters full of sentimental declarations of love while all the time betraying him. The so-called Baroness Gravay de Livernière, one of the most shameless and accomplished swindlers of her time, wrote in her diary the following remarks about a youth of 18, whom at 48 she was endeavouring to marry. " Such a practical man! He only loves me because he hopes for the patronage of my friends. Ah, memories! when I think of him I recall the gallant cavalier who wrote:

> "' Pour avoir de noble dame
> Obtenir le doux baiser,
> Je vais brûlant d'une flamme
> Que rien ne peut appaiser.' "

Just because these women are moral lunatics and wanting in deep, true feeling, they fall easily into exaggerated sophistries, like the coward who in conversation boasts of imaginary theatrical courage.

Intelligence.—The intelligence of female criminals varies much. Some are very intelligent, while others are not remarkable in this respect. As a general thing, however, their minds are sufficiently alert; and this is one reason why they do not commit so many impulsive crimes (as men).

To kill in an explosion of bestial rage is compatible with the intelligence of a Hottentot; but to plan poisoning demands a certain ability and astuteness. And the crimes of women are almost always deliberate.

Impulsive female criminals who revenge themselves for a small offence by some act out of all proportion to its cause (like Closset, Rousoux, &c.), or women of great physical strength like Bonhours or P., may have only average intelligence, but the ferocious criminals who commit a multiplicity of crimes are generally very able.

M. (a case mentioned by Ottolenghi) had a remarkably active mind, very fertile in ideas, although her education had been scanty. She was greatly addicted to writing down her notions, and either scribbled them as best she could or dictated them to her companions; and when we remember how undeveloped are the graphic cerebral centres of women in general, this must be taken as a significant proof of mental superiority. For the rest, M.'s intelligence is sufficiently demonstrated by the fact that at 17 she had organised for herself and others a vast and profitable system of prostitution.

Brinvilliers, Lafarge, and Weiss had also acute minds, and wrote extremely well. Jegado was described by a witness as seeming a fool, but being really fiendishly clever.

Tiquet had been for many years distinguished for

her wit among persons of the best society. And the women who are induced to commit crimes through greed are usually well endowed with ability. Mercier, in spite of being subject to a religious mania which often caused her to make grave mistakes, had really remarkable business capacity. She had often amassed considerable sums of money by her commercial enterprises, and easily remade them when lost.

Lyons, the celebrated American adventuress and thief, must have possessed a very superior intelligence. She enriched herself by robbery in America, and came to Europe to continue the same system out of sheer love for it. Arrested *in flagrante* by the police of Paris, she succeeded in obtaining her liberty through the intercession of the British and American ambassadors. Equally able were many others, such as the pretended Countess Sandor, who wrote for newspapers, and in the disguise of a man captivated the daughter of a wealthy Austrian nobleman and obtained her in marriage, living with her for several months and extorting money from her father, until at his instigation she was arrested and her real sex discovered. Other instances are Bell-Star, who during many years led a band of outlaws in Texas and organised expeditions against the government of the United States itself, and finally the so-called Gravay de Livernière already described, whose real name was never discovered out of the seven or eight aliases which she had assumed; who at the age of 48 fascinated a youth of 19 to such an extent that he would not give her up even when she had been sentenced; who simulated the birth of a child, and for a long time passed for a cousin of the Queen of Spain.

P. W., who was guilty of stabbing and probably of poisoning, managed political newspapers, organised political conspiracies, and published novels and poems.

Madame Tarnowsky also remarked with reference to Theodosia W., a celebrated receiver of stolen goods in St. Petersburg, that in the management of her business she required much astuteness and discernment in order to distinguish between her different customers, who were sometimes poor wretches bringing their last possessions to pawn, sometimes real thieves, and sometimes spies.

Another proof that born criminals are often of great intelligence lies in the frequent originality of their crimes. M., already alluded to (Ottolenghi), enriched herself by a remarkable combination of prostitution, pandering, and blackmail. Lacassagne induced her accomplice in the murder of her illegitimate child, to take all the guilt upon himself by promising to marry him as soon as he had worked out his sentence, but when he presented himself to exact the fulfilment of her agreement, she murdered him with the assistance of her brother. Gras not having money enough to marry an artisan, caused the latter to throw vitriol at another lover of her own, who was in delicate health, her plan being to marry him when thus disfigured by persuading him that no other woman would take him, then to ruin his already shattered constitution, and, on being left a rich widow, to marry the man of her heart.

The superior ability of born criminals is explicable

when we remember that these women are often weak and physically incapable of satisfying their perverse instincts. If they have sufficient astuteness they can still triumph in the struggle for life, but in the contrary case they become prostitutes.

Writing and painting.—These two accomplishments are almost totally wanting in the born criminal. We have never found any tattooing or other design containing an allusion to crime, nor even any special sorts of embroidery which yet ought to be the graphic form peculiar to female offenders. The only instance we remember of the symbolic drawings in which male criminals indulge is that photograph, already described, of the lover of Pran. . . ., which she had adorned with two crosses and a death's head. The design was completed by a date, namely, that on which she intended to attempt his murder out of revenge for his having abandoned her. She held the document in high esteem, and kept it always by her in prison as a memento of her deed.

The born criminal is rarely inclined to write much. We know but of three instances among them of memoirs: those of Madame Lafarge, of X., and of Bell-Star, while male criminals are greatly addicted to these egotistic outpourings. Madame Lafarge, the woman X., and Bell-Star, particularly the last, were certainly endowed with superior intelligence, but among male criminals even those whose mental equipment is less than mediocre, there have been many who wrote memoirs.

Very rare also are poetesses, such as the mistress of the brigand Cerrato who dictated verses to him.

The most characteristic document ever written by a female criminal is the confession of her sins drawn up by the Marchioness of Brinvilliers, and which was one of the gravest witnesses against her at her trial. In it we find, first, that intensity of religious sentiment which feels the need of defining the sense of one's own guilt by giving it the life and weight of written words; next, the absence of foresight peculiar to the criminal, and finally that aberration of moral perception which confounds as equally wicked omissions of mere formal religious duties and monstrous crimes like parricide or incest.

Mode of execution of crimes. Deliberation.—Another proof of the frequent ability of born criminals is the deliberation with which women so often accomplish their crimes, and which, whether we regard it as an effect of weakness, or as suggested by the reading of romantic literature, is equally an evidence of intellect above the average.

The means taken to accomplish an end, even a comparatively simple end, are often most complicated. We have already described the elaborate plan conceived by Gras to obtain wealth and marry her lover.

Princess X., in order to remove the husband of the woman of whom she had need for her own vile purposes, carefully and lengthily prepared a meeting between the friend herself when with her lover and the friend's husband, in the hope that the jealousy of the latter would favour her own desires; and later she induced the friend, whom she had then determined to poison, to write a declaration of suicide which would guard the Princess herself from detection.

M., who wished to supplant a friend as lady's-maid in a family, first tried to turn her employers' minds against her by calumny; then when this failed, she calumniated the employers themselves to the servant by accusing them of cheating their domestics out of their salary. This device also proving useless, she next stole the key of the house from her friend, profited one evening by a moment when the latter had gone out leaving the front door open, to introduce herself furtively and hide under the other's bed. When the friend was asleep, M. stabbed her, and fled, shutting the house door after herself. The next day she returned, and calmly proposed to the mistress of the house to nurse the wounded woman until her recovery, and on the mistress hesitating to accept the offer, M. promised if she would do so, to reveal the name of the aggressor.

R. B., wishing to kill her husband, prepared, while he slept, a large cauldron of boiling water, then woke him, saying that somebody in the street was calling to him, and as he went, still half asleep, to the window, she pushed him into the cauldron.

It is clear that to conceive such complicated plans there is need of a certain amount of imagination which may supply the place of want of force. Muscular strength, were it present, would facilitate the execution of the crime, and its absence necessitates tortuous and indirect action. This is so true that women of masculine force, like Bonhours, who dressed herself in men's clothes and enjoyed wrestling with men, or like P., who could wield a heavy hammer, do not show this deliberation in their crimes, but settle matters with a resolute blow from a knife or a club.

One curious point in all this deliberation is that it proves itself often defective even in the case of the cleverest criminals. The plans hit upon even when most elaborate are constantly absurd and impossible, not to say mad. Morin, in order to rob and kill her enemy, devised a scheme for inveigling him into a house outside Paris which she had rented for the purpose. Once there, she intended to have him dragged down into a cellar and tied to a post, with nooses, carbines, pistols, and swords disposed all about to frighten him and superinduce in him the proper frame of mind for listening to a document composed in an inflated style which his daughter was to read aloud to him, and the object of which was to persuade him to sign certain bills of exchange. At the same time two ruffians dressed up as ghosts were meant to contort themselves, and utter terrific cries, thus giving the final touch to a scene which had been suggested by a novel of Mrs. Radcliffe's.

In the same way the born criminal constantly endeavours to prepare a preventive *alibi*, or proof of innocence; but her ideas, however ingenious, are often quite unadapted for their purpose. Madame Lafarge, for instance, who during her husband's malady put arsenic into his drinks instead of gum, used to make a point of being seen eating gum herself.

Buisson, while engaged in murdering an old man, was scratched by her victim, and as soon as she reached home she hanged her cat, then went with an air of anger to tell her friends that the brute had sprung at her face. Madame Meyron caused her husband to be stabbed in his bed by her lover, then drew up the bed coverings, called her friends, and, showing the corpse, said that death must have resulted from vomiting of blood.

Instigation.—The female born criminal does not always commit her crime herself. Often, unless she be endowed with masculine strength of muscle, or her intended victim be another woman, or her contemplated crime an insidious one, such as poisoning or incendiarism, her courage fails. The letters of the women Béridot and Avéline to their lovers are full of laments at weakness. Lavoitte said to her accomplice, "If I were a man I would kill that rich old woman myself." Here we see the cowardice of a weak creature at the thought of a struggle with one stronger than itself. Moral shrinkings there are none; the woman simply has recourse to instigation. For the born criminal is especially to be recognised by the fact that in a joint crime the part played by her is that of an *incubus*, to use an expression of Sighele's: she eggs on her accomplice to the deed with an extraordinary refinement of wickedness.

Fraikin employed Devilde, a paid assassin, to murder her husband, and when his courage had failed him for the third time at the moment of execution, she angrily exclaimed, "A man must be a fool to let so excellent an occasion escape him." At the fourth attempt she made him drunk, then conducted him to her husband's chamber, hid herself at the foot of the bed, at the same time showing him a note for a thousand francs, and at the decisive moment she still had presence of mind enough to admonish the murderer not to seize her husband by the hair, as he wore a wig.

Albert, whose paramour, Lavoitte, instigated him to murder an old woman, thus recounted the wiles by which she persuaded him: "She began by describing all the wealth of the woman, and the little use she made of it. I resisted, but the next day Philomene returned to the charge, arguing that in war one kills one's neighbour, and that there is no harm in it—then, why should that horrid old woman not be killed? 'God will pardon us,' she added, 'for He sees our misery.'"

Madame Simon tried to kill her weak husband by encouraging him to drink, and obliging him morning and evening to imbibe a mixture prepared by herself of brandy, gin, and other deleterious compounds. Afterwards she proposed to each one of her innumerable lovers to commit the murder, promising one of them *five francs* (!) and her hand; and at last Mérangal, a weak, half-crazy youth, was induced by her to accomplish the deed, for which she armed him with her own hand.

Madame de Brinvilliers, wishing to persuade one of her lovers against his conscience to commit a crime, said to him, "*What can it matter to you whether that old woman lives or not? You do not even know her.*"

Obstinacy in denial.—A peculiarity of female

offenders, and particularly of the born criminal, is their obstinacy in denying their crime, no matter how convincing the proof of it may be. The male criminal, when denial no longer serves him, usually confesses, but the woman only protests her innocence the more strenuously, the more obviously absurd her asseverations become.

D'Alessio, Rondest, Jumean, Saraceni, Béridot, Pearcy, and Daudet persisted in denying everything. Madame Lafarge maintained her guiltlessness to the end, and proclaimed it in the memoirs which were to survive when she was gone.

Jegado, in the teeth of all evidence, continued to assert that she did not even know the nature of arsenic, and that her one fault was to be too kindly disposed towards people in general ; and this attitude she persisted in to the end.

Even when they do not deny altogether, they invent excuses for themselves so elaborate and absurd that even a child would not believe them, but the criminal reiterates them imperturbably.

Madame Dacquignié declared that she had killed her husband in self-defence, although she bore no marks of violence. She maintained that she had only inflicted one blow on him, yet the corpse had six wounds.

Madame Lafarge, to excuse herself, invented a theft of diamonds of the most complicated and absurd description.

Madame Hoegli asserted that she had only inflicted on her daughter the usual corrections which a mother may give her child : if the daughter was suffocated, that was an accident.

Dépise, who had wounded her lover in an ambuscade, pretended that he had beaten her, thrown her down, and encouraged his dog to bite her.

Prager maintained that she had her brother armed with a revolver in her husband's room only that he might take possession of certain letters which would have compromised her in her divorce suit (but which she would not admit contained any proof of her adultery): as to the revolver—it was intended simply to frighten her husband.

Sometimes, when being tried in court, these women change their line of defence two or three times, and they asseverate each new statement with undiminished ardour, and without apparently ever reflecting that the variations in their story will influence the judges against them.

Madame Goglet, who set fire to her house in order to burn her old husband, said at first that the guilty party was a stranger whom she had fired at without hitting him. Next she asserted that she was not the true Madame Goglet, but a great friend, who exactly resembled her, and had undertaken to nurse the old man in his real wife's place. And finally, when the husband swore to her identity in court, she did not hesitate to affirm that he had become purblind in consequence of a shock.

"The female delinquent," observes Rykère, "is more sophistical and argumentative than her male prototype. She finds pretexts and excuses which astonish one by their fantasticality and strangeness."

Pasteur Arboux also remarks, "Not only do women when they fall into crime fall deeper than men, but they lie with greater coherence and audacity. They are bolder in the stories which they tell, and more hypocritical."

In short, the denials and excuses made by female offenders are marked by absurdity and elaborateness. That is to say, there is the same deliberation about them as we noted in the crimes of women. It is clear that if these criminals persist in their denials in the teeth of the most irrefragable proofs, this can only be because they are but little imbued with the sense of truth, and fail to conceive the state of mind which evidence produces in their judges. The logic of fact not penetrating to their own brains, they cannot feel the force of an irrefutable circumstance, and they believe others to be in the same case as themselves. The same feebleness of logical faculty explains the complicated lies which they invent in their own defence, and of which they fail to perceive the absurdity, patent though it be to others. Add to this the action of auto-suggestion which, when the lies have been repeated often enough, ends by converting them into half truths, and does so all the more easily that female criminals have very short memories for their own deeds. In a brief period the recollection of what they have done grows dim, and the delinquent then, freed from the sense of her crime, is able all the better to fix her attention on the story which she is telling. The image of the truth already faint is replaced in her mind by the imaginary narrative. A lie costs but little mental fatigue, and is consequently all the easier to repeat. The female offender does not waste her energy in inventing a plausible lie, but continues to reaffirm what she has already said without hesitation or failure, and she sometimes succeeds thus in influencing judge and jury to such a degree as to impose on their credulity with a fable of the most fantastic description.

Revelation of crime.—To the long list of contradictory circumstances which we have met with in the course of this work, we must now add another. We have shown that the female delinquent is obstinate in denying her guilt when pressed with questions by the judge. We have now to show that she often reveals her own guilt in a perfectly spontaneous manner: a singular psychological phenomenon for which there are many causes. One is that need to gossip and that incapacity for keeping a secret characteristic of the female sex. Gabrielle Bompard, for instance, while travelling with Garanger, began telling him many things about Eyraud, and on arriving in Paris, where all the newspapers were speaking of Eyraud and herself, she could no longer refrain from revealing her own identity and that of her accomplice. The woman Faure who threw vitriol at her lover would never have been discovered, so well had she taken her precautions, if she had not herself confided the secret to a female friend. Where an act of vengeance is concerned the temptation to tell is doubled through the keen joy which the avenger feels in her deed, and her desire to intensify that joy by confiding it to others. Nor must we neglect to take into account the habitual featherheadedness and imprudence of the female criminal who does not realise the peril to which she exposes herself by alluding publicly to her act. Sometimes the confession assumes a different form. The female criminal is impelled, indeed, to incriminate herself, but her want of foresight does not go so far as to make her reveal her intended crime before it is accomplished.

Her need to talk about it finds satisfaction by indirect means. She will show herself full of anxiety concerning the health of the man whom she intends to poison, telling her acquaintances, with every sign of sorrow, that she is sure he is about to die, even when he is still quite well. And when at last he sickens, but the truth is not yet suspected, she exhibits great concern, and is always predicting the worst.

Madame Lafarge, after she had sent her husband the poisoned tart, went about saying that she was in fear of receiving a black-bordered letter; and she inquired for how long a period widows in that part of the country habitually wore mourning. Hagu, after poisoning the wife of her lover Rogier, said, during the illness of her victim, "I tell you that she cannot live long. Is it possible that so young a man could remain with a woman who hates him?" Jegado, as soon as one of her victims fell ill, and before anybody suspected aught but a slight indisposition, would say, "He will die. Be sure of it. That is a mortal illness. Send for the priest," and so on.

All such speeches serve to resuscitate in the mind of the female offender the image of her crime, and afford her an after-taste of the voluptuous joy which she feels in evil-doing. Jegado's conversation turned always on death: "Her talk," said one person, "was a perpetual reminiscence of deceased persons."

As we have already mentioned, women, unlike men, do not embody their crimes in writing or drawing; hence the more imperious longing to invoke the memory of their acts by narrating them.

A woman talks of her crime just as a man will revive the recollection of it by written allusions, or by some drawing or engraving on an utensil, &c.[1]

Very singular is the confession which a woman sometimes makes to her lover. The female delinquent will reveal her crime to the man she loves, even if he neither questions nor suspects her. She will even sometimes force him to accept written proofs of her guilt, thus furnishing him with a weapon against her, of which she feels the full gravity when her mad but brief passion is over, and which often leads her to commit a fresh crime in order to rid herself of an inconvenient witness. V. confided to Signorini, her lover, that she had stolen some Government coupons; and later, when tired of him, she killed him to save herself from being accused of the theft.

Menghini, in a letter to her latest lover, D'Ottavi, avowed the murder of her husband, and when D'Ottavi left her she induced her preceding lover to kill the confidant, who had now become dangerous.

We have in all this a natural consequence of the tendency to mutual confidences which prevails among lovers, and especially of the need which every woman feels, when in love, to give some extraordinary proof of devotion to the man of her heart. The greater the pledge of love, the more the woman desires to bestow it; and what more can she do than to make

[1] *See* "Uomo Delinquente," vol. i.

a confession of guilt which by its very nature places her liberty and her life at the mercy of her lover? And here we have a fresh example of the habitual reckless imprudence of the female offender. She never reflects that her love is always of short duration, but invariably believes that it will be as lasting as it is intense. This, joined to that absence of moral convictions which causes her to regard the gravest crimes as a mere trifling lapse, furnishes the only possible explanation of her conduct. Otherwise, how could she make up her mind to confess her crime to a lover in whom (even supposing him to be momentarily attracted by an avowal which lifts the woman, through her wickedness, out of the ranks of the commonplace), it must nevertheless in the long run inspire only horror and aversion?

In other cases jealousy, a spirit of revenge for having been abandoned by her lover, drives the female criminal to accuse her accomplice. "The woman," writes Joly, "who is, or believes herself to be, betrayed, is merciless in denouncing her accomplices." Sometimes the betrayal results not from passion, but from a spirit of astute calculation. The woman finds herself threatened with the detection of her crime, and by abandoning her accomplice she hopes (especially if young and good-looking) to earn the indulgence of the law for herself. The fickleness of the female sex must also be taken into account. A woman adores a man as a god, and is willing to die for him during a few months; then her affection turns to hatred, and she hands him over to justice without the least hesitation. According to

Guillot this inconstancy forms the greatest danger for all associations of malefactors. Bompard unhesitatingly sacrificed her accomplice, who was also, in part, her victim. Bistor was arrested on information received from the woman Perrin, his associate in crime, just as the police were about to pigeon-hole the case.

In consequence of this frequent deliberate or involuntary betrayal of associates on the part of female delinquents, the more intelligent criminals of the opposite sex are wary of trusting them.

In the band of malefactors captained by Chevalier and Abadie there was a regulation to the effect that only two women, the mistresses of the leaders, should be admitted.

Synthesis.—In general the moral physiognomy of the born female criminal approximates strongly to that of the male. The atavistic diminution of secondary sexual characters which is to be observed in the anthropology of the subject, shows itself once again in the psychology of the female criminal, who is excessively erotic, weak in maternal feeling, inclined to dissipation, astute and audacious, and dominates weaker beings sometimes by suggestion, at others by muscular force; while her love of violent exercise, her vices, and even her dress, increase her resemblance to the sterner sex. Added to these virile characteristics are often the worst qualities of woman: namely, an excessive desire for revenge, cunning, cruelty, love of dress, and untruthfulness, forming a combination of evil tendencies which often results in a type of extraordinary wickedness. Needless to say these different characteristics are not found in the same proportion in everybody. A criminal, like Bonhours or P., will be deficient in intelligence, but possessed of great physical strength; while another, such as M., who is weak physically, triumphs over this obstacle by the ability with which she lays her plans. But when by an unfortunate chance muscular strength and intellectual force meet in the same individual, we have a female delinquent of a terrible type indeed. A typical example of these extraordinary women is presented by Bell-Star, the female brigand, who a few years ago terrorised all Texas. Her education had been of the sort to develop her natural qualities; for, being the daughter of a guerilla chief who had fought on the side of the South in the war of 1861–65, she had grown up in the midst of fighting, and when only ten years old, already used the lasso, the revolver, the carbine, and the bowie-knife in a way to excite the enthusiasm of her ferocious companions. She was as strong and bold as a man, and loved to ride untamed horses which the boldest of the brigands dared not mount. One day at Oakland she twice won a race, dressed once as a man and once as a woman, changing her dress so rapidly that her ruse remained unsuspected. She was extremely dissolute, and had more than one lover at a time, her admirer *en titre* being always the most intrepid and daring of the band. At the first sign of cowardice he was degraded from his rank. But, however bold he might be, Bell-Star dominated him entirely, while all the time having—as Varigny writes—as many lovers as there were desperadoes in four States. At the age of eighteen she became head of the band, and ruled her associates partly through her superior intelligence, partly through her courage, and to a certain degree through her personal charm as a woman. She organised attacks of the most daring description on populous cities, and fought against government troops, not hesitating the very day after one of these raids to enter some neighbouring town unaccompanied, and dressed—as almost always—in male attire. Once she slept in the same hotel as the judge of the district, without his once suspecting her identity or even her sex. And as during the *table d'hôte* dinner he had boasted that he would undoubtedly recognise Bell-Star if he ever met her, and would arrest her on the spot, the following morning, when mounted, she sent for him, told him who she was, called him a fool, and after lashing him twice across the face with her whip, galloped away. She wrote her memoirs, recording in them her desire to die in her boots. This wish was granted, for she fell in a battle against the government troops, directing the fire to her latest breath.

Another Napoleon in petticoats similar to Bell-Star was Zélie, a Frenchwoman by birth. She was extremely intelligent, spoke three languages perfectly, had extraordinary personal fascination, and even from childhood showed herself perfidious and profligate. Her adventures having carried her to the brigand country of North America, she became the leader of a band of malefactors. With a bold and audacious air, and her revolver in her hand, she was always the first to face danger, and when quarrels arose among her companions she would throw herself into the midst of them and make them lay down their arms. Laughing she crossed perilous mountain-paths where others feared to follow her: neither epidemics, earthquakes, nor war availed to cow her. She eventually died in a lunatic asylum in France, a prey to hysteria.

M. R., a case described by Ottolenghi, was a thief, a prostitute, a corrupter of youth, a blackmailer, and all this at the age of 17. When only 12 she robbed her father in order to have money to spend among her companions. At 15 she fled from home with a lover, whom she left almost at once for a career of prostitution. With a view to larger gains, when only 16 she organised a vast system of prostitution, by which she provided young girls of 12 and 15 for wealthy men, from whom she exacted large sums, of which only a few sous went to the victims. And by threats of exposure she managed to levy costly blackmail on her clients, one of whom, a highly-placed functionary, was dismissed from his post in consequence of her revelations. She was extremely vindictive, and committed two crimes of revenge which serve to show the strange mixture of ferocity and cunning composing her character. One of her companions having spoken evil of her, she (who was then only 16 years of age) let a little time pass, then coaxed her enemy to accompany her outside the gates of the town. They reached a deserted spot as evening fell, and M. R. suddenly threw the other girl on the ground, and while recalling her offence proceeded to beat her violently with a pair of scissors and a key, nor desisted until her victim had fainted; after which she quietly returned to town. "You might have killed her," somebody said. "What did that matter?" she replied; "there was nobody to see." "You might have employed a hired assassin." "I am afraid of those," was the answer. "Besides, on principle one should do things oneself." "But with a key you could never have killed her" (went on the other). "If one beats the temples well," M. R. replied, "it is quite possible to kill a person even with a key."

She conceived on another occasion such a violent hatred to a brilliant rival that, enticing her into a café, she furtively poisoned her coffee and thus caused her death.

It would be difficult to find greater wickedness at the service of a vindictive disposition and an unbridled greed. We may regard M. R. as an instance in which the two poles of depravity were united. That is to say, she was sanguinary (for she went about always with a dagger in her pocket, and stabbed anybody who offended her in the least) and at the same time inclined to commit the more cautious and insidious crimes, such as poisoning, blackmail, &c. And we consequently find in her an example of the law we have already laid down, to the effect that the female born criminal, when a complete type, is more terrible than the male.

CHAPTER XIII.

OCCASIONAL CRIMINALS.

THE born offender is more completely and intensely depraved than any other, but the case is quite different with the occasional criminals who form the large majority of female delinquents. In them perversity and vice are of a milder form, and there is no want of the higher virtues of the sex, such as chastity and maternal love.

1. *Physical characteristics.*—The first thing to be observed is the absence of any characteristics or features denoting degeneration. As we saw already 54 per cent. of female offenders are absolutely normal in these respects, and even as regards the special senses they show no peculiarity, 15 per cent. having fineness of taste, and 6 per cent. fineness of smell.

2. *Moral character.*—The same may be said of their moral equipment. Guillot unconsciously described the occasional criminal exactly when recording his observations on female prisoners, in the following words :—

" The guilty woman, with a few exceptions in which all vices are combined, is more easily moved to penitence than men, recovers the lost ground more quickly, and relapses into crime less frequently."

And he quotes a lady visitor of St. Lazare who, speaking of the female prisoners, said: "When one knows them it is easy to love them:" thus showing that their natural perversity is not excessive.

"The writings on prison walls in the male cells," continues Guillot, "breathe violence, impiety, threats, and obscenities; those in the female cells are much more reserved, and speak only of repentance and of love." And he gives a few examples:—

"In this cell where my love perishes, far from thee, my adored one, I moan and suffer."

"John loves me no longer, but I shall love him always."

"You who enter the cell, called *souricière*, if not separated from your loved one you only suffer one-half."

"What should my heart find to say to you in this mournful cell, unless it expresses all its pain and agony, its longing and despair at the thought of my loved one?"

"Henrietta once loved her lover more than any woman ever loved, but now she detests him."

"I swear never to begin again, for I am sick of men; love brought me here, for I killed my lover. Beware of men, they are liars all."

"The judgment of men is nothing—only God's matters."

"God is so good, He pities the unfortunate."

"Mary, our Lady, Holy Virgin, I throw myself at your feet, and place myself under your protection."

And in these female criminals the sense of chastity is very strong. In France, for instance, they shrink with horror from the idea of going to St. Lazare where they might come into contact with prostitutes.

Macé refers to occasional offenders and not to the shameless and dissolute born criminal in the following remarks:—

"The women are reluctant. They are alarmed at the idea of St. Lazare, because associating with it an indelible brand of ignominy and disgrace. They see themselves brought into contact with the degraded of their sex, and no woman enters willingly on the road to that prison."

Guillot also noted the antagonism existing between prostitutes and delinquents in St. Lazare.

The latter hold venal women in horror; but it must be confessed that the aversion is mutual, for prostitutes boast that they have never stolen.

The born criminal, on the other hand, cannot despise the prostitute, for she is herself equally unchaste.

Guillot remarks upon the strong maternal love existing in occasional offenders, and which contrasts with that utter absence of the sentiment in the born criminal, so amply demonstrated already by us.

"In St. Lazare," says Guillot, "maternal jealousy frequently breeds rivalries and jealousies. Every mother wishes her own child to be considered the handsomest, the strongest, and to be most admired, most caressed. The birth of an infant is an event which turns the whole prison upside down; and insubordinate offenders, who would not submit to prison regulations even when threatened with solitary confinement, have shown a lamb-like docility on being threatened with separation from their child."

And not only chastity and maternal love, but other gentle qualities are present to prove how little the occasional offender differs from her normal sister.

Guillot, for instance, remarks upon the species of affection and the extreme trustfulness of this class of women towards their advocates, especially if young and good-looking. The lawyer becomes a kind of protector, inspiring rather a chimerical confidence and a filial respect and attachment.

One prisoner wrote on the wall: "I am in prison, charged with a theft of 2,000 francs: but it is of no consequence—I have a lawyer."

Here, then, is an example of the need of protection and the confidence in the other sex, which we have described as characteristic of the normal woman, but which are entirely wanting in the born criminal, who, semi-masculine, tyrannical, and selfish, demands not help or protection from anybody, but the simple satisfaction of her own passions.

This confidence in the lawyer is only a form of the feminine need of protection, which finds a stronger expression in love. Love among occasional offenders is much more disinterested and profound than among born criminals—in whom, indeed, it is a mere shallow impulse born of unbridled selfishness.

"They" (occasional offenders), writes Guillot, "know quite well how to distinguish between the unhappy woman who testifies in court against her lover while thinking to save him, as in the Pranzini trial, or while seeking to exculpate herself, as in the Marchandon affair, or with the object of freeing herself from the yoke of a monster, as in the Prado trial, and the woman who from cowardice consents to take part in a conspiracy against her lover. They pity the first class for having to do what they would do themselves under similar circumstances, but the action of the second class revolts the sentiments of tenderness and generosity of which these women are still capable."

For instance, Gabrielle Fénayron, while confined in St. Lazare, could never show herself in the prison court, because, had she done so, the other prisoners would have ill-treated her.

Occasional criminals are consequently capable of the spiritualised love which is especially womanly; but in the born criminal there is only sensuality and lust.

In order, however, to understand exactly in what the degree of criminality of these occasional offenders consists, we must make a psychological examination of the occasions which have led them into crime, and which may be divided into several heads.

3. *Suggestion.*—In many cases the origin of her reluctant crime in such a woman is suggestion on the part of a lover, or sometimes of her father or brother.

A prison-sister once said to us, pointing to the women, "These are not like men. They do not commit crimes out of evil passions, but to please their lovers. They steal or compromise themselves for men's sakes, without having sometimes any direct interest in the act."

Sighele [1] remarked that among the distinctive signs of these occasional crimes is the length of time necessary to make the suggestion bear fruit, together with uncertainty of execution on the woman's part and her speedy remorse when the deed is done.

A certain L., whom her lover wished to induce to kill her husband, took from him a bottle of sulphuric acid, promising to make her husband drink it; but at the moment of pouring the poison into a glass of wine she felt her courage fail, and, dropping the bottle, confessed.

Guiseppina (Josephine) P., a fatherless girl of 17, was seduced by a man much older than herself, who afterwards married her. The marriage turned out unhappily, and after the birth of a daughter, whom the husband repudiated, the couple separated. The woman, thrown on her own resources, was reduced from wealth to a mere pittance of thirty francs a month; and she became the lover of a certain Guillet, a brutal and avaricious peasant, who obtained great influence over her, and in order to get possession of her husband's property induced her to assist in murdering him.

Josephine had yielded, but when arrested showed herself penitent and confessed the crime. "God will forgive me," she said, "because I have been so unhappy. I had no means of existence, I was alone and starving. My own family would give me nothing, and it was then this man (Guillet) ruined me. He is the origin of all my misfortunes and of my crime."

---

[1] "Coppia Criminale," 1893, and "Archivio di psichiatria," vols. xiii. and xiv. Turin.

M. R., who showed none of the graver signs of degeneration, and was industrious and honest, resisted the profligate designs of her father, and turned a deaf ear to her brother, who wished her to support him by prostituting herself, but fell in love with a man of bad character, and fled from home in his company. The pair were soon reduced to misery, for the woman could find no work, and the man looked for none; and eventually the lover proposed that they should commit burglary upon a jeweller, threatening to abandon the woman if she refused. For a time she resisted, then, after two days of utter want, consented, but only to show herself uncertain and inefficient in the commission of the offence, so that she was arrested without any difficulty. In prison she showed herself penitent and made a full confession. There was, however, something masculine in her force and energy of character, and still more in her absence of maternal instincts. For she was pregnant, but said openly that she should take no care of her child.

"Women are the cause of most of the offences committed by men," writes Guillot, "but they are often ignorant of the means by which their caprices have been satisfied; or if they have suspicions they stifle them, not daring to protest, and either yielding to threats or allowing themselves to be blinded by love. They become, in fact, docile slaves."

The majority of women who commit abortion have done so under suggestion; infanticides, on the other hand, showing, as we have seen, a greater similarity with the women who err from passion. As Sighele well observes, abortion is hardly ever the act of the woman only. Generally it is her lover who forces her to it to avoid the scandal which would otherwise result. Fouroux, for instance, induced his mistress, who was the wife of his friend, an officer in the navy on foreign service, to commit abortion. Georgina Boges, a woman of very weak character, almost without any individuality of her own, was so much under the influence of her lover (who was also her mother's) that she helped him to kill her child. Before the judge she was still so much dominated by her partner in sin and by her mother that she tried to exculpate them by taking the whole blame of the crime upon herself.

Desirée Ferlin, a girl of weak health and character, extremely gentle, was violated by her own father, and at his suggestion had recourse to abortion; but when arrested refused to speak of her father until forced to do so, and then tried to defend him. A girl named Lemaire was also twice forced to commit abortion by her father; but in her case terror, and not simple suggestion, was the agent. She hated her father and tried to resist him, but in vain, for he was a man of the worst description, who forced her to lead a life of utter isolation, and was in the habit of brutally beating her. Once, because she had broken loose, he made her kneel on the edge of a scythe to ask his pardon.

Sometimes it is not the suggestion of a despotic lover, but the example of an acquaintance which supplies the impulse to the act. A woman finds herself suddenly pregnant, and would be glad to escape from so compromising a condition, but has no clear ideas on the subject, nor has formed any definite resolution. She meets a friend who was once in a similar position and has more experience; who gives the address of an expert midwife, and testifies to the simplicity and security of the method recommended. Nobody will know anything any more than in the friend's case. The perplexed woman ends by being persuaded, and a fixed resolution succeeds to her first vague desire. Here is a letter found among the papers of a midwife, and furnishing a good example of the way in which such an idea is formed gradually by suggestion in the midst of many doubts:—

"MADAM,—My friend, Mrs. X., tells me I may confidently address you and count upon your discretion. I have to tell you a very delicate thing: I am pregnant and in despair. I am sure my lover would abandon me if I had a child, and that would give me pain. He does not know my condition, and I do not wish him to know it. My friend assures me that you will be able to relieve me without danger and without anybody's knowledge. Please make an appointment and believe in my eternal gratitude."

In other cases it is want and the claims of an already large family which suggest the expedient. "Why bring another unfortunate being into the world?" This is the feeling, the reasoning of the mother who loves the children she has already, and would love the new-comer if it were not destined to add to the existing misery of the family. Her idea is no proof of perversity, especially as she desires to get rid not of a living thing, but of something invisible and intangible, which has for her as yet no existence in reality. In this connection we may recall the case in which Zola was on the jury and which he related to a reporter of the *Figaro*. "A woman was in the dock who in three confinements had had four children. One day she found herself again pregnant. Her husband, a porter, earned very little. In despair the woman went to call on a neighbour to whom she related her trouble. Then suddenly an idea came to her. 'If I could only get rid of it!' she said. The neighbour can give her no advice, but knows of a woman who can. Together they seek out this woman in a washhouse, and the deed is done, in return for the sum of four francs and a half, which is all the porter's wife can dispose of. And now behold all three at the assizes! Would you have had the heart to condemn those three women who had nine children among them, and who stood there in tears? *I* had not the heart."

Now here is a case in which the criminal is an artificial product, the outgrowth of a suggestion, and absolutely analogous to the examples furnished on a much larger scale by hypnotism.

It is true that, as in hypnotism, the subject only responds to the suggestions which are in harmony with his character; and the women who are induced by another will than their own to commit offences have certainly had a latent tendency to crime. But the tendency is not strong enough for them to have sinned spontaneously; and this is the point wherein they differ from the born criminal. They are offenders, indeed, but offenders on a reduced scale, and they possess only some of the characteristics of the born criminal. In one case the maternal sentiment will be deficient, in another there are dissolute tendencies, facility for falling in or out of love; and sometimes there is even less departure from the type of the normal woman, crime being resorted to with difficulty and followed by intense remorse.

In short, there are degrees by which we pass from the born criminal to the woman of moral life, and each degree offers the example of a more or less complete occasional offender.

Suggestion, as we have seen, emanates almost always from a lover, the reasons for this being partly sexual and partly due to the confidence which women have in men. Another factor, as in the case of M. R., is the capacity for an intense if not enduring affection, and the influence which a man naturally acquires over the woman to whom he is joined by illicit affection. More rarely suggestion emanates from a woman.

Giulia Bila was bound to Maria Moyen, a woman of equivocal life, by affection of an intensity such as is rarely seen, and was so entirely under her friend's influence as to consent without difficulty to execute the vengeance which Maria had planned against a lover who had abandoned her. Giulia was filled with indignation equal to Maria's, against the betrayer, who was always represented to her in the blackest colours, and felt such a hatred to him that she easily adopted the suggestion of throwing a bottle of vitriol in his face. But her offence was hardly committed before she was filled with horror and remorse. She allowed herself to be arrested, and weeping, averred, what of course was true, that she had not been her own mistress when accomplishing the act.

Fernande K., a German woman of the most malignant character, organised in Paris a band of female domestic thieves whom she ruled with a rod of iron, commanding them as a general commands his soldiers.

She picked up all the servant-girls who had been dismissed for a first small offence (such as thefts of little value) and found some difficulty consequently in engaging themselves again; procured them situations by forging certificates, and forced them to commit robberies of as much value as possible in each house, the proceeds being brought to her for division, with a lion's share for herself.

Not one of her tools dared to disobey her, or to defraud her of even a small part of the spoils by keeping anything back from the division.

Rondest, that ferocious born criminal, who, as we have seen, murdered her mother so as not to be obliged to support her, had a friend in whom she gradually inspired just the same hatred for the mother as she was possessed by herself. The friend, regarding the elder woman as a personal enemy, beat and insulted her, and constantly repeated Rondest's own phrase, "I have to support you," just as though she had been the daughter *in propriâ personâ*.

This is a form of contagious hatred and crime analogous to what experts in mental affections describe as contagious delirium (Sighele), and the phenomenon is unknown among normal women.

Friendship is a form of suggestion, as Sighele has shown, and in certain cases it results in the total absorption of the weaker personality in the stronger one.

Why do we find this friendship and this suggestion in the criminal class? We have already explained the absence of friendship between women by the latent animosity of one to the other; but there is an even stronger reason. Friendship is not possible without suggestion, and suggestion can only work when between two persons there is a marked psychical difference. Now normal women are monotonous; they resemble one another, and cannot be acted upon by suggestion: consequently friendship with its dominion of the stronger over the weaker is impossible to them. On the other hand, criminals, being products of degeneration, develop variations which sometimes amount to monstrosities; consequently between any two of them there may be such a difference in character as lends itself easily to suggestion, the born criminal, that malignant semi-masculine creature, being able to influence the criminaloid, in whom bad instincts are latent, being indeed mere exaggerations of normal impulses.

4. *Education—bad results of it.*—The occasions which present themselves to draw the naturally moral woman into crime are multiplied now by the higher education conceded to females, but of which they can make no use by earning their bread in offices or professions.

Many women of intelligence find themselves with nothing to show in return for much expense and labour. They are reduced to want while conscious of not deserving it, and being debarred from the probability of matrimony owing to the ordinary man's dislike to a well-instructed woman, they have no resource but in suicide, crime, or prostitution The chaster ones kill themselves; the others sell themselves, or commit thefts.

Macé relates that many governesses are to be found in St. Lazare imprisoned for thefts of gloves, veils, umbrellas, pocket-handkerchiefs, and other articles necessary for them to make a good appearance in school, and which they cannot always earn enough to purchase. They have been driven to the offence, consequently, by the exigencies of their profession. "The number of governesses," he says, "who have no pupils is so great that a certificate, whether high- or low-class, becomes the cause of suicide, of theft, or of prostitution."

M., the daughter of an eccentric, unpractical mother, received a high literary but incomplete education, crowned by a university degree, which only unfitted her for real life. At twenty-three she found herself an orphan, ruined by family reverses, and with an idle brother who refused her all help. After various vain efforts she accepted a post of teacher in an elementary school in the country, but was dismissed, at the unanimous request of the inhabitants, on its being discovered that she was a Protestant. Then, alone in the world, without means of existence, and haunted by the memory of more prosperous days, she began buying articles of jewellery in shops, where she obtained credit in virtue of the former position of her family, and either resold them at half-price or pawned them. A series of such frauds finally brought her to prison, where she died before her trial, worn out by misery and shame.

5. *Excessive temptations.* — Sometimes offences, especially offences against property, are committed by normal, or nearly normal, women through sheer excess of temptation.

We have observed that in the normal female the sense of property is not very strong. Richet relates that the articles accidentally found and brought to the Municipal Office in Paris are almost always thus restored by men; and a cultivated lady, Mrs. R., once confided to the writers that it is very difficult for women to play without cheating. So weak a respect for property will naturally yield to strong temptation. Their offence will even appear to them in the light of an escapade rather than a crime, and we must admit that they can commit it without being deeply depraved.

"Women," as Joly truly remarks, "have a floating idea that they may do anything to men, since it is always open to them to pay with their persons."

Shoplifting, which has become so common since the era of huge establishments, is a specially feminine offence—temptation being furnished by the immense number of articles exhibited, and which excite the desires of women who can only afford to buy a few. We saw that fine things are not articles of luxury for women, but articles of necessity, since they equip them for conquest; and therefore the huge shop, with its manifold and various seductions, betrays them into crime. An inspector of the *Bon Marché* told Joly that out of 100 female thieves 25 per cent. are habitual offenders who rob whenever they can, 25 per cent. are impelled to the act by want, and 50 per cent. are, as he expressed it, *monomaniacs*—that is to say they are women often in a good social position and of easy means, but who yet cannot resist the temptation of so many beautiful things displayed before them.

Of this class a certain proportion are true kleptomaniacs.

Macé calculated that in the thirty principal shops of Paris there are five thefts committed every day, while in the provinces the number amounts to a hundred thousand; and he affirms that out of every hundred thieves there will be one poor woman for ninety-nine rich or fairly well-to-do, the reason being that women in society come into contact with luxury, feel the need of it, and are consequently more subject to temptation.

Zola has given a good description of this form of dishonesty in his " Bonheur des Dames."

Ladies who cannot spend, or do not need to do so, go all the same to the great sales, as an engineer will go to an exhibition of machines, just out of interested curiosity. Little by little a fever possesses them, and they end either by buying far beyond their means or accomplish a dexterous theft.

Domestic thefts committed by maidservants are almost all to be included under the head of occasional crimes. Girls come up from the country and enter houses where the great or relative well-being which reigns seems to them a sign of enormous wealth. They are badly paid, yet are given money, plate, and other valuables to handle, which awake in them the greed innate in every woman. A small malversation in the daily expenditure, or the theft of a trinket or a piece of silver, seem to them rather an irregularity than a judicial crime. "Forty-nine per cent. of female thieves," writes Madame Tarnowsky, "belong to the class of domestic servants, and return to service in their intervals of liberty from prison; 34 per cent. are general servants—that is to say, they receive no training and take low wages." Our theory with regard to occasional criminals receives confirmation from this enormous proportion of domestic servants among female thieves.

Given, then, this feeble organic shrinking from theft, and stealing soon becomes a habit if the occasions for committing it be repeated: the occasional offender becomes an habitual offender, and goes to swell the ranks of the systematic female thieves who are always practising upon their employers.

Balzac, in the following words, described this evil as it existed in his day:—

"With a few exceptions, cooks, male and female, are domestic thieves, shameless thieves whom we pay. ... Once women of this description wanted forty sous for the lottery, now they take fifty francs for their savings bank. They plant their toll-house between the dinner-table and the market-place, and the Municipality of Paris itself is not so successful in exacting its dues. Fifty per cent. is levied on all eatables, and presents demanded from the tradespeople as well.

"The richest shopkeepers tremble before this new tyranny, and seek silently but invariably to conciliate it. Anybody attempting control is met (by these women-servants) with insolence and abuse, or is grossly calumniated.

"We have indeed now reached a stage in which servants demand particulars regarding their employers, as the latter formerly did about them."

Madame Grandpré assures us that the evil is much greater in Paris to-day. She mentions maidservants who have so enriched themselves as to become persons of consideration in their neighbourhood, and who, worse still, instruct in their own practices young girls freshly arrived from the country.

Madame Grandpré cites as an example the story of a servant-girl whom she became acquainted with in St. Lazare:—

"She had come to Paris to seek a situation which would enable her to support two little brothers of whom she was very fond. She was very ignorant, but was engaged in the house of rich people, who paid her ill and nourished her badly, besides setting her to do the most menial tasks under the control of the upper servants, whose tyranny was, as usual, all the greater for being exercised in petty ways.

"One evening, when the girl was weeping over the humiliations and hardships of her position, in her own room, a fellow-servant, older and more experienced, went to console her. She won the girl's confidence, and in reply to her complaints of misery, taught her various artifices by which she could add to her salary, and which the other, seeing small harm in them, consented to after only a little hesitation. Eventually she had to go to prison. 'And yet,' she said, 'she (the fellow-servant) does the same thing, but she is not in prison; on the contrary, she is respected in the neighbourhood, and all the tradesmen bow to her.'"

Another proof that thieves are occasional criminals, differing but little from the normal woman, is furnished us by the observation of Madame Tarnowsky, who remarks on the difference in industry between prostitutes and thieves. The latter, when in prison, can be employed in various ways; they are prudent and put by money; they are also more tenacious than prostitutes, and can concentrate their minds better: thus showing their freedom from many of the fundamental qualities of the real criminal.

6. *Desertion and corruption of infants.*—Neglect during infancy, and desertion on the part of parents, are among the causes which most conduce to dishonesty in women, who begin by being occasional thieves, then on leaving prison, either finding it impossible to work after their long period of idleness, or failing to overcome the prejudices of employers against those whom justice has branded, are transformed into habitual offenders.

The male child only learns respect of property from teaching and example, and much more fatal consequently is desertion in the case of the female infant who is naturally less honest even when well educated and surrounded with every advantage.

The effect is well described by Madame Tarnowsky in her remarks upon Russian female thieves, of whom the majority spring from the people, whose habits are careless and spendthrift.

"The future thief (female)," writes the lady, "grows up without learning to work, and is left to run about idle in the midst of all the temptations of the streets. She is often cold and hungry, for at home there is neither food nor fire; and she finishes one day either by prostituting herself for a dainty, or by stealing some article for which her longing has grown during long hours of idleness, and then she goes to prison to expiate the crime of having been born of poor and vicious parents.

"Her first period of detention ended, she goes forth rich in knowledge acquired from her companions in prison, and promising herself to profit by what she has learnt, but to be wary and not let herself be caught again.

"After her first theft she has ceased to hold communication with her family, who, in any case, could only starve and ill-treat her; and crime consequently becomes a necessity of her existence."

7. *Abuse and blows.*—Other occasional offences committed by women are blows and abusive language.

Owing to the latent antipathy of women towards one another, they are subject to mutual hatreds which arise and grow from trivial causes, and, thanks to the sex's superior hastiness of temper, lead easily to insults and assaults. Abuse and blows appear, indeed, to be for women what, in barbarous days, homicide was for men—namely, a natural method of resenting injury.

"A little water spilt upon the stairs," writes Macé, "will set two women quarrelling. One slaps the other; the slapped one flies to the police court and causes her enemy to be condemned to a fine, in default of paying which she is taken to prison."

Such incidents happen every day between neighbours, or competing retail shopkeepers; between caretakers and tenants, between portresses and servant-girls, between servant-girls themselves, and so on. Nor are ladies of higher condition strangers to such methods, only that *they* often resort to modes of vindictiveness which do not always lead to a court of law.

8. *Mendicity.*—Even begging, which in men is almost always a result of degeneration, a congenital tendency developed by vagabondage and idleness, is sometimes in women an occasional delinquency.

As we have pointed out already, women are less inclined than men to commit suicide from want, and one reason of this is that when reduced to misery they resort with less difficulty to begging, either because they are by nature more pliable to circumstances, or because more moved by maternal affection. Macé tells the story of a widow with two daughters who, when no longer able to earn even a franc a day by sewing trousers, because one of the girls was ill and had to be nursed, sent the other one out to beg. The child was arrested, but would not give her address until she had exacted a promise that she should not be sent to prison. The Prefect of Police went to visit the case and found the family in a squalid garret, and the mother determined not to be separated from the sick girl whom she dreaded to see die like her husband in a hospital. The spectacle seemed so pitiable to the officer that, instead of taking legal measures, he left a donation of 100 francs. Macé says that in the case of women the police constantly have not the courage to commit women for begging; for even they, so little given to a liberal interpretation of the law, feel that it would be inhuman to treat what they recognise for an occasional and involuntary offence, in the same manner as they visit the vagabond propensities of the true degenerate.

9. *Characteristic local offences.*—It is the *occasional* nature of women's offences which explains a fact otherwise in contradiction with the monotony prevailing in all the physiological and psychical manifestations of the sex, the fact, that is, that in different countries different sorts of female criminals abound. There are, in short, ethnological variations in the criminality of women of more marked extent than variations in any other branch of their psychology, but the reason is that different social conditions in each country offer opportunities for different sorts of crime.

In Sweden, for instance, infanticide is most common, the reason being that in that country women are employed to draw sledges, and are consequently at the mercy of brutal men during journeys outside the towns and in districts removed from authority. They find themselves pregnant and have recourse to infanticide as the only means of saving their reputation, and concealing a shame of which the causes are accidental and an incident of their calling. A special opportunity breeds a special class of offence, and the offenders, who are quasi-normal, would have broken no laws had the condition of their life been different.

According to the anonymous author of the "Scandales de St. Pétersbourg" infanticide and abortion are common incidental crimes among the upper classes, the occasion for them arising from the dissolute habits of the men, and the facile morals of the women in the midst of a society which is so strangely composed of barbarous and civilised customs.

The writer in question says: "It is especially the women of the upper classes who have recourse to this offence. Sometimes they are young girls anxious to save their reputations; sometimes married women, who, for one reason or another, do not wish to become mothers. Specialists both male and female have a very large practice. The facility with which abortion is practised is all the greater that neither husbands nor lovers are at all scrupulous in this respect, and regard the act as only slightly if at all criminal.

Again, according to the same authority, a still more common offence among Russian women is simulation of birth or the substitution of one infant for another —and here the cause is that for various social and legislative reasons marriage is costly and difficult— consequently even moral women have to consent to unions where they have no other guarantee—a feeble one for the most part—than the love and loyalty of the man.

Very often the latter after some years grows weary of his companion, and especially if there are no children he is ready to avail himself of the absence of a legal tie. Then it is that the woman conceives the idea of avoiding desertion by simulating a birth which may revive her husband's love by awakening the paternal sentiment in him. There was a celebrated law-suit in St. Petersburg, wherein the parties were an extra-legal wife and a very rich, very avaricious banker, who so cruelly ill-treated his companion that she sought to soften her lot by pretending to make her husband a father.

She managed the ruse so well as to deceive him completely; and he made her a handsome donation. This great success induced a feeling of remorse in her, and she imprudently made a full confession of the deception she had practised. Her husband was furious and brought an action against her, of which he was himself the chief victim, since it covered him with public ridicule.

In the same way shoplifters were for a time a French speciality, for as long, at least, as the huge emporia of fashion were French exclusively; and even now the evil must be greater in France than elsewhere, if we may judge by the fact that almost all our examples of the offence come from French writers. The reason of this preponderance is that, by common report, the French shops are the biggest and the most attractive in the arrangement of articles for sale; consequently they are the most tempting.

Another occasional offence, specifically local, is abortion in the United States, where it is so diffused that public opinion has ceased to condemn it.

In proof, we have the advertisements of doctors and female midwives who practise chiefly in this branch and recommend their establishments in newspapers and on posters.

Not long ago one of them caused a leaflet "*to ladies*" to be distributed in the streets.

This phenomenon is due undoubtedly to the ever larger share which women are beginning to take in professions and business, thanks to the natural development of capitalism, and which, by rendering maternity a positive misfortune, causes abortion to be almost a social necessity. And public opinion is so alive to this truth that the act in question is no longer regarded as either dishonourable or criminal.

10. *Synthesis.*—Occasional offenders, who form the majority of criminals, may be divided into two classes—one which includes the milder sorts of born criminals; and another which differs but little from the normal, which may indeed even be described as consisting of normal women in whom circumstances have developed the fund of immorality which is latent in every female.

To the first class belong above all offenders through *suggestion*, and who are guilty of bloodshed or offences against the person; the second class includes offenders against property.

In their eyes theft is often a matter of as little moment as it is to children; it appears to them in the light of an audacity for which account and compensation are due to the owner of the article taken, but not to abstract justice, the representative of society. They look upon it, that is to say, as an individual rather than a social crime, just as it was regarded in the primitive periods of human evolution, and as it is still regarded by many uncivilised nations.

CHAPTER XIV.

HYSTERICAL OFFENDERS.

IN the asylums for the insane hysteria is most common, and chiefly contributes to differentiate insanity in the male from insanity in the female. [In Italy in 1888 there were 4 hysterical males and 788 hysterical females, the latter thus forming one-tenth of the insane (64·82).] But in our official criminal statistics hysteria does not exist. Salsotto, by exercising extra care in investigation, found it among the graver female criminals, but only in a few instances. In the prison of Turin we find it in 3·9 per cent. of the inmates, the maximum being 10 per cent. among the poisoners and assaulters, with 7·2 per cent. in murderesses, 4·0 per cent. in women guilty of rape, and 3·0 per cent. (the minimum) in infanticides. All the other figures are uncertain. I myself have seen hysteria, but very rarely in prisons, and never to so grave a degree as one would imagine *à priori.*

As a general thing it seems connected with crime because it gives rise to sensational trials which fix public attention, and lend an exaggerated importance to the affection. Add to this that hysteria, as in all cases where I was consulted, is often adduced by the accused or her counsel; but the real thing is not there, only a coarse imitation. This may be attributable to the lower culture and greater inactivity of the women of Turin who ever outside prison offer fewer instances of general paralysis and hysteria (both maladies to which abuse of excitement largely contributes) than are to be found elsewhere. It is impossible, for instance, to compare in this respect our women to those of Paris or even Rome.

1. *Psychology.*—We need not give the physical characteristics of hysteria. They can be studied in the second volume of "L'Uomo Delinquente," pp. 327-30.

In a good half of hysterical women there is sufficient intelligence if little power of fixing the attention; but their disposition is profoundly egotistical, and their absorbing preoccupation with themselves makes them love scandal and a public sensation. They are excessively impressionable, consequently easily moved to choler, ferocity, to sudden and unreasonable likes and dislikes. Their will is always unstable; they take delight in evil-speaking, and if they cannot draw public attention by baseless trials and scandalous forms of revenge, they embitter the life of those around them by continual quarrels and disputes.

A still higher degree of hysteria leads to false witness, and they stir up law and authority against the pretended culprits.

This is a symptom which begins sometimes even in childhood.

(*a*) What is of more importance for us is the

facility of hysterical women to undergo hypnotic suggestion, so that the will of the hypnotiser replaces that of the patient, and he can make one side of the brain act quite contrary to the other side, evoking cheerful images in one part and sad ones in the other, so that he has but to place the patient in an attitude proper to a particular idea, and the idea itself is suggested.

In hallucinatory suggestion the organs are modified as in real suggestion. Let an imaginary bird be placed on the top of a tower, and the patient's pupil dilates to watch it, then narrows as the bird is supposed to descend. Consecutive optical images can also be evoked. If the subject is told to look a long time at (imaginary) green he afterwards sees red.

Patients can be persuaded that they are made of glass, that they are birds, that they have changed their condition or their sex, and they proceed to perform appropriate acts. Complete amnesia and paralysis may be suggested, and the peculiar exaggerated reflex actions of the tendons follow. Real fixed ideas, strange, impulsive, even criminal, may be evoked; the patient can be made to kiss a cranium, can be induced to kill a third party at some stated, distant period, and to do it in the perfect belief that he is acting according to his own will, so that he will give reasons sometimes for the act, reasons which are naturally spurious. It follows that crimes may be committed; and many things done, especially in a cataleptic condition, become explicable.

The hypnotised hysterical subject, in short, is an obedient automaton, without any initiative of his own he follows the will of another. Moreover, during each of these hypnotised states he forgets what he has done in the preceding one, and remembers it only when brought back to the same state, which is an important thing to remember. For where one offence succeeds to another, and imputations are made of deeds which the offender has forgotten because committed in his hypnotised condition, he must be hypnotised anew before his responsibility can be made apparent. It happened, for instance, that a man was accused of an offence against public decency which he denied, and thus aggravated his position. Motel, however, remembered that he was subject to the somnambulistic trance and hypnotised him, with the result that before the judges he ingenuously confessed the offence.

(*b*) A still more salient characteristic of hysteria is mobility of mood. The subject passes with extraordinary rapidity from laughter to tears, "like children," says Richet, "whom you will see laugh immoderately before their tears are well dry."

"One hour," writes Sydenham, "they are irascible and discontented with everything; the next they are cheerful, and follow about their acquaintances with a tenacity equal to the affection which they first had for them."

"Their sensibility is exalted by the most futile causes. A word will grieve them like some real misfortune, such as unkindness from their husband, the death of their children, and so on. Their impulses are not wanting in intellectual control, but are followed with excessive rapidity by action."

"Moral impressions," writes Schüle, "dominate them because they become organic. An idea will bring about a convulsion, and often one notices in them a sudden incoherence, a sudden confusion of mind, which passes after a long sleep. (This is absolutely like what happens in epilepsy.)"

Reflection is replaced by reflex action, so that they will conceive an antipathy to beautiful things and take a sudden liking to some disgusting object.

In the hospital (writes Huchard) they seek one another just like epileptics, one might say; but jealousy springs up at once, they denounce one another, conspire one against the other; friendship is hardly born before it dies and is transformed into quarrels.

Imitation is an absolute contagion among them, and they organise puerile revolts, laugh and complain about trifles. When one girl puts on a flower all the others do the same, and usually they are very fond of brilliant colours.

Although of such a changeable disposition they are subject to fixed ideas, to which they stick with a kind of cataleptic intensity. A woman will be dumb or immovable for months under pretence that speech or motion may hurt her. But this is their only form of perseverance. They are indolent and idle by nature, but can be persuaded to work. They make great projects then and work actively for some days, then sink once again into idleness.

(c) They have a special handwriting, or rather a special tendency to vary in their handwriting, which is sometimes very large and sometimes very small, according to their psychical condition (Binet). This is a peculiarity which we observed also in epileptics.

(*d*) They have a mania for lying. "The scriptural expression, *Homines mendaces*," says Charcot, "seems intended for them. They simulate suicide, maladies, anonymous letters. They lie without need and without object: they cultivate it as an art." "And," continues the same authority, "one is astonished at the sagacity and tenacity of their fictions, especially where the doctor is concerned. They observe, for instance, that anuria attracts his attention, and they will prolong the pretence of it, and pretend to have ejected urine from their ears, their eyes, their nose, and they will feign fecal vomitings."

A girl accused herself of having thrown a man into the river, and the water was about to be dragged and the girl brought to trial when a doctor revealed that the whole story was an invention dictated by hysteria.

In all grave cases, as Schüle remarks, hysteria causes a moral perversion, of which the germ may be perceived in excessive egotism—in the desire to do evil for evil's sake.

(*e*) Another peculiarity is their great tranquillity notwithstanding the apparent gravity of their illness: they are paralysed, blind, drawn up without being at all alarmed, even when unaware of how easily they may be cured.

(*f*) The cases of theft and arson are most common among hysterics at the period of menstruation.

(*g*) They are remarkably erotic. It is true that this is denied by some. Legrand says that they depart from virtue less out of lasciviousness than from a spirit of adventure, or a desire for unknown emotions, or a sudden flash of passion brief and not strong ; but I would remark that even in such cases the sexual element is latent ; and for the rest, if very many are apathetic, others are most excitable.

Legrand out of 83 hysterics found 12 per cent. who prostituted themselves without necessity, and three committed monstrous excesses. Moreover, all the criminality of the hysterical subject has reference to sexual functions. Where they invent calumnies the greater part turn upon assaults. " Some hysterical women," writes Schüle, " during the honeymoon will leave their husbands and run away with a casual acquaintance."

I would add to all these peculiarities yet another, which has been well described by L. Bianchi—that is, the mania of hysterics for writing anonymous letters, or letters with a borrowed signature, some of which are addressed to themselves. It often happens that they persuade themselves of the authenticity of these productions, and become the victims of their own deceit. Naturally it is still easier for them to delude others.

The man Conte, for instance, by means of letters which he wrote with his own hand, persuaded the authorities that a prelate had tried to murder him, after which he gulled and cheated his doctor (who had defended him during his trial and cured him of hysterical attacks by hypnotism), and extracted from him a large sum by pretending that he was about to make a good marriage ("Archivio di psichiatria," vol. vii. fasc i.). And we shall see that almost all accusations of assault are supported by anonymous or forged letters (*see* following pages).

2. *Delirium.*—Hysterical, like epileptic subjects, suffer often either from melancholy or monomaniacal delirium—indeed, according to Morel, they show this symptom the oftenest when the other special morbid phenomena of their malady are wanting.

The maniacal affection is accompanied by hallucinations and impulses, by a continual need of agitation and change of movement, by the desire to break and throw down all that comes in the way. It will make a sudden apparition in the midst of rude health, last but a short time, and depart without leaving any trace. All at once a person will leave a ball-room and throw himself into the river. A girl will break all the plates and pour boiling water on her brother's neck while he is dining, then fly from the house to a wood, where she is found building an altar with stones for the celebration of her own marriage. Often these crises are periodic, thus offering another analogy to epilepsy.

3. The forms of hallucination are the same as those which haunt drunkards, such as rats, serpents (especially red); and, as in drunkenness, lively images alternate with melancholy ones (Morel).

4. *Suicide.*—Suicide is more often attempted or simulated than put into execution. It is almost always automatic and causeless, and is attempted all at once and very ostentatiously *coram publico*, instead of quietly as is the case with other suicides. One will take laudanum after warning the police. Another jumps into the river when a boat is passing.

5. *Flights.*—Another point in which the hysterical

person resembles the epileptic is in taking flight and setting out on the strangest journeys, sometimes consciously and sometimes not.

A woman will go away for two or three days, either abandoning herself to prostitution, or simply wandering about, after which she will return home and sometimes boast of what she has done, or sometimes keep silence.

Hysterical women, like drunkards, are calm in prison, and do not protest against punishment.

6. *False accusations.*—Many women accuse their servants of theft either to enjoy their disgrace and have them put into prison, or out of feminine vanity or hatred.

But the most common form of calumny is criminal assault, which accusation is often brought against a public magistrate, or a father even, but more frequently still against a priest or doctor.

Usually the accusation is so absurd that it cannot be believed; but often it succeeds; and the means adopted for making it consists almost always of letters, anonymous or otherwise.

An unmarried woman of 25, of good family, pursued a priest with love-letters in the following terms: " My beloved, where are you? Nobody knows us. Your Laura, who kisses you ardently." A short time afterwards the innocent priest was accused by the lady of having corrupted her.

A girl of 18 declared to the King's Proctor that she had been criminally assaulted several times by priests, her cousin aiding. She went into the most minute particulars, declaring that she was praying alone in the church one evening, not having noticed that the congregation had dispersed.

The priest came, invited her into the sacristy, then proposed that she should accompany him to Spain. When she resisted his proposals he cut himself in two places in order to induce her to listen to him. She fainted, and on coming to her senses found he had taken advantage of her, and so on, and so on.

On another occasion she averred that her cousin had taken her to a convent where the nuns shut her up all one night with a priest.

The accused parties were brought up for trial, and the absurdity of the girl's charge having been proved, she was accused in her turn. She persisted, however, in her story, composed verses in the priest's honour, and showed letters containing declarations of love, which she affirmed were written by him.

Finally a medical examination, which ought to have preceded instead of following all these proceedings, demonstrated the utter baselessness of the tale, and proved the girl to be suffering from hysteria, heightened by jealousy of her cousin, whom she thought the priest favoured unduly.

General D. M. had a daughter of 16, called Maria, who complained that Lieutenant P., when seated near her at table, had addressed unbecoming remarks to her. From that moment anonymous letters rained upon the house, containing declarations of love for the general's wife and threats against the daughter; and finally arrived a missive, also anonymous, which warned the general that an attempt had been made to dishonour his daughter. The lieutenant was forbidden the house, and the day after his dismissal the nurse found the young lady stretched upon the ground, half strangled by a handkerchief, and dressed only in her night attire, which was stained with blood. She declared that the lieutenant had come to her room in the night and tried to criminally assault her, and had wounded her with a knife; and the family received a letter purporting to be from the officer and boasting of his deed. He was arrested, and although it was proved that the anonymous letters were not his, although others were received continually while he was in prison, and experts found a great resemblance in them to the handwriting of the girl, whom the doctors also proved to be suffering from hysterical anosmia and ambliopia, the poor young man was condemned by the jury to ten years' imprisonment.

An hysterical woman stole linen from a hospital, and even from her own press, and hid it with much care. When brought up for trial she succeeded in having it believed that she had found, or been presented with, the articles she had stolen.

Out of 83 hysterical accused, 21 had made false accusations, 9 of which were of criminal assault, besides 3 who bore false witness.

A girl, whose case is related by Legrand du Saulle, showed hysteria at puberty, and at the same time was so devout that she wished to enter a convent. At 20 she began a series of fantastic calumnies, accusing a priest of having seduced her when he had never even seen her.

After her marriage she took to drink, and used to

beat her husband. She eloped with a shopman, and finally was imprisoned for attempted homicide.

A famous instance is the woman Glaser's, who deceived doctors and judges, and passed for being mad, dumb, subject to hallucinations, a forger, a thief, and calumniator without anybody ever being able to discover how far it was all true, and whose case was the despair of the great expert Casper by obliging him to reverse his judgments.

Maria V. (aged 23) was found unconscious, deeply cut in a regular manner all over her face and body, her hands tied, her mouth gagged with a handkerchief, and her eyes tied down with the strings of her cap.

She accused four young men whom she minutely described of having reduced her to this condition when she resisted their attempts at criminal assault; but the case was proved in court to be all an hysterical invention.

Another woman burnt her hand with live coals in order to accuse another of the act.

Maria H., a woman of 26, when jilted by her promised husband Martin, fell into convulsions and syncope, but eventually recovered. One morning all the vines of a magistrate were found cut, and Maria accused Martin and his brother, who were condemned for the offence. At the end of some months she exhibited wounds on her person, and accused an uncle of Martin's, who was sentenced to five years' imprisonment. In a short time new wounds were followed by new accusations, this time against another uncle of Martin's, who had all the inhabitants of the place against him, Maria, the pretended victim of a whole family, having become a popular idol; and it was only after she had stolen articles from a family which she entered as servant that a suspicion of her *bonâ fides* in the other matters began to arise. Later she married a vine-dresser, who shortly afterwards died of poison; and a forged will finally resulted in her being sentenced to prison for life. (Legrand du Saulle, "Les Hysteriques," 1884.)

A lawyer relates how a girl of 12 charged a proprietor of Gratz with rape, and caused him to be put in prison for a year, and he would have remained there longer, only that a servant accused of stealing by the same person was proved innocent through the missing watch being found in the latter's own trunk. Later the police were informed that the aforesaid proprietor out of revenge caused stones to be thrown every night against the windows of the house where the girl lived with her mother, but when they went there at midnight they found the denouncer throwing the stones herself.[1]

7. *Stealing.*—Another very frequent offence among hysterical subjects is stealing.

Out of 83 accused of various offences, 17 had been guilty of this; and, as we have seen, Legrand du Saulle found 50 hysterical women in 104 who had been caught stealing in the shops of Paris.

C. H. went to a neighbouring village to watch her husband, of whom she was jealous. She did not find

[1] "Aus den Papieren lines Vertheidigen," von Dr. Julius Kosiek. Gratz, 1884.

him, and the idea occurred to her to steal fowls in the house to which she had gone. She stole 21, and sold them so cheaply that the buyer himself accused her of theft. She confessed, and at the same time made a hearty meal, and talked to everybody of what she had done. When arrested she threatened to kill herself.

Another hysterical subject, aged 20, penetrated into shops by means of false keys, and carried off whatever of value she found.

A., the daughter of mad parents, at 15, during menstruation, imagined herself surrounded with enemies. She fled into the fields, stole everything she could find, and threatened to burn and to poison wholesale.

At the end of 10 to 15 days she quieted down, and declared that she had yielded to an irresistible impulse.

During 8 years she seemed cured, then after a pregnancy she had a return of the symptoms, then showed erotic tendencies and fell into prostitution.

Stealing in the big shops is a special thing caused by the great crowd and the immense stock.

Like epileptics, hysterical subjects as a whole traverse the whole gamut of offences. Out of 88 I found—

```
21 guilty of calumny.
17    ,,     theft.
14    ,,     suicide.
10    ,,     prostitution.
 4    ,,     arson.
 4    ,,     poisoning.
 3    ,,     swindling.
 3    ,,     homicide.
 3    ,,     infanticide.
```

3 guilty of calumny and false witness
2 ,, stealing of infants.
1 ,, abuse of children.
1 ,, offence against nature.
1 ,, exercise of medicine.
1 ,, offence against decency.

8. *Multiple crimes. Murder.*—We have said that the impulses of hysterical women are always like those of big children; but it is strength to do greater evil which is wanting in them as in all women. For the rest they can often surpass their sex, and then become terrible, worse than men.

And there are not wanting instances in which one woman will be guilty of crimes of different sorts. One will wound, rob, poison, burn, and bear false witness. Another will prostitute herself, steal children, calumniate, and steal.

A certain U., a peasant woman, was hysterical to a high degree. Very beautiful, she became the mistress of one who ill-treated and starved her; then, in complicity with another, a young lover, she robbed him, and finally one night, while he was asleep, she, unassisted, mutilated and almost killed him with a reaping-hook. Before the judges she invented a story of an imaginary struggle, and succeeded in having herself acquitted.

The woman Bompard was hysterical, and so was the woman Zélie, of whom we have already spoken.

But the most classical example of hysteria is offered by the woman Z., who was at once a thief, a prostitute, an assassin, and a calumniator. Her story is the same as that of all the morally insane or born female criminals.

She was a woman of 20, the child of parents of small morality. Her father drank and had a bad character; her sister led a profligate life; her mother —a foundling—was helpless and complaining.

Z. was branded with hereditary signs—very thick, black hair, black eyes, a big mouth, very prominent cheekbones, and frontal microcephalia.

From her early school-days she was the torment of her companions. A profligate between the age of 14 and 17. When only 14 she quarrelled with and worried her fellow-workers in a shop where she had been placed, and where she also behaved in a bestial and dissolute manner. She stole and accused two of her companions of theft, besides falsely accusing her master of adultery. She stole some lace and hid it under the bed only that she might discredit a fellow-worker who had never done her any harm, and who was dismissed in consequence of the charge. She also tried to poison another employer who had always been kind to her; and in a sort of delirium of perversity she arrived at the pitch peculiar to hysterical women and born criminals of doing evil absolutely without any reason. She would cut the bells, or make her own room filthy and then accuse her mistress of it.

She formed a violent friendship with a woman named Lodi, of handsome appearance and rather light conduct; but even here she was moved by the envy which consumed her. She wished to see her friend covered with jewels so as to annoy another woman, and also probably to prepare the way for a future attack upon her character. Later she turned against her, and showed in calumniating her an exaggerated and baseless hatred.

She became the mistress of an old man, and robbed him until, in spite of his fear of her (a fear that he confessed to the police), he dismissed her. But she contrived to return one night, and in that night the old man was killed by repeated blows on the head. Nobody was in his room but Z., who suddenly roused the street by her shrieks, and was found hanging out of the window in her nightdress. She declared that she had been alarmed by the presence of two assassins, then of one who had disappeared entirely. The state of the lock of the house-door, which had evidently been vainly forced from the inside, showed that she herself had tried to fly. When the absence of any other aggressor, and the fact that she was found to have hidden the old man's purse in her stocking, and his jewels in her clothes, made it impossible for Z. to persist in her first lie, she then admitted having helped the murderers, but averred that she was only the accomplice of a paid assassin hired by a certain Pallotti, who had instigated her to commit the deed so that he might be freed from a debt of 1,800 francs which he had contracted for jewels to give his mistress (Lodi). And she told this story in such minute detail that Lodi and Pallotti were arrested, although perfectly innocent.

In prison Z. showed a singular piety. She was hardly admitted before she asked to go to confession, and she dictated prayers in verse to the Madonna. But at the same time she wrote letters bearing the impress of conviction to Pallotti, accusing him of having taken part in the murder.

Before the judge and at the assizes she showed herself shamelessly mendacious, contradicting herself without blushing, and saying, when everything else failed, "*Let Pallotti tell.*" She looked him full in the face in court and said, "You have made me suffer. You have little to gain by it. You will gain nothing."

It should be observed also that she showed no real emotion, only an affectation of fear. But a few hours after the murder she remembered having left a ring in her victim's room, and she remained throughout quite unmoved, even when shown the blood-stained hammer with which experts declared that the deed might have been done even by the hand of a woman.

I may be mistaken, but when I recall many similar instances I can but think that a motive and an element of calculation in this woman's crime was the prospect of being able to calumniate Lodi, whose great fault consisted in being beautiful and beloved, and in having shown affection to Z. herself.

I may remind the reader of that hysterical woman of Buonvecchiato who asked to be allowed to beat her dog, and when asked her motive by the doctor, said, "*It is because I always see him caressed by others.*"

9. *Poisoners.*—Naturally poisoners are not wanting among hysterical criminals.

Maria J. had cases in her family of hypochondriacs, lunatics, and suicides. Left an orphan, and leading rather an agitated life, she fell ill, and, thinking herself affected with blindness, sought medical advice and in this way became acquainted with certain poisons which she conceived the desire of administering to others. Although comfortably off she became a sick-nurse; and one day, being with a lady, an invalid whom she carefully tended, she prepared her something to drink.

Strange symptoms followed, the patient's eyes and eyelids being paralysed, and her stomach oppressed. Maria then gave her another mixture, an effervescent, which produced delirium during three days.

The same mixture given to another lady had the same effect, namely, delirium and vomiting; and some sweetmeats which Maria insisted on the invalid swallowing also caused instantaneous sickness.

When the doctors issued orders she listened most attentively and promised obedience, but they were no sooner gone than she began to abuse them and ill-treated the patient.

Later she became directress of a school, and took upon herself the care of a young girl. Under pretence that a journey would do her charge's health good she took her away, and gave her the usual sweetmeats, whence followed delirium, vomiting, and the victim's death. In this way she poisoned nine people; and the curious thing was that she foretold, in conversation with her friends and neighbours, the death of her victims and the symptoms they would present, thus offering the best proof of her own guilt.

When arrested she confessed her crimes, and admitted that she had administered atropine and morphia, with no other object but that of making medical experiments and procuring rest for the patients.

10. *Saints.*—Among hysterical women we also find saints, ecstatics, and fasting girls, like Koerl and Louise Latean.

11. *Analogies of hysteria with epilepsy.*—The reader will have observed how much analogy there is between hysteria and epilepsy. The convulsions of hysteria are so like epileptic fits that they can only be distinguished from them by the scarcity of urea, by the presence of hysterogenic zones, especially in the ovary, pressure on which will sometimes cure an attack; by the beneficial effects of a continuous current; by hydropathic treatment; by the smaller effect of bromide, and by the absence or merely slight degree of fever (which is, however, present sometimes).

Wettkowski ("Klin-Wochens," Berlin, 1886) did not observe any rise of temperature in hysterical sufferers. Rousseau found only a low degree—oscillating between 1·10 and 1·5. The attack is followed by a fall, which hardly ever reaches 39°; but Rousseau says that the same patient may have different temperatures according to the attack ("Progrès Med.," 1888, vi.).

If in hysterical subjects the degenerative characteristics of epilepsy be wanting, all the functional peculiarities, the lateral action, and dulness of sense are very much more marked. Here again Briquet and Morel observed that where convulsions or other typical symptoms are absent, psychical phenomena are common. There is a relation between hysteria and the sexual organs, but the same, if in a lower degree, may be said of epilepsy; and if hysterical patients are more liable to be cured at the critical age, on the other hand the cases in which hysteria makes its first appearance in youth appear quite incurable, and thus correspond, physiognomically, as in every other point, with epileptics and born criminals.

In both maladies there is intermittence, sometimes regular, sometimes lasting years; and we have masked forms of hysteria in which the affection shows itself in malignancy, idleness, love of calumniating, cheating, suicide, exaggerated vanity, continual travelling, excessive, precocious, anomalous altruism, impulsiveness, brief lapses of consciousness, giddiness, &c. (*see* above). The analogy is present also in those rare cases of excessive altruism which we noted in criminals from passion ("Uomo Delinquente," vol. ii. part ii.), and also in some rare instances of epilepsy (Idem, part i.).

The similarities in a psychological sense are so many that I have preferred to give the textual words of authors, so as not to be accused of partiality.

Etiologically the relation between epileptics and dipsomaniacs is quite certain.

And the hysterical subject offers parallel peculiarities to the epileptic, the infant, the born criminal, and the morally insane in the variability of his symptoms, in his desire for a change of place, in his need to do evil for evil's sake, in his gratuitous mendacity (lying for lying's sake), in his causeless irascibility.

And here I perceive that these pathological symptoms of the hysterical patient throw light on certain characteristics of the born criminal to which I did not draw sufficient attention. Chief among these is their continual gratuitous mendacity.

Valentini writes: "*Thieves lie unprovoked the instant they open their mouths; they lie without knowing why, from second nature; and they do it unconsciously even when they have no wish to deceive.*"

Delbrück also observes that old inmates of prisons tell lies without motive. And Moeli says "that criminals tell lies even *after* they go mad, so ingrained is the habit in their minds, just as an artist will continue to have ability in his art." And the mendacity of children is notorious.

Epileptics are also sometimes distinguished by the letter-writing mania. And I alluded to the morally insane who address love-letters to themselves. Variations of character are common to the hysterical and the epileptic—and epileptics, even while hating and quarrelling with one another, are gregarious among themselves; and they also are capable of that double personality which in some hysterical persons constitutes a true second life. Finally a persistent or intermittent piety will cause both classes to attain to absolute saintliness (Saint Paul, Saint Theresa).[1]

12. *Calumny.*—The feature, however, which distinguishes hysterical women from all others is the intensity of their mania for calumny, and the success with which they apply it. The reason is simple. Women—even bad women (and they are the most frequently hysterical)—have less strength and less capacity than men for deeds of violence, and are consequently more inclined to crystallise their bad

[1] See "The Man of Genius," part iv.

impulses into calumny; also they are more subject to that auto-suggestion which incarnates an idea and transforms it into action. Like the hypnotised subject described in my "Studies on Hypnotism" (3rd ed.), they profess and proclaim the false with the same intensity as an honest person will affirm the true, especially as women, like children, are less impressed with the sense of truth, and more easily disregard it. Moreover, when hysterical they are possessed by their own lie, which presents itself to their minds with a force of conviction greater than truth can bring; and they are subject besides to that species of exaltation which the hypnotised experience at every stage, and whence suggestion derives its overmastering force. Finally (as Schüle says), "they have such an unbridled fancy that truth and falsehood, facts and desires, are all one, all equally true to them, and they consequently often misrepresent in perfectly good faith."

Hysterical women furnish us with the saddest cases of calumny, of swindling, of triumphant mendacity, not only among the ignorant masses, but also in the stern halls of justice where it is not always given to those presiding to distinguish truth from the falsehoods which hysteria affirms with such superabundant energy.

That which has struck me most in studying the psychical anomalies of hysteria, and the more celebrated trials to which it has given rise, is that the subjects of this affection, like epileptics, would be indistinguishable from the born criminal, except that their malady lends a peculiar virus, a fatal point to their deplorable capacity for evil, so that even if (as I do not maintain to be the case) most criminals were hysterical it would never be wise to set them at liberty.

Even their great undeniable susceptibility to suggestion must not be allowed to plead in their favour since as a general thing they can only be influenced for evil, never for good. We saw this in the case of Gabrielle Bompard, who fell into the hands of an honest man (*see* above), but deceived him continually.

A still more remarkable instance is offered by the following case:—

A young married woman leading a profligate life robbed a man of his purse. He perceived the loss, and returning to the house he had just left proclaimed it. The woman professed herself astonished and indignant at the charge, but the police when summoned found the missing sum almost intact hidden in the chimney. The thief was taken to prison, and fright and rage produced in her such strong hysterical convulsions that four robust people could hardly hold her. One of the writers came upon the scene after some hours, and by a simple compression of the bulbs and the application of a small magnet cured the convulsions entirely, but they were followed by profuse uterine hæmorrhage, which was probably due, like the attack, to psychical disturbance.

After vainly trying a tepid enteroclisma we hypnotised the patient and suggested that the hæmorrhage should cease. It did so as if by magic, like the convulsions; and when two days later both symptoms returned they were cured immediately by the same method, so that the good nuns (in charge of the prison) regarded us as sent by the Evil One. Now here was an opportunity to try hypnotism as a means of obtaining a confession of guilt, so we continued our experiments in suggestion for some time, and were able to conjure away a headache and a mood of deep melancholy; we even obtained, though only for a brief period, transposition of the senses and believed we had dominated the patient completely. But when we ordered her to make a sincere confession of guilt she immediately began over again the string of lies which she had told (naturally in vain) to the magistrate; relating, namely, that the man had invented the story of the stolen purse out of revenge for having been repulsed by the prisoner's young sister, how the money found was honestly come by, &c.

The proof that she deceived us unconsciously (persisting, that is to say, in the habitual mendacity of her waking moments) lies in the fact that when told next day by a companion that she had spoken of her offence, and believing that she had betrayed herself, suspecting also (for the hysterical are always suspicious) that we were acting for the police and not out of mere scientific interest, she informed us resentfully that she had invented lies to deceive us and had never been hypnotised at all. And later, when suffering from bad hemicrania, she refused to be hypnotised anew, and we naturally did not insist, since the will of the patient had to be respected, and we were satisfied with the results already obtained.

Suggestion in this case was strong enough to cure convulsions and hæmorrhage, but it could not extract a secret which the patient was interested in keeping, nor alter by one fraction the mendacious tendencies which were thus proved to have an organic basis deeper than that of any other hysterical manifestation.

13. *Hysterical prostitutes.*—Seeing that the only differences between the born criminal and the hysterical woman consist in the superior mendacity and volubility of the latter, and in a frequently paradoxical preoccupation with sexual matters, it becomes clear that the reason why epilepsy shows itself rarely among prostitutes is that it is replaced by hysteria.

Legrand du Saulle observed that 12 per cent. of hysterical women took to prostitution out of sheer dilettantism, without any pressure from misery; and Madame Tarnowsky found that 15 per cent. of prostitutes were hysterical. She included under this head the few who showed intelligence and cultivation, as well as those who loved excitement, and others greedy and vain who appropriated everything they found. Most of the number were extraordinarily precocious and profligate, having begun their career as early as the age of eight, and they also showed the special changeableness of hysterical subjects by passing from one lover to another and hating the old ones profoundly. Thirteen per cent. had real attacks of hysteria.

We know that psychical hysteria, like epilepsy, may show itself unaccompanied by true convulsions, and is then only the more cynical and indecent, and it is consequently very probable that the number of prostitutes with an hysterical basis is infinitely larger than we have hitherto imagined to be the case.

CHAPTER XV.

CRIMES OF PASSION.

An analysis of crimes of passion disproves yet another of the many popular fallacies regarding women. The inferiority of the weaker sex to the other in this respect is not so much numerical as that the female offenders differ from the genuine type of the male criminal in their nature, which has more analogy with the born female delinquent on the one hand and the occasional criminal on the other. But crimes of passion have, nevertheless, much in common in both sexes.

1. *Age.*—Naturally, as among men, so among women, the offenders are chiefly young.

The age at which the crime is committed is usually that of the fullest sexual development: Vinci was 26; Connemune 18; Provensal 18; Jamais 24; Stakelberg 27; Daru 27; Laurent 22; Hogg 26; Noblin 22; and the female political criminals were also young (Sahla 18; Corday 25; Renault 20).

Rarer, yet not exceptional, are the cases in which crimes of passion resulting from love have been committed at an age comparatively advanced, by women in whom youth and sexuality have a shorter cycle.

The woman Lodi, whose conduct had been good up to middle age, finally fell in love with a fellow-servant, and at his instigation robbed her master of bonds for 20,000 francs, all of which she handed over to her lover without keeping a penny for herself.

Dumaire killed her lover when she was 30; Perrin at the age of 40 tried to kill her husband.

2. *Characteristics of degeneration.*—If we except a greater development of the maxillæ, and greater virility than usual, female offenders from passion have no special physiognomical characteristics nor signs of degeneration. Madames C. H. B.,[1] Charlotte Corday, — Perowska, Helfmann, Vera Sassulich, — Kulischoff,[2] were all very handsome.

3. *Virile characteristics.*—It is remarkable that female offenders of this class have also some masculine traits of disposition; such, for intance, as the love of firearms.

Mesdames Clov. Hug. and Dumaire amused themselves habitually with revolver practice. Madame Raymond always carried a dagger and a pistol, having, said the husband, acquired the habit at Hawaii, where all women do the same. Nevertheless, it is difficult to understand why she should have persisted in it after many years of residence in Paris. Madame Souhine was described by the witnesses as having a haughty, energetic, and resolute character. Madame Dumaire, according to Bataille, who was present at her trial, was resolute, outspoken, logical.

---

[1] *See* Lombroso, "Uomo Delinquente," vol. ii. pp. 117, 168.
[2] Lombroso and Laschi, "Crime Politique," vol. ii. p. 177, Plates VI., VII.

Finally, many women, contrary to the usual tendencies of their sex, occupy themselves with politics and become religious and political martyrs. Madame Daru was a Corsican, Noblin a native of the Basque provinces; that is to say, both belonged to semi-primitive nationalities in which the woman is habitually rather virile, and both showed muscular strength in the commission of their crime, for Daru killed her lover with blows from a knife, and Noblin strangled her rival.

Sometimes the female offenders of this description take a strange pleasure in dressing themselves as men —like B., for instance, who assumed men's clothes when attempting her schemes of revenge on her husband's mistress. It is true that masculine qualities are not always found in criminals alone, as is proved by the instance of Mrs. Carlyle, certainly the purest and most angelic of women, who yet as a child climbed walls and gates and loved to box with her schoolboy companions, from whom she got usually less than she gave.

4. *Good feeling. Affection. Passion.*—In the women who commit crimes of passion there is great intensity of feeling. Indeed, their affections are infinitely more ardent than those of normal women, and they never show the absence of domestic sentiments which we noted in the born criminal.

Ellero, speaking of the incendiary, R. Antonia says: "There was but one opinion about her: all bore testimony to her being an excellent wife, a most loving mother, and filled with compassion for all the needy and the suffering. Her heart was indeed greater than her head, and her notion of good and evil was blood of her blood, a pure instinct, and, for that very reason, was not very wise. Not once but many times she had induced her husband to go security for the family of her sister who was threatened with financial ruin."

B., who had a virile physiognomy, but otherwise few abnormal features, was a most affectionate wife, an exemplary mother, and of such immaculate conduct, that a memorial in her favour was unanimously signed by her neighbours after she had been arrested.

Myers, who killed her faithless lover, eventually became an exemplary mother. Ottolenghi noted in B. R. a strong moral sense and very chaste instincts. She proved these, in fact, by her assertion that what disgusted her in her husband was not so much his coarseness nor his repulsive appearance as the idea that he had been her mother's lover.

Madame Daru adored her children and maintained them by her own incessant toil, while her husband spent his substance in riotous living.

The infanticides—who are mostly criminal from passion—are, according to Cère, almost the only female offenders who, when married in the penal settlements, become excellent mothers of families.

"Often," writes Joly, "in St. Lazare we have infanticides of the gentlest dispositions, in whom it is quite evident that there is no absence of maternal love. A little time ago there was an infanticide—a pretty girl, neither an idiot nor depraved—who used to make dolls out of the house-linen, and carry them in her arms like infants."

Despine tells the story of a girl who, directly her child was born, threw it down a lavatory; but when it was brought back still alive, felt maternal love awake in her, so that, taking the infant, she warmed it, nursed it, and showed herself the tenderest of mothers.

The chief quality of Madame Souhine was an extreme independence which made her prefer to die with her children rather than live on charity.

Madame Du Tilly, an excellent wife and mother, had but two ideas—to provide for her children and to prevent her improvident husband from ruining himself and his family.

Jamais, even when in the greatest want, remained chaste and pure, and wrote to her absent lover, " I keep myself for you." Madame Dumaire, who had provided for herself by a rather equivocal marriage, on being left a widow showed herself generous, and assisted her relatives.

5. *Passions as motives for crimes.*—The passion which most often betrays such women as we have described into crime is love. Strangers to the coldness of the normal woman, they love with all the intensity of Heloise, and take a real delight in sacrificing themselves for the man they adore, and for whom they are ready to violate prejudices, custom, and even social laws.

Vinci for her lover sacrificed the long hair which was her only beauty.

Jamais sent her soldier-lover money and gifts, although she had to support herself and two children by her toil.

Dumaire was disinterestedly but passionately in love with Picart, whom she assisted by paying for his studies, never demanding that he would marry her if only she might continue to live with him.

Spinetti married a man of bad character, whom she vainly tried to reclaim, and whom she, herself once rich, eventually consented to wait on like a servant.

Noblin was so devotedly attached to Sougaret that, although herself naturally of good instincts, she would not leave him even after discovering him to be a criminal. Three times, to please him, she committed abortion, and finally accomplished a crime which was repugnant to her natural goodness.

This intensity of love explains why almost all such women have formed illicit connections without being, for that reason, impure. Virginity and marriage are social institutions adapted, like all customs and institutions, to the average type—that is to say, in this case, to the sexual coldness of the normal woman. But our offenders love too passionately to submit to such laws. They are like Heloise, who refused to marry Abelard for fear of injuring him, and declared herself proud to be called his mistress.

The greater number of infanticides are to be ascribed originally to an imprudent passion which overrides respect for social usage. Grandpré gives an instance in the infanticide who in a short time fell hopelessly in love with a stranger who had come to her neighbourhood during the summer season, and whom she met in the country roads.

From this point of view, then, the woman whom

passion betrays into crime is very different from the born offender who violates the laws of chastity from lust and love of pleasure and idleness. But all such good and passionate women have a fatal propensity to love bad men, and they fall into the power of frivolous and fickle, sometimes depraved lovers, who not only abandon them when tired of them, but often add to the cruelty of betrayal the still greater cruelty of scorn and calumny.

The motive for crime, then, in the woman becomes very strong, and is hardly ever limited to the mere pain of desertion. Such women as Camicia, Raffo, Harry, Rosalia Leoni, and Ardoano were betrayed after vows of fidelity; and in the instance of Leoni there was the additional fact of the opprobrium arising from the accusations of her lover, who declared that he was one of thirteen.

Vinci, who had sacrificed her hair for her lover's sake, was taunted by her rival, who took advantage of the ugliness consequent on the loss of the adornment to supplant her.

Jamais was cynically deserted by her lover when, her occupation failing, she could no longer supply him with money, and received, moreover, letters of an insulting nature from him.

Madame Raymond was betrayed by her husband and by her most intimate friend. She discovered the intrigue and, for once, forgave it; but later learnt that the intercourse continued, and found letters from her rival full of insulting allusions to herself. An almost similar instance is that of Guérin.

Madame T., an affectionate wife and mother, who

for many years had led a comparatively happy life, all at once finds herself and her children deserted, and the house despoiled by her husband, who has fallen in love with a prostitute.

To all these causes we must add the unjust scorn of the world which visits on the woman what it calls her sin, but which is only an excess of love, dangerous in a society where the dominating force is egotism. Derision, and often the inhuman severity of relations, add to a sorrow which is already profound. Jamais, for instance, was repulsed by her dying father, who would not receive her last kiss; and Provensal was the recipient of a letter from her brother, who reproached her with having dishonoured her family and become a stranger to it.

Such impelling causes are secondary in the cases which we have been considering, but become the principal motive of crime in infanticides, who are, however, also moved by a kind of desire to revenge themselves on the child for the infidelity of the father. "When it was born," said an infanticide to Grandpré, "I reflected that it was a bastard, that as his child it would be base like him, and my fingers closed round its neck."

Statistics prove unmistakably all that we have advanced by showing that illegitimate births and infanticides are in *inverse*, and not as might be expected, in *direct* ratio; that is to say, that infanticide is most frequent in districts where, illegitimate births being rarest, they are regarded with most severity.

Fear of shame impels to crime, and hence the

difference in the statistics of infanticide furnished by towns and rural neighbourhoods:—

		1851–55.	1875–80.
France	Country	32	35
	Town	21	22

		Country.	Town.
Italy	1885	34	17
	1886	40	19
	1887	32	18
	1888	37	20

These differences are evidently owing to the greater facility which the towns offer for concealing the shame. These crimes from passion are consequently determined by public opinion and its prejudices, just as in old days men had to exact vengeance for injuries to themselves and their families under pain of being dishonoured.

Sometimes crime arises from revolt against ill-treatment and excessive humiliation.

B. R., who tried to poison her husband, had been married by her wicked mother to that mother's lover, a brutal, disgusting old man with whom she would not live, and who, out of revenge, used to beat her cruelly, leaving her without food, and forcing her to occupy a garret open to all the winds of heaven.

Spinetti, who had made so many sacrifices for her vile husband, on being beaten by him and ordered to rob her master of some valuables, cut his carotid artery with a razor.

C. H., calumniated atrociously by a man who accused her of having led a dissolute life, prosecuted him for libel and killed him in the assize court, when exasperated at his success in having the suit remanded by means of a legal artifice.

6. *Maternal and domestic love.*—More rarely than the other causes which we have detailed, the incentive to crime is some injury inflicted on the woman's maternal or domestic affections.

Madame Du Tilly, a most affectionate wife and mother, found herself abandoned by her husband and insulted by her rival in his love, a milliner. The honour of the family and its well-being were being ruined little by little, but the worst prospect of all to her was that if she died her children would have the other woman for a stepmother. To avert such a catastrophe Madame Du Tilly determined to disfigure her rival by throwing vitriol in her face.

In a similar case Madame T. inflicted a hailstorm of blows upon the prostitute for whose sake her husband had sold everything, even the domestic utensils.

Madame Daru, a very well-conducted woman, was exposed to continual brutality on the part of her drunken husband. One day, when he had threatened both herself and the children with a knife, she fled with her little ones from the house, then, returning when the man was asleep, stabbed him to death.

Another woman, whose portrait Macé gives, a person of refinement, education, and gentle nature, who had fallen from prosperity into extremest want, committed a theft that she might pay her son's school-fees. When arrested she refused to give her name in order not to dishonour the boy, and her identity would never have been known had a lawyer in court not recognised her. She died a few days later of a broken heart.

One is disposed to wonder at first at the rarity of offences committed through maternal love, since that is woman's strongest sentiment. But maternity is, so to speak, a moral prophylactic against crime and evil; for a mother hesitates to commit an offence which might separate her temporarily or permanently from her child. The idea of such a risk leads her to forgive injuries inflicted on the child himself rather than resort to violent means of revenge; and she will urge the child to forgiveness in preference to losing him as she might do if he resented his wrongs.

Moreover, maternity is pre-eminently a physiological function; while criminality, even when induced by passion, is pathological; and it is rare for the two things to be confounded.

Maternity is an intense normal feeling, and cannot therefore become a perturbing element; but the case with love is different.

In the normal woman love is weak, and only becomes intense when it has reached the stage of a pathological phenomenon.

This theory finds confirmation in the fact that maternity is largely a cause of madness. The proportion of cases in which domestic sorrow has produced insanity is as follows:—

	Percentage.	
	Men.	Women.
In Italy (1866–77)	1·60	8·40
In Saxony (1875–78)	2·64	3·66
In Vienna (1851–59)	5·24	11·28

In Turin three times more women (12) than men (4) go mad from the loss of a child; and grief at sterility will render three women insane as against no man.

There is yet another restraining factor which accounts for the small number of crimes arising out of maternal passion. A woman regards her child as a part of herself, providing for him and resenting in her own person the injuries inflicted on him, especially while he is little and cannot provide for himself. But when the child grows up and can look after himself, he separates from his mother, and she, while following his actions, his struggles and attempts, with affectionate interest, no longer feels bound to interfere as protectress or avenger. A wrong to her child will grieve her profoundly, but it will no longer excite her as in his infancy. To a certain degree, in short, she recalls the behaviour of female animals who abandon their little ones as soon as they can fly or walk alone.

And if a crime committed out of maternal love is possible only when the children are small, for this very reason it must be rare, since an infant not having entered upon the struggle for life has few enemies, and is exposed to few injuries or persecutions. Almost the only person against whom they have to be protected or revenged is a bad or careless father, and he fortunately is not a very common phenomenon, elementary duty to his family not being the relation in which the civilised male shows himself most frequently wanting.

7. *Dress and adornment.*—It is a singular fact that connected, and sometimes even confounded into a whole with maternal love, is that passion for dress which we found so characteristic of the born criminal. Madame Du Tilly confessed that one of the things

which most exasperated her against her husband was that he arrayed his mistress in her garments. Madame Raymond was irritated by the frequent presents of jewellery made by her husband to his paramour, and which contrasted with his avarice towards his wife. T. told us that she went to visit the kept mistress of her husband with a heart full of rage, but no intention of assault; but when she saw the woman wearing her own wedding-veil she leapt upon her and killed her with blows.

Sometimes the same irritating effect is produced by objects which have some peculiarly dear or sacred associations of ideas.

8. *Analogies with male criminals.*—Up to this point the analogy between male and female criminals from passion has been nearly perfect, but we have now to consider certain characteristics which, while essential to the type of the male offender, are only found in some women. Such, for instance, is the almost instantaneous explosion of vindictiveness following on the provocation. Madame Guérin, hearing that her husband was at Versailles with his mistress, flew there and stabbed him. Madame Daru, on being threatened, together with her children, more seriously than usual one evening by her drunken husband, waited till he was asleep, then thrust a knife into his heart. Spinetti cut her lover's throat immediately on his making the proposition which we have already described; and similar instances of rapid action are offered by Provensal and Jamais.

Only in some women, again, does sincere and violent remorse follow on their crime. Noblin ran shrieking through the village roads and spontaneously gave herself up to the authorities. Madame Daru tried to commit suicide, but her courage failing she gave herself in charge. A. B., after setting fire to her house to obtain the insurance money, remained paralysed at the idea of what she had done. It was only at the instigation of her brother that she went to claim the money; she took what the agent gave her without remark, then made a full, unasked confession. Madame Du Tilly only wished to disfigure her rival, and was horrified to hear that she had caused her the loss of an eye. Of her own accord she paid her a large indemnity, and continually asked if she were in further danger, showing great pleasure when the doctor gave a good account of his patient.

And only in occasional instances is the suddenness of the impulse betrayed by the choice of any weapon within reach, as in the case of Madame Guérin and Madame Daru; injury being even inflicted sometimes with the teeth or the fists, as in the example of Madame T., who attacked her husband's mistress with these natural weapons.

Finally, it is occasionally only that we find uncertainty in the execution of the crime, as in the cases of Jamais and Provensal, who fired off several shots without aiming properly at their respective victims, whom they barely touched.

9. *Differences between the two sexes.*—The women are as a rule not previously quite immaculate. Often they have bad traits which contrast with the exaggerated goodness of the male criminal, and cause them to approximate on the one hand to the born criminal,

and on the other to the occasional criminal. Frequently they brood for months and years over their resentment, which is even susceptible of alternations of forbearance and even liking towards their victim.

That is to say, that often premeditation in the woman is longer than in the man; it is also colder and more cunning, so that the crime is executed with an ability and a gloating which in the deed of pure passion are psychologically impossible. Nor does sincere penitence always follow the offence; on the contrary, there is often exultation; and rarely does the offender commit suicide.

That B., to whose excellent conduct, as we have seen, the whole neighbourhood testified, and who was so good a wife and mother, on learning that her husband had a mistress, hid a stick under her skirts one night, and after lying in wait for the couple, fell upon them with threats, and finally beat them.

The husband later formed an intimacy with another woman, a servant in his house; and towards her B.'s conduct was very hesitating. Sometimes after a furious scene she drove her away—sometimes, especially when short of cash, she allowed presents and money to enter which could only come from her rival.

But in the midst of these alternations of behaviour B.'s resentment simmered and rose ever higher as her husband's ill-conduct plunged the family into greater want. Finally, one day when he had carried off the last penny, and she learnt that the paramour was in a neighbouring clandestine establishment, B. dressed herself as a man, and, on pretence of being a client, sought out the servant and beat her ferociously. Here the delay in the explosion, the preceding periods of acquiescence, the manner of the offence, all differentiate this woman (of a nature really good) from the true passionate criminal.

Madame Laurent, on discovering that her husband had an intrigue with the servant-girl, dismissed the latter; but the memory of the affront rankled ever more in the mind of the wife, who at the end of *six months* sought out the offender and killed her. No man guilty of a crime of passion would have deferred his vengeance so long. The use of vitriol, too, which as we saw was employed by Madame Du Tilly (and others), is opposed by its insidiousness and inhumanity to the nature of the true crime of passion. The refinement of cruelty in the method, and the coolness necessary to its employment (for the fluid must be well aimed), are contrary to the supposition that the woman is very much excited at the moment of execution.

B. R., whom we have already described as married to a former lover of her mother's, a brutal old man who beat her and made her suffer cold and hunger, at the end of her patience one day mixed some sulphate of copper, given her by her lover, in her husband's food. But when her husband, who found the dish bitter, ordered her to give it to the fowls, she obediently threw it away at once. A few days later her husband, after a fresh quarrel, found a piece of *polenta* of a suspicious colour and accused her of an attempt on his life, to which she at once confessed. Here, then, is another example of a slow and deliberate crime (for such is the nature of poison) suggesting itself as a means of getting rid of a justly detested husband.

A peasant woman of Bergamo (also of irreproachable morals), being betrayed by her husband, dressed herself in men's clothes, and accompanied by an old hag of her acquaintance, hid herself in a wood till the rival passed, then fell upon her and wounded and disfigured her (the elder woman aiding). Here passion was the origin of the crime, and the criminal, as we have seen, was of good moral character: nevertheless the disguise, the premeditation, the studied barbarity of vengeance, and, above all, the choice of an accomplice, distinguish the offender from her male prototype, who always executes his deeds of passion unaided.

The crime of Madame Raymond showed great coolness and power of calculation. She went to the house where her husband and his mistress were in the habit of meeting, and to gain admittance resorted to a very clever stratagem. She rang the bell and slipped under the door a note addressed to her husband, and which said: "Paul, open. Lassimonne (the mistress's husband) knows everything. He is on his way. I come to help you. Do not be afraid."

Madame Brosset was separated from her husband for incompatibility of temper, but jealousy tormented her all the same. One day she repaired, armed, to his habitation, and finding him there with another woman (a little humpback), she stabbed him to death. Even Madame Daru, who is one of the most genuine types of the criminal from passion, was not prevented by anger against her husband from planning to kill him with most security during his sleep.

Dumaire, if on one side akin to criminals from passion, on the other resembles the born delinquents. She had led a profligate life, but was intelligent and frugal enough, strange to say, to have enriched herself by her gains; and she showed the utmost disinterestedness of character in relieving the wants of her relatives, and so on.

She fell in love with Picart, and was faithful to him for many years; had a daughter by him; helped him in his studies; and did not ask him to marry her, but only to continue to live with her.

But Picart, on finishing the course of instruction for which she had paid, contemplated leaving her to marry a rich heiress, and then Dumaire killed him. The purity of her passion and the unworthy conduct of her love would incline one to regard her crime as impulsive, but against this theory we must place the long premeditation (shown in the warning addressed to Picart's family, "If it be necessary to kill him, I will do it"); the absence of remorse evident in her declarations to the judge that if the crime were to be done again she would not shrink from it, since she preferred to see her lover dead than married to another; and finally her resolute, energetic way both of committing the offence and justifying it, which contrasts with the stormy but uncertain and hesitating action of true passion.

Dav. . . . was seduced by a sergeant whom she passionately loved, and who had promised to marry her. He deserted her when she was pregnant, and she threw vitriol over him.

Now here was no *cocotte* or prostitute, who alleges desertion as the cause of a vengeance to which she has been really moved by egotism. Here is a girl who had been gravely injured, and in whose offence passion was a strong factor.

Nevertheless, there are in the case certain particulars opposed to the crime of pure impulse. Before seduction she threatened her lover with death should he desert her, thus showing that theoretically she had already conceived the deed before anything had happened to provoke it. Also she sought out her lover in a low masked ball to which she went accompanied by another man, thus showing some lightness of conduct; and finally she chose vitriol as her weapon, because, as she declared, she wished her victim to feel all the pain of death; and, so far from evincing remorse, she eagerly asked the prison doctors if the man were dead.

Equally balanced between the two sorts of crime (that ascribable to impulse and that proper to the born delinquent) is the deed of the girl Santa, who three times at a distance of months endeavoured to wound her most unworthy lover (who had seduced and abandoned her), and finally did kill him with a knife.

Clothilde Andral, an actress (who certainly was not new to equivocal adventures), became the mistress of an officer who eventually deserted her and her child. She was left in great want, made all the greater by the fact that she could not nurse the infant; and at last, exasperated by misery, by the sufferings of her child, by the base conduct of her lover, who never even answered her letters, she threw vitriol at him, but only wounded him slightly.

In this instance, again, the previous impure life of the woman and her long preparation (for three times at long intervals she came to spy upon the officer) are against the theory of mere passionate impulse; but, on the other hand, the motive for the offence was a grave one, and the sentiment from which it sprang was not ignoble.

In all these cases, then, we find not the sudden fury of passion which blinds even a good man and transforms him temporarily into a homicide, but a slower and more tenacious feeling, which produces a ferment of cruel instincts and allows time for reflection in preparing and calculating the details of the crime. It may be said, in answer to this, that the women we have described are naturally very good; and it is true that they differ but little from normal women. But this apparent contradiction diminishes when we reflect that the normal woman is deficient in moral sense, and possessed of slight criminal tendencies, such as vindictiveness, jealousy, envy, malignity, which are usually neutralised by less sensibility and less intensity of passion. Let a woman, normal in all else, be slightly more excitable than usual, or let a perfectly normal woman be exposed to grave provocations, and these criminal tendencies which are physiologically latent will take the upper hand. But then the woman does not become a criminal through the intensity of her passions (these being colder in her), but through the explosion of a latent tendency to crime which an occasion has set free. That is to say, a normal or quasi-normal woman may commit a crime of passion without being a typical criminal from impulse. Her passions are weaker (than the man's), yet strong enough to drive her to a criminal act when some outrage to her dearest feelings sets free her latent tendencies to crime. Her deed then is ascribable partly to passion and partly to an innate depravity (*malvagità*), which yet does not detract from the fact that the offender is generally a good and even a very good woman.

The same may be said of those offences in which passion enters as a very important factor, but would be impotent unaided to produce the particular effect, to achieve which the suggestion of a man is necessary. Lodi stole at the instigation of her lover, who threatened to leave her if she did not obey him. Noblin was the mistress of a man called Sougaret, who one day confided to her that he had committed a crime. After many years of life in common Noblin found herself deserted for another woman, and in her grief she threatened Sougaret with the revelation of his terrible secret. He had confided this also to his new mistress, and in order to save himself he conceived the idea of getting rid of one woman and binding the other to him by making her an accomplice in murder: and it was the latest mistress that he determined to sacrifice. For a whole month he incited the reluctant girl to the deed. "He drove me on," she related, "torturing me for weeks, now exciting my hatred by telling me how much the other loved him, now defying me to strike her and reproaching me with cowardice. I hesitated a whole month, but he returned constantly to the charge, telling me I could not love him since I would not kill the other woman."

We see, then, that passion alone would not be sufficient to produce a crime, but must be reinforced by suggestion. This only means in other words that suggestion is necessary in the case of women whose criminal tendencies are more latent, but for that reason profounder and more tenacious. A man who commits a crime when driven to it by strong passion, may have a great natural repugnance to the offence, which is momentarily suffocated by feeling; but a person who, even when under the influence of passion, is induced by suggestion to commit a deed of blood— that is, with leisure to calculate and to feel a horror of the action demanded—must have a lower degree of organic repulsion to crime. The latent fund of wickedness existing in the normal woman renders possible a hybrid form of criminal impulse which admits also of complicity.

10. *Crimes of passion from egotism.*—Egotistic criminal impulses prove even better that crimes of passion must be the effect of a slow fermentation of the wickedness latent in the normal woman. There is a class of pure, good, affectionate women in whom the only motive for their crime is the egotistical sentiment of jealousy bred in them by illness, accident, &c. Their offence may be regarded as originating partly in passion; but it lacks a grave cause, and is also entirely unprovoked by the victim; thus showing an analogy with the deeds of the born criminal.

We will proceed to instance a case which happened in Belgium. A man loved and was loved by a dowerless girl whose cousin, an heiress, was herself in love with the same individual. The man, good at heart, but weak, and alarmed at the idea of a struggle for life, decided eventually to engage himself to the heiress. She, a short time before the date fixed for her marriage, fell dangerously ill; and as on her death the cousin would succeed to the property and be in a position to marry the man of her choice, the dying woman was so possessed by jealousy that she determined to destroy her promised husband's chances of happiness by taking away his character. She swallowed a very valuable diamond, and then confided to her father that the young man had stolen it. After her death her father, who regarded the confidence as an effect of delirium, looked, partly from scrupulousness, into her jewel case, and found the ring without the diamond. The young man was then arrested and would have been condemned only that, fortunately for him, common report accused him of having poisoned his affianced in order that her cousin might inherit. The authorities ordered an autopsy, and the expert found the diamond in the body of the dead woman.

Mrs. Derw—, very happily married and much attached to her husband, was attacked by phthisis and brought in a few months to the verge of death. Her love for her husband turned to violent jealousy: she made him swear again and again that he would never marry a second time, never look at another woman; she implored him to die with her, and one day, after receiving from him fresh assurances that he would always be hers alone, she snatched a loaded gun from the wall and shot him dead.

Madame Perrin, bedridden for five years and incurable, became extremely jealous of her husband, reproached him perpetually with his infidelities, and finally determining to put an end to the situation, she called her husband to her bedside and wounded him with a revolver which she had hidden under the sheets. The crime, she declared, had been premeditated for a long time.

In all these instances the motive for the offence is the noble feeling of love; and the offenders are naturally good women. Yet they are impelled to crime by an outburst of the wickedness latent in every woman, by the sharp pangs of a jealousy which resents happiness in others as a personal injury. The sudden destruction of their own felicity renders them unwilling that others should marry the man they are leaving. No doubt the motive is a strong one: their sorrow is great; and in normal circumstances they would have remained excellent women. But all the same the offences we have detailed prove the likeness between women and children, since they might be described as offences committed by big children of developed intelligence and passions.

The crime then is one of passion, but is entirely egotistical, since it springs from jealousy and envy instead of from the sentiments called by Spencer *ego-altruistic*, such as love and honour, which drive men to crimes of passion.

And it is worth while to note here that Marro[1] states jealousy to be the cause of madness in 17 per cent. of women as against 1·5 per cent. of men, which shows the preponderance of the feeling in the female sex.

[1] "Madness in Women," 1893.

CHAPTER XVI.

SUICIDES.

1. To complete our study of crimes from passion we must investigate suicides; for, even setting aside legislative and juridical considerations, the affinity and analogy between criminal impulses and suicide are so great that the two offences may be considered as two branches of the same trunk.

Suicide resembles crime in its variability, but the number of deaths self-inflicted is four and five times less among women than among men.

Here are the percentages:—

	Men.	Women.
Italy (1874–1833)	80·2	19·8
Prussia (1878–1882)	83·3	16·7
Saxony (1874–1883)	80·7	19·3
Wurtemberg (1872–1881)	84·6	15·4
France (1876–1880)	79·0	21·0
England (1873–1882)	75·0	19·0
Scotland (1877–1881)	70·0	30·0
Ireland (1874–1883)	73·0	27·0
Switzerland (1876–1883)	85·0	15·0
Holland (1880–1882)	81·0	19·0
Denmark (1880–1883)	78·2	21·8
Connecticut (1878–1882)	70·0	30·0

And if out of all these figures we separate the suicides caused by passion from the others, we find the same proportion as among crimes of passion.

2. *Suicides from physical suffering.*—The smaller number of suicides from passion (among women) is, so to speak, prefigured in the smaller proportion of suicides from physical suffering, that is to say, the revolt of the organism under pain.

Out of a hundred suicides of both sexes the proportion resulting from physical suffering is as follows (Morselli):—

		Men.		Women.
Germany (1852-1861)	... ...	9·61	−	8·08
Prussia (1869-1877)	... ...	6	+	7
Saxony (1875-1878)	... ...	4·61	+	6·21
Belgium	... ...	1·34	−	0·84
France (1873-1878)	... ...	14·28	−	13·56
Italy (1866-1877) ...	... ...	6·70	+	8·50
Vienna (1851-1859)	... ...	9·20	+	10·04
,, (1869-1878)	... ...	7·73	+	10·37
Paris (1851-1859) ...	... ...	10·27	+	11·22
Madrid (1884)	... ...	31·81	−	31·25

There is consequently a *relative* superiority of the woman in this respect in Prussia, Saxony, Italy, Vienna, and Paris; and an inferiority in Germany, Belgium, France, and Madrid.

But even the superiority is relative, for the quotas give the proportional percentages of the suicides in both sexes; and the greatest difference is found in Vienna, where the suicides of men stand to those of women as 7·73 to 10·37—that is, as 1 to 1·34; and as suicide among men is always 3 to 5 times more frequent than among women, we see that, in reality, when the figures for the two sexes are compared, the number of suicides from physical pain is infinitely greater among men than women. Women feel pain less than men, consequently are less impelled by it to suicide, in spite of the fact that they are more frequently exposed to physical pain—are physiologically bound to endure it, indeed. And as physical sensibility forms the basis of moral sensibility, and physical pains may almost be described as the passions of the organism, we find ourselves face to face here with the original reason why women commit fewer suicides from passion than men.

3. *Want.*—Want is also a cause which drives more men than women to suicide. The percentages of suicide from want are low in both sexes relatively to the total of self-inflicted deaths; and this inferiority is doubled and tripled by the fact that women commit suicide two and three times less frequently.

The proportion per cent. of suicides from want is as under:—

	Men.	Women.
Germany (1852–1861)	37·75	18·46
Prussia (1869–1877)	—	—
Saxony (1875–1878)	6·64	1·52
Belgium	4·65	4·02
Italy (1866–1877)	7	4·60
,, ,, (financial reverses)	12·80	2·20
Norway (1866–1870) ,,	10·30	4·50
Vienna (1851–1859)	6·64	3·10

These results are the more striking inasmuch as the probability of falling into want is as great for the one sex as the other—that is to say, that loss of means almost always affects a husband and wife, or a father and daughters, &c., &c. Women, however, bear misery much better than men, and that for many reasons.

Woman represents the median type of the species, and can consequently adapt herself much better to varying social conditions. As Max Nordau remarked, the difference in nature between a duchess and a washerwoman is only superficial, so that a duchess can adapt herself to new surroundings and become a washerwoman much more easily than a man can transform himself under analogous conditions.

We have all seen women of high rank who have easily accepted the position of maids or companions, &c., but a man who has to descend from a high place does not bend with such facility beneath the iron hand of destiny; more often he breaks. Moreover, a woman having fewer needs and a lower degree of sensitiveness is better adapted than a man to support not only moral suffering, but even physical privations, such as insufficient food, absence of comforts, and so on.

There is the additional fact, too, that in cases of financial ruin the woman has often only an indirect responsibility, and is consequently much less overcome by remorse than the man. Maternity, again, has a beneficent influence, for a mother who sinks into poverty is less affected by the grief of ruin than impressed with the necessity of providing for her children, whom she cannot leave on the streets, while a father, in the paroxysm of his pain, much oftener forgets the innocent victims of his errors and his faults.

Finally, a woman having less pride than a man has less difficulty in resorting to begging, an expedient to which the sterner sex often prefer death; and it frequently happens that a woman, with her weaker moral sense, will have recourse at last to the facile relief offered by prostitution. It follows from all this that many more factors are necessary before a woman can be driven by want to suicide.

When poverty, in her case, has reached the acutest stage of privation, when all means of relief fail, and age or innate chastity render prostitution impossible, then she also is impelled to commit this form of suicide from passion.

"I have tried in a thousand ways to find work," wrote one before her self-inflicted end, "and I have only met with hearts of stone or vile characters to whose infamous propositions I would not listen."

A beautiful young girl left a letter saying that she had nothing left, all she possessed being in pawn. "I might have had a well-stocked shop," she added, "but I prefer death to the existence of a fallen woman."

4. *Love.*—Love contributes largely to suicide as to crime. The statistics of female suicides from love show a preponderance in this respect over the sterner sex, the percentages being as follows:—

	Men.	Women.
Germany (1852–62)	2·33	8·46
Saxony (1875–78)	1·83	5·18
Austria (1869–78)	5·80	17·40
Vienna (1851–59)	5·89	14·13
Italy (1866–77)	3·80	7·50
Belgium	9·53	12·08

Exceptions to the rule are, however, furnished by—

	Men.	Women.
Prussia (1869–77)	12·50	8
France (1856–68)	15·48	13·16

These figures show that the passionate woman flies to suicide as a relief to the disillusions and the pangs of love; and this fact, through the well-known law of antagonism between suicide and crime, must tend to diminish considerably the number of crimes committed from passion.

This predominance among women of suicide over homicide for love is in perfect harmony with our view of the nature of love in women. We saw that in women love is a species of slavery, a sacrifice gladly made of the entire personality. These elements, even when very strong, sometimes allow egotistic sentiments to triumph in the average woman, but are so exaggerated in passionate natures that ill-treatment on the part of their lover only increases their fury of self-sacrifice.

In such natures it is evident that the most violent love cannot impel the subjects of it to crime. To suppose, for instance, that Mrs. Carlyle, Mademoiselle Lespinasse, or Heloise would have killed the object of their adoration because neglected or ill-treated, is a psychological absurdity, since their love and devotion only grew more intense under ill-treatment. There are many ignorant Heloises who, when putting an end by suicide to the agony of an ill-requited affection, express in their last words a feeling of self-sacrificing devotion towards the man who should inspire them only with vindictiveness.

A girl writing to her lover says: "You have deceived me. During two years you swore to marry me, and now you desert me. I love you, but I cannot survive the loss of your affection."

Another writes, under similar circumstances: "I have done everything morally possible to live without the affection which comprised my whole life; but the effort is beyond my strength. Certainly my fault is great, and my memory will be cursed even by my child, the very thought of whom sets all the chords of my being vibrating; but still without the other half of myself, without him whom I have lost, my life is insupportable. I had thought of throwing myself at his feet, but he would have spurned me. I pray that he may pardon my injustice of character, my violence, and only remember the happy hours which he passed with me."

One of two deserted women wrote to her friend: "Assure him (the lover) that I pray for his happiness, and die adoring him."

Another said, "Death will soon divide us. I hope thus to make you happy."

"What have I done," asked yet a third, in her last letter to her faithless lover—"what have I done to deserve this misfortune? Perhaps you desert me because I loved you more than my life?"[1]

Desertion, in short, awakes no resentment against the deserter. He is looked upon as lost through death, which causes so much grief, that for the woman no other consolation is possible but to die in her turn. And she dies when she does not go mad.

Marro, in this respect, has furnished the following figures:—

	Men.	Women.
Unrequited love causes madness in	1·5 per cent.	2·5 per cent.
Betrayed love	0·3 ,,	1·7 ,,
Desertion, or the death of husband or wife	0·6 ,,	3·2 ,,

[1] Sighele, "Evoluzione dall' omicidio al suicidio nei drammi d'amore." "Arch. di psich.," 1891. Brierre de Boismont, "Du Suicide," 1860.

the proportion being doubled and sextupled for women.

Now, if we connect all these remarks with the frequency of virile characteristics in female criminals from passion, we shall find ourselves in possession of the key of our enigma. Women who kill their lovers from passion have a virile strength of sentiment. And this is the reason why even the woman guilty of a crime of passion so rarely offers the complete type of her class. Love alone does not excite her to crime: she is less moved by it than by egotistical sentiments which disillusion has set fermenting. Pure, strong passion, when existing in a woman, drives her to suicide rather than to crime. If the contrary be the case, then either her natural latent fund of wickedness has been set free, or virility of disposition has infused into her feelings a violence, and consequently a capacity for murderous assaults, to which the true woman, the finished woman, is a stranger.

The true crime of love—if such it can be called—in a woman is suicide; all her other crimes of passion are of a hybrid sort.

It is remarkable that marriage causes more suicides among men than women. Fourteen women commit suicide when deserted by their husbands, and the same number when widowed against fifty men in the first case and forty-one in the second.

This fact is partly explained by the predominance of maternal over conjugal love already insisted upon, and partly by the circumstance that, as we have seen, so many women go mad from love. We must take into consideration that the love which drives women to violent measures is frequently illicit or legally forbidden. And matrimony, like all social institutions, having been created for the average specimen of humanity, the woman who tranquilly casts anchor in the port of marriage belongs to the great army of normals, and loves too feebly to commit suicide when widowed. On the other hand, the passionate woman finds in the very barriers erected by society to the satisfaction of her instincts, the rock on which her love and her life go to wreck. Hence the number of passionate women who commit suicide or go mad.

5. *Double and multiple suicides.*—In a double suicide the predominating partner is almost always the woman. Where two lovers commit suicide, thus expiating what is generally an infraction of social laws, the woman is usually the more resolute.

In the Bancal-Trousset case it was she who, after reading *Indiana*, conceived the notion of dying with her lover. *He* resisted, and she reproached him, saying, "You do not love me enough to make this sacrifice." Bancal ended by consenting, but when the time came he hesitated to open her veins, and she urged him to it, begging him to make haste. When she fainted, Bancal felt a horror of his deed and tried to stop the bleeding, but Trousset, determined to die, insisted that he should give her poison, and, when that was not enough, that he should stab her. "Make an end of it," she said; "you must kill me."

Similarly in the case of C. M. and P. L. it was

with the girl that the idea originated, and as he hesitated and began to weep, "Child," she said, "you have no courage. See! I will kill you and then myself. It is time to finish with pretences."

Brierre de Boismont relates that a young girl of tranquil nature, who was in the habit of reading neither romances nor plays, on hearing that the parents of her affianced refused their consent to the marriage, became all at once possessed with the idea of a double suicide. She urged the young man to it with affectionate caresses. "I am determined to die," she said, "rather than give you up. Give me also this proof of love."

Bertha Delmas and Emile Gasson had engaged themselves to one another without thinking of the military service which he had to perform. The day of his departure came, and he left, consoling himself with the idea that at the new year he would be able to see his promised bride again. But when the moment arrived his leave was denied him in punishment for an infraction of discipline. When the girl learnt this, she pawned her earrings for nine francs, and wrote to him to come at all costs, as she could no longer live without seeing him. Gasson deserted and rejoined Bertha, with whom he passed a week. But as he was in constant danger of being arrested, Bertha conceived the idea of suicide, persuaded him to consent, and fixed the day and hour for the deed. He was continually for putting it off, but she ordered him to fire. The attempt failed, and when Gasson was brought up for trial, the contrast between his character and the woman's shone forth as clear as noonday. He was timid, irresolute, stammering, and showed that he had been under the influence of suggestion. She, resolute, firm, virile, proved by her attitude that she had planned and prepared everything.

R. C., of Turin, was forced by her parents to marry a rich man whom she disliked, during the absence on military service of her previous affianced. She was in despair, and when her lover returned on a day's leave she fled with him to San Bernardo. They spent a few hours there; then, tying their feet and hands, threw themselves into the lake. The woman left a letter for her family, in which she said that she had been constrained to make a marriage she detested, and that rather than be unfaithful to her husband, or false to the man she loved more than life, she preferred to commit suicide.

Not many years ago in Ivrea dwelt two large, patriarchal families of neighbours. The day came when a son of one household had to leave for Turin to finish his studies. He begged his mother to prepare a particular dish for his supper; he joked with his father; but when the evening arrived he had disappeared. A daughter of the other household, between whom and the youth there had long been great affection, had asked her mother for the same dish. She arrayed herself for the first time in a dress that she had purposely embroidered many months before, and said, "Do I not look like a bride?"—then by the evening she also had disappeared.

The two fathers, seized with the same suspicion,

met at dawn, and having found a letter from the student, in which he declared that he preferred death to separation, they ran to the canal, and, causing the water to be turned off, found the girl and boy locked in each other's arms, and smiling as if death had found them in the happiest hour of their lives. The girl's mother, searching her room, found a diary in which the fatal determination was already recorded, and wherein the writer alluded with pleasure to the thought of "that day."

Moralists and theologians may say what they will, but in this money-making, sordid age, such incidents, so far from inspiring us with horror, fill our eyes with tears and our hearts with the deepest compassion; for they prove that we can still feel strong, ideal disinterested passions, and are even ready to die for them.

Suicide for love, which as we see is so common, has certainly a physiological root, being the effect of an elective affinity strengthened by the reproductive organs and the peculiar repugnance to separation induced by these in the molecules of the organism.

The Indian Suttee has a physiological root which accounts far better for the rite than any masculine tyranny or than the sanction which religion usually accords to any time-honoured custom. (The Vedas, indeed, prohibit suicide.) We know that when the English first attempted to put an end to the barbarous usage, or at least to prevent the priests from encouraging it, they met with great opposition. Lieutenant Earle endeavoured to dissuade a widow, who was smilingly preparing to ascend the pyre, by urging her at least to try the effect of the flames by first holding a finger in them; and she, with a smile of scorn, plunged the member into a lighted oil-lamp, and watched it burning unmoved. "You may say what you choose," she replied to the officers, "but I must belong to him and to nobody else; I loved him and could not love another." She went seven times round the pyre, then mounted it, and laying her dead husband's head on her breast, herself set fire to the pile, of which in a few hours there remained but a heap of ashes, over which the Brahmins were muttering their prayers.

The truth of the explanation we have offered is proved by the fact that in countries where there is no religious ordinance of the kind—as, for instance, in China—yet childless widows will hang themselves publicly, believing that they go to join their dear deceased at once. In New Zealand the daughter of the conqueror Hongi, seeing her father returning from battle unaccompanied by her husband, jumped into his boat, snatched his sword, and after running sixteen prisoners through, tried to shoot herself, but being wounded merely, proceeded to strangle herself, and thus went to join her husband in the land of shades.

We see, then, that it is almost always the woman who conceives the suicide, and carries it out with most resolution.

In a double suicide—that of R. F. and G. B.—it was the woman who fired the first shot which killed her lover. And Bourget, in the "Disciple," makes the man fail in courage at the supreme moment, while his companion never wavers in her fell intent.

All this is quite natural. Love being, even in the normal woman, a very important element, even though as a rule she does not feel the sentiment with excessive intensity (we may here recall the celebrated dictum of Madame de Staël), for the passionate woman it must necessarily constitute almost her whole existence. To separate her from her lover is to kill her; while a man, even when very much in love, finds life too attractive on other sides to feel that his whole existence is shattered because deprived of the object of his affections. The exasperation of unsatisfied desire may bring him for a moment to accept suicide as a condition of appeasing himself; but the desire past, as Bourget well divined, his joy in life, and in all the aims in which the loved woman has no part, reassert themselves.

That is why so many men, like the Robert Greslou of the French novelist, hesitate to commit suicide when the impelling cause is removed, while the woman only shows herself more determined than before. Add to all this that in illicit connections, such as those which we have been considering, women risk social consequences of much greater moment to themselves than to their lovers, and under these circumstances the resolution to commit suicide is reinforced by the reflection that their families, their husbands, their whole world, in short, is lost to them.

A class of suicides peculiar to women is that of a mother who, reduced by want or other causes to despair, kills her young or infirm children and then herself.

Madame Arresteilles, who adored her son of 29, an epileptic idiot, fearing that the rest of the family might treat him harshly after her death, killed him and committed suicide. Madame Berbesson also killed her daughter, whom she worshipped, who had gone mad and was to be sent to an asylum; then, unable to support the idea of separation, the mother put an end to herself. Madame Monard, worn out by the brutality of her husband, who continually beat herself and her two children, tried to kill the latter. Madame Souhine, a very respectable working woman, whom the imprisonment of her husband and an industrial crisis had reduced to the greatest misery, sold all she had, bought good dresses for her children, gave them a comparatively sumptuous repast, and then when they were asleep she strangled them and tried to commit suicide.

These women were all very moral; and their act, although it looks at first sight like infanticide followed by suicide, is in reality, so to speak, only the completion of their own self-inflicted death. To die alone and leave their children is impossible for them, the children being almost an organic portion of themselves, so that to leave them seems like killing themselves but in part. An affectionate mother does not think her own sufferings ended if those of her children must continue, and the proof of this is that these infanticides followed by suicide always take place when the children are small or unable to look after themselves—that is, imbecile or otherwise incapable. For maternity is a function which exists for the protection of the weak, and a mother feeling that her children are a part of herself, as long as they are unable to provide for themselves provides for them by every means in her power, such means including at times the pathological phenomenon which we are at present considering.

When the child grows up the mother can separate from him, and although she continues to love him (thus differing from the lower animals which abandon their offspring), she no longer feels bound to him by that common life which, so to speak, makes of two beings but one organism.

Madame Souhine, when asked why she had killed her children before trying to kill herself, replied: "I wished to go with them."

This view is confirmed by the fact that when the child is still young enough not to be, as we might say, entirely disjoined from his mother, but sufficiently old to undergo *suggestion*, then his mother does not actually kill him, but persuades him to commit suicide in her company.

E. and E. B., whose cases were examined by Garnier, persuaded the one, a boy of 13, the other, a boy of 10, to kill themselves at the same moment as their respective mothers put an end to their own lives.

Sometimes, however, the double maternal suicide is determined not by misfortune leading to despair, but by more egotistical sentiments, and the crime then becomes analogous to a suicide of the passionate-selfish sort, and is the equivalent (offered by natures of another kind) to the infanticide committed by good women and affectionate mothers. E., a prey to neuropathic affections (persistent headache, giddiness, insomnia, nightmare, &c.), and of a very melancholy temperament, belonged to a family originally noble and rich, but fallen into decay, and was married to a man of good instincts, but inferior in education to herself and in poor circumstances. The woman was fretted by the existence she had to lead in one room, which served as bedroom, sitting-room, and kitchen, and where constant poverty reigned. She perpetually accused her husband of ill-treating her, although such was not the case, and finally, in a moment of greater irritation than ever, she decided to kill herself and the son whom she adored. If, instead of being a woman not naturally bad, but neuropathic, she had been wicked and wanting in maternal love, she would have revenged herself for all the privations and pains of her life by tormenting her child, as did Madame Stakembourg, and perhaps by poisoning her husband. But being of a better nature, she chose suicide in company with the boy, thus yielding to an egotistical impulse instead of to the ego-altruistic feeling which constitutes the sentiment of maternity.

Double suicides in two women are extremely rare.

We have found one incomplete instance in the death of Olga Protaffow and Vera Gerebssow They were very intimate friends and lived together in extreme poverty. Tired of their misery, Vera made her friend promise to kill her if within two months their condition should not have improved. Olga promised, and when the two months were over, after much hesitation, kept her word. The rarity of such an act corresponds entirely to the rarity of female suicides from friendship, and is to be explained by the same cause—the small degree of friendship which women can feel for one another.

Double suicides among married couples are also extremely rare; and for the third time we have to observe that matrimony being an institution adapted to normal women, such women, with their weak passions, naturally pay but a small toll to suicide, while, on the other hand, passionate women find in the customs, the prejudices, and the laws of marriage the very rock on which they perish. We know of only one very sad case of a double suicide of husband and wife, which happened at Bologna. A youth of 20, an only son, adored by his parents, of great intelligence, loved by his companions, admired and encouraged by an illustrious living poet, and to whom a magnificent literary future seemed promised by the examples of talent which he had already given, died suddenly during an epidemic of diphtheria; and his parents, thus deprived of their one great object of affection, committed suicide together by asphyxia a month later. In this instance the intense paternal and maternal love of the pair had bred a new bond of union, a kind of second love for their son into which entered all the pride and all the hopes they had centred on this offspring of the mutual tenderness of their youth: and in this sentiment we must seek the explanation of such a strange phenomenon as a suicide between two old people.

6. *Suicides from madness.*—Confirmatory at once and explanatory of the affirmation that suicides from passion are comparatively rare among women, is the fact that 50 per cent., and sometimes more, of suicides in the female sex are due to madness.

These are the statistics:—

	Suicides from Madness.	
	Men.	Women.
Germany (1852–61)	30·17	50·77
Prussia (1869–77)	23·50	44
Saxony (1875–78)	26·59	48·40
Austria (1869–78)	8·20	10·80
Belgium	41·22	81·94
France (1856–68)	15·48	13·16
Italy (1866–77)	16·30	27·50
Norway	17·90	28·40

These differences can only be partly explained by the predominance among women of causes producing acute mania, such as puerperal fever, which affects them exclusively, and pellagra, which attacks them in preference. Together these two causes counterbalance or exceed the effects of alcoholism in the other sex; but the fact remains that violent passion in a woman leads rather to madness than to suicide or to crime. Only when grief is so intense as to produce hallucination or delirium, only when an extreme anomaly has stirred her spirit to the depths, does the woman resort to suicide equally with the man, and even more than the man. This phenomenon in respect to suicide is analogous to that which we observed with regard to crime. An infinity of variations in the character, passing from a slight hyperesthesia and vivacity of passion to positive madness, may conduce to suicide; and the woman, as less sensitive and less variable than the man, must contribute fewer examples of those suicides from passion which in men arise from the multiple variations, the numerous slight psychical anomalies which occur in this or that individual.

Woman being less variable remains more normal, but when anomalous is almost always so to a graver degree, being then, indeed, an example of a double exception. And that is why in her case suicides from passion, which represent slight variations of character, are rare, while more frequent are suicides from madness arising when anomaly has reached its highest point.

The woman, as distinguished from the man, in other words, stands at one or other extremity of the pole, being either perfectly normal or excessively anomalous. And when the anomaly is excessive, suicide and madness are one. Consequently women are very rarely criminal when compared with men, but when criminal they are infinitely worse. That is to say, the two poles are respectively normality and extreme degeneration, and the intermediary variations which should connect the two do not exist.

CHAPTER XVII.

CRIMINAL FEMALE LUNATICS.

1. *Statistics.*—In Italy, between the years 1871–86, there were 1,753 criminal male lunatics and 96 criminal female lunatics, being 5·6 women against 100 men, which is a lower proportion of women than that found among criminals, these being for the decade 1870–79 as 7·3 women against 100 men.[1]

From Sander and Richter's observations we learn that out of 1,486 male lunatics 13·9 per cent. were criminal, while out of 1,462 female lunatics the criminals were 2·6 per cent.[2]

In some recent investigations made together with Busdraghi, one of the writers found the following figures:—

Out of 100	incendiaries	...	63 males	...	37 females.
,, ,,	homicides	...	75 ,,	...	25 ,,
,, ,,	thieves ...	...	62 ,,	...	38 ,,
,, ,,	guilty of rape	...	30 ,,	...	0 ,,

And these had all gone mad out of prison.

This smaller proportion of lunatics among female criminals is certainly ascribable to two causes—one being the minor degree of alcoholism (drink, as

[1] V. Rossi, "Criminal Lunatics in Italy," 1887.
[2] Drs. Sander and Richter, "Die Beziehung Zwischen Geisterstorung und Verbrechen," Berlin, 1886.

we shall see, furnishing the largest contingent of male criminal lunatics), and the other, the smaller prevalence of epilepsy, together with the tendency which that disease when existent in women has to assume the forms of prostitution or lasciviousness, both offences which, however reprehensible, are less criminal and less dangerous, and therefore do not lead to sensational trials and jealous reclusion. Ninety-nine out of a thousand of our female criminal lunatics were prostitutes, and 212 servants, or of no profession.

Out of 24 female criminal lunatics observed by Sander 11 were thieves, 6 prostitutes, 2 beggars, and 2 swindlers.

As to the nature of the madness, the following results are given for the decade 1870-79, in Italy :—

Melancholia and monomania of persecution	33
Mania	22
Imbecility and idiotcy	10
Hallucinatory monomania	7
Megalomania	2
Suicide	4
Moral folly	4

showing an evident prevalence of the forms (hallucinatory monomania, melancholia, suicide) generated by prison life, and on account of detention, or of those congenital affections, such as imbecility and idiotcy, which ought to guarantee the subject from incarceration ; while the diseases so common in the male criminal, such as epilepsy and moral folly, are rare.

Esquirol says that even among moral women the most common forms of madness are melancholia and furious mania.

In Italy, however, the female melancholics were

CRIMINAL FEMALE LUNATICS.

inferior to the male as 1,657 to 3,414, but the female maniacs (especially furious maniacs) are as 1,843 to 1,836.

If among the minor criminals, who form the largest proportion of the incarcerated, there is but little madness, the contrary is the case among the worse sorts of criminals.

Salsotto studied the cases of 409 female criminals in the prison of Turin, and found that 53, or 12·9 per cent., out of the number were affected as follows: Epilepsy 11 (2·6 per cent.), hysteria 19 (4·9 per cent.), alcoholism 13 (3·1 per cent.), and idiotcy 10 (2·5 per cent.).

The proportion of the different crimes to madness was as follows (adding the figures given for male criminal lunatics by Marro):—

```
26 p. c. in murderesses    (130) — male criminal lunatics 40 p. c.
25    ,,   poisoners        (20) —    ,,         ,,        —   ,,
30    ,,   wounders         (10) —    ,,         ,,        26  ,,
20    ,,   guilty of assault(10) —    ,,         ,,        23  ,,
15    ,,   swindlers        (20) —    ,,         ,,        23  ,,
80    ,,   incendiaries      (4) —    ,,         ,,        85  ,,
16    ,,   guilty of rape   (25) —    ,,         ,,        33  ,,
 0    ,,   thieves          (90) —    ,,         ,,        31  ,,
```

Here there is an evident prevalence of madness among the worse criminals, and a certain parallelism with the males.[1]

---

[1] The various species of mental disorder were distributed as follows:—

Out of 130 murderesses—

    5 epileptics, being 4 per cent.
    9 hysterical, ,, 7·2 ,,
    6 drunkards, ,, 5 ,,
    1 somnambulist, ,, 0·9 ,,
    2 crétines, ,, 1·8 ,,
    2 idiots, ,, 1·8 ,,
    1 religious maniac, ,, 0·9 ,,

At Broadmoor the greatest number of lunatics are to be found among the homicides and wounders (103 in 141); next comes incest, 19; parricides 6, and burglary 3.

The greater number of female lunatics are married women, while the greater number of male lunatics are single (*see* "L'Uomo Delinquente," vol. ii.); and this fact confirms the observations made on healthy criminals in all countries.

The lunatic asylums for females receive more inmates in summer (25) than in winter (21), while the figures for spring and autumn are respectively 11–14. The statistics of male criminals are about the same.

Out of 100 infanticides—
    2 epileptics, being 2 per cent.
    3 hysterical, ,, 3 ,,
    3 idiots, ,, 3 ,,
    3 drunkards, ,, 3 ,,

Out of 10 wounders—
    3 hysterics, being 30 per cent.

Out of 10 guilty of assault—
    1 epileptic, being 10 per cent.
    1 hysteric, ,, 10 ,,

Out of 20 poisoners—
    2 hysterics, being 10 per cent.
    2 epileptics, ,, 10 ,,
    1 drunkard, ,, 5 ,,

Out of 20 swindlers—
    2 hysterics, being 10 per cent.
    1 epileptic, ,, 5 ,,

Out of 4 incendiaries—
    3 crétines, being 80 per cent.

Out of 25 guilty of rape—
    3 drunkards, being 12 per cent.
    1 hysteric, ,, 4 ,,

We may conclude that the history of female criminal lunatics is that of female criminals in general. And the same may be said of the characteristics of their madness, which simply serve to accentuate the nature of their crimes.

2. *Premeditation.* — Although to a less marked degree than in the male, the graver cases of moral insanity or congenital criminality in females present all the most essential features of epilepsy (*see* following chapter). And the ability displayed in the commission of the crime, its premeditation, the steps taken to establish an alibi, and the efforts at dissimulation, are equal and sometimes greater than similar phenomena in the simple criminal.

One of the most extraordinary instances of ability was given by Euphrasie Mercier, who carried through a series of most complicated forgeries in order to gain possession of the fortune of Madame Ménétrier, then killed her victim, and destroyed all trace of the corpse; doing the whole thing so well that, in spite of all the efforts of the rightful heirs and of one of the best police systems in Europe, the crime was only discovered at the end of two years, when a nephew of the murderess revealed it. And yet Mercier was a mystic and a monomaniac, religious, but mad probably from her birth, being the daughter of a religious lunatic, who believed that he could cure all illnesses. And her sisters and nephews and nieces were afflicted with the same delusions (Ball, " De la Responsabilité partielle," 1886).

A lady of wealth, aged 26, with no hereditary history, after becoming a prey to fixed melancholia, stole sheets, &c., from patients whom she tended as a nurse, and effaced the marks to escape detection. She protested remorse, but relapsed again immediately (Savage).

There are (says Savage) pathological female thieves who steal, knowing what they do. They feel, especially at certain periods, an irresistible temptation to thieve, or to break things, or to plunge their hands into particular liquids. Nothing will deter them from the accomplishment of their desires, which they achieve, if by no other means, then through violence. There are women whose appetite can only be appeased with stolen food. (*See* also vol. ii. of "L'Uomo Delinquente.")

One peculiarity of the female criminal lunatic, which is, however, only an exaggeration of her normal state, is that her madness becomes more acute at particular periods, such as menstruation, menopause, and pregnancy.

Esquirol, Algeri, Schroter, and Ball have all noted instances of this peculiarity, which sometimes exhibits symptoms resembling epilepsy. In other cases there will be morbid irritability, melancholy, erotic excitement, delusions as to sins committed, persecutions undergone, &c.

Brouardel has recorded many examples of incendiary and homicidal impulses in pregnant women, and relates the case of one, the mother of five children, who sent poison to one child who was at school, and after despatching orders for the youngest one, who was with a wet nurse, to be brought to her, threw herself with the remaining three down a well.

"In short," writes Icard, "when in this state a woman is capable of anything. Passionately loving mothers will cut their children's throats; and others, naturally good, will pose as victims, and invent infamous calumnies against their dear ones; while chaste women will talk and act in the most indecent manner."

"A kind of animal instinct reigns supreme in the pregnant woman (writes Cabanis, vol. iii. p. 344), and may drive her to any excess. And the same phenomenon is possible at the first return of menstruation, and during the nursing period."

We see, then, that another characteristic of the female lunatic, and consequently of the criminal lunatic, is an exaggeration of the sexual instincts. These which in male lunatics are almost always in abeyance, lead in women, even in very old women as in quite young girls, to the most disgusting and unnatural excesses. ("Arch. di psich.," vol. vi. p. 219.)

Marro writes, "The majority of female lunatics at the period of menopause are subject to erotic delirium. They have ideas of strange marriages and monstrous births, and are subject to sudden obscene delusions. One will be seized with a delirium of jealousy; another feels herself swarmed over by little imps, who hang on to her apron, play her every kind of trick, pinching and pricking her. Hallucinations, in short, abound, presenting every variety of delirium springing from the one basis of sensuality." " Under the influence of mania" (writes Schüle) " women relieve themselves by incessant chatter, in which there is a mixture of true and false perceptions, and especially of momentary fantastic ideas accompanied by grimaces and erotic gestures."

Nymphomania transforms the most timid girl into a shameless bacchante. She tries to attract every man she sees, displaying sometimes violence, and sometimes the most refined coquetry. She often suffers from intense thirst, a dry mouth, a fetid breath, and a tendency to bite everybody she meets, as if affected with hydrophobia, and sometimes she even shows a horror of liquids, and feels as if she were being strangled.

One of the writers knew of a case in which these morbid erotic symptoms appeared in a woman, previously absolutely chaste, after an attack of diphtheria. The instance remains unique (Lombroso, "Amore nei pazzi," 1880).

More common is a milder form of the same mania in which the subject shows either an excessive cleanliness or an excessive dirtiness, also a tendency to strip herself, or tear off her clothes, or to talk of her own marriage, or that of other people (Emminghaus, "Allgemeine Psichopathologie," 1878). Sometimes she is taciturn, melancholy, obstinate; the presence of persons of the opposite sex heightens her breathing, makes her pulse beat more rapidly, gives her a more animated expression. At first reserved, she will later throw off all restraint, and only think and talk of sexual things.

Female lunatics in general surpass their male prototypes in all sexual aberrations and tendencies, and, after long years of observation, I am disposed to agree with Hergt ("All. Zeit. Psych.," xxvii.), who affirmed that two-thirds of female lunatics suffer from maladies of the reproductive organs, which, by increasing reflex action and impairing psychical activity, bring on convulsions and produce abnormal sensations, which are transformed into illusions, hallucinations, delirium, or obscene impulses.

A third characteristic of the female lunatic compared with the male is greater acuteness and impulsiveness, so that in the Italian statistics furious mania in women is as 669 to 524 in men.

Krafft Ebing remarked also that in women madness is usually more turbulent and indecent in its manifestation than in men. Briefly, in female criminal lunatics we find to a more marked degree that which we had already noted in the ordinary female criminal, namely, an inversion of all the qualities which specially distinguish the normal woman; namely, reserve docility and sexual apathy.

CHAPTER XVIII.

EPILEPTIC DELINQUENTS AND MORAL INSANITY.

1. *Epileptic delinquents.* — We have discovered the same relation between moral insanity and epilepsy in women as in men; the difference, however, being that both maladies are infinitely rarer in the female prisoner.

Marro in the same connection shows that motor epilepsy also is one-third less frequent in female than in male delinquents. According to his statistics, during six and a half years, out of 23,333 male criminals in the prison of Turin, there were 0·66 per cent. of epileptics, and 0·22 similarly affected out of 3,358 female offenders; while, if we take the averages of the calculations made by Morselli and Sormani, we find from 0·25 to 0·27 of male epileptics in Italy, and 0·27 in France (Charvin) among the normal population.

Much rarer is psychical epilepsy or epileptic madness, as we may convince ourselves by studying the statistics of epileptic lunatics in the prisons.

According to the decennial statistics of Beltrani Scalia, and the investigations of Virgilio Rossi

("I. Pazzi criminali," Rome, 1891), out of 349 criminal lunatics confined in the Italian prisons between 1880 and 1891, 25 were epileptic, and 35 morally insane; while out of 36 *female* criminals none were epileptic, and only three morally insane.

Between the years 1866 and 1882 out of 877 male lunatics in penal establishments, 9 were epileptic and 49 morally insane; and out of 20 female lunatics, none were epileptic, and only one was morally insane.

In Germany in 1881 there were 22 epileptics among 65 male lunatic delinquents (or 33 per cent.); out of 24 female lunatic delinquents, 3 were epileptic (12 per cent.).

This fact, which is very important as regards the criminality of women, is observed also out of prison in the ordinary mad-houses.

In Italy, in the year 1878, according to official statistics, there were in the different mad-houses 1,658 cases of frenetic epilepsy, of which 1,041 were men, and 617 women (100 men as against 59·1 women); in 1886–88 the female epileptics were 58·0 as against 100 males; and the predominance in this respect of men over women appears more marked in Southern and Central, than in Northern Italy.

	Men.	Women.	Out of 100 Men.
N. Italy	515	351	68·1
C. Italy	312	192	61·4
S. Italy and the Islands	214	74	38·0

Male epileptics constitute 8·7 per cent. of all maniacs, and female epileptics only 5·8 per cent.

In Germany, Sommer found that out of 100

epileptics, 60·7 belonged to the masculine, and 39·3 to the feminine sex.

In Servia, in the asylum of Belgrade, there were in 1890 16 male and 6 female epileptics.

In New South Wales (according to statistics furnished us by the Government of Australia), between 1887 and 1891 epilepsy was noted as determining madness 111 times in men, and 70 times in women.

The greater number of male epileptics to be found in the asylums is all the more significant that the longevity of males so affected is less than in females. As Köhler justly observes (" Lebensdauer der Epileptiker ; Allg. Zeitsch f. Psych," 1877), female epileptics usually die after the age of 25, and male epileptics earlier.

Nevertheless, in France and England the majority of writers maintain that epilepsy is more common in women. Gowers thinks that the proportion among 100 epileptics is 53·4 males for 46·6 females. Esquirol believes that the number of female epileptics surpasses the males more than 1·3. But neither the first nor the second writer give the exact number of lunatics *received* into the asylums ; and it is this number, far more than that of the living denizens at any given moment, which we ought to have, for the reason already mentioned, that women live longer than men.

The extraordinary difference which we have noted is not in harmony with the observations made upon motor epilepsy, and can only be explained by the fact that the cerebral cortex is in women much less irritable than in men with respect to the psychical centres, although there may be equality of the motor centres in the two sexes; and the reason lies in the inferior psychical activity of women.

Tonnini remarked that epilepsy in the female more often causes dementia and imbecility than madness; that is to say, it produces fewer psychical anomalies just as it produces fewer degenerative anomalies, there being 16 of these in women as against 27 in men, while the contrary happens with female lunatics, their anomalies being more numerous than those of male lunatics, in the ratio of 8 to 12.

One of the writers, having already demonstrated that the greater part of sexual psychopathic phenomena, especially the graver and more monstrous forms, are epileptoid varieties which, beginning at puberty, continue throughout the life of the individual, we must conclude once again from their almost total absence in women (who yet in a life of prostitution would have so many occasions, pretexts, and reasons for such excesses), that the particular cortical irritation which results in psychical epilepsy is much less common in the female than in the male.

In short, the predominance of the male sex over the female is evident once more even in that moral insanity which, as we have proved, presents so many affinities with congenital criminality and physical epilepsy.

The subject of criminality in the female receives illumination from this rarity of epilepsy and moral insanity among women. It explains why they are so much oftener merely occasional criminals, and why, even when criminals from passion, they hardly ever commit their crimes in one of those sudden impulses which are always partly epileptoid; also why, in common crimes, they exhibit a premeditation, a gloating that are the very antithesis of the offence which springs instantaneously from an epileptic movement. It throws light on the tardy action of the female offender, and while confirming the theory of the relation between congenital criminality and epilepsy, serves also to explain sexual differences.

On the few occasions where a woman is a born criminal, I have always discovered in her as in her male prototype the symptoms of an epileptic tendency; and naturally these are the more marked the graver the offence.

Out of 405 women condemned to prison in Turin for important crimes, Salsotto found epilepsy in 2·6, which is 13 times higher than the results furnished by minor offenders. For instance—

In 20 poisoners	epilepsy was present in	10	per cent.
10 guilty of murderous assault	,,	,,	10	,,
20 swindlers	,,	,,	5	,,
130 murderesses	,,	,,	3·9	,,

while in

100 infanticides	,,	,,	2	,,
10 wounders	,,	,,	0	,,
25 offenders against morals	,,	,,	0	,,
90 thieves	,,	,,	0	,,

Here, then, we see epilepsy prevalent in the worst congenital criminals, while it gradually diminishes and disappears as we reach the class of occasional offenders.

Again, among the worst criminals the motor forms of epilepsy are rarer and less frequent than with men, while the psychical forms predominate, as in the following instances:—

T. P., aged 19, a painter's model, expelled from France, where she had been a year in prison for homicide, repeated the offence of stabbing so many times that she was confined on 26 occasions in one year in the prison of Turin. She was 1·59 m. in height and weighed 54 kgs. Her lower jaw was much developed; she had orbital margins, prominent cheek-bones and sinuses, a regular nose and ears, black hair (scanty from long-standing scald), very large, sparkling dark brown eyes; enormous median incisors (with diasthema), and canine lateral teeth sloping internally and backwards like all the other lateral teeth. The total circumference of her cranium was 570. Its probable capacity, 1616. Cephalic index, 84. She was tattooed with the entire name of an Italian lover, whom she had known in Paris, and a date, both ornamented, and on her left arm bore the initials of another lover, and the words, "*J'aime Jean.*"

General sensitiveness: she felt the Faraday current at 66 mm. on the right side (normal 70) and at 55 on the left. Sensitiveness to pain: 30 on the right side (normal 36) and 30 on the left. Tactile sensitiveness: 2 mm. on the right, 2·5 on the left; in the tongue, 1·5. Great meteoric sensitiveness: she showed much irritability during atmospheric changes. Magnetic sensitiveness: she felt a strong burning sensation when the magnet was applied to her forehead. Sense of taste, small. Sense of smell, dull. Sight: 30·20 in both eyes. Exact chromatic perception. Hearing: she perceived a watch at 140 cm. on the right and 131 cm. on the left.

She had been very precocious, and was a mother (of a dead child) for the first time when only 16. Her movements were easy, prompt, and very rapid; and her muscular agility most remarkable. Her muscular force was exceptional, the dynamometer marking 55 on the right and 50 on the left; and although bound she succeeded in tearing the straitwaistcoat which had sometimes to be applied to her. Her greatest force lay in her teeth, with which she could reduce wood, glass, and other things to the smallest pieces. Her voice was sonorous and harmonious; her perception and ideation rapid. She could remember distant events, but not recent ones. She was very dissolute, and chose her lovers among the worst characters. When she had money she consumed it in drinking, smoking, and gluttony. Of a mule-like obstinacy, she was also extremely capricious, and demanded the satisfaction of every fancy which she took into her head even when in prison. Her hatred knew no limits, and she gloated over revenge with voluptuous delight. Having been betrayed by one of her lovers, she tattooed his name and the date of her acquaintance with him on her right arm, at the same time swearing vengeance on him. And one day, having enticed him to visit her, she spat in his face a paste composed of glass and tobacco, which she had kept in her mouth, and which blinded him completely. Another lover, having beaten her when drunk, she allowed him to fall asleep, and then set fire to the mattress on which he was lying.

When she entered prison for the 26th time in one year she was covered with wounds, but would not give up the name of the man who had attacked her, saying that she wished to work her own revenge, and she did not conceal even from the judge the intention of wounding her assailant as soon as she should be at liberty again. She always carried a knife, which she used on the smallest provocation and with the utmost indifference. She was quite insensible to the consequences of the wounds she inflicted, and recalled with pleasure a man whom she killed, as we shall see, in Paris. She often found that to stab was not satisfaction enough, and preferred to blind her victims.

She was, however, kind to her female companions when in need, and she was passionately fond of children. While not really a thief, she appropriated with great facility anything which came in her way. She spoke French and Piedmontese slang with great facility, and sang forbidden songs in a pleasing manner.

Prison life had no terrors for her; on the contrary she dominated the situation and insisted on the best treatment.

Born near Caserta, she was stolen by some strolling mountebanks at the age of two years; and grew up without knowing that she was not among her own kindred. Having quickly learnt to sing and dance, she was forced under pain of merciless beatings to beg through the streets, and began this life at 14 years of age. At last, when with her companions in the neighbourhood of Paris, she learnt that the man whom she had always regarded as her father did not stand in that relation to her, and was, on the contrary, deeply in love with her. Frightened and much grieved, the girl escaped and went to Paris. She lived for some days by singing, then became the mistress, for two years, of a young man, a model, from Catanzaro, by whom (at 16) she had a dead child. She eventually left her lover, who, she discovered, had been unfaithful to her; and from that moment she began the habit of carrying about the knife which she wielded, often in drunken affrays, with such facility.

She killed a painter who had refused to pay her, and it was after her imprisonment for this crime that she began to be a model; but her life became ever more profligate and bestial, and she frequented the worst company. Even when out of prison her unruly conduct caused her to be arrested for wounding alone 12 times in one year. The police said that she ought to be arrested every day. In affrays she almost always came out victorious, being so active and daring as to put men as well as women to flight. When in prison she clamoured and shrieked for days together, and broke everything within her reach. No punishment sufficed to correct her. The slightest cause would provoke this condition, the only way of calming which was to give her something that she wanted. She only remembered the crisis very confusedly when it had passed, but sometimes an allusion to the outbreak provoked a fresh one in her.

At intervals of two or three months she had been seized with true motor epilepsy, to the great terror of her cell-companion (whom it may be mentioned in passing she had corrupted).

Another of our examples is M. B., aged 47, whose type of face is Mongolian. Capacity 1,426; touch somewhat dull, 2·8 on the right side, 2 on left (left-handedness); slight sensory deadness, also slight insensibility to pain; sight affected by peripheral scotomata in the internal superior quadrant.

From her early youth she had drunk 5 or 6 litres of wine a day, and eight wine-glasses of aquavita. At the age of 20 she stole a thousand francs, which she squandered in articles of adornment and in wine. Later she wounded a lover who had left her for another woman, and strung herself up to the act by drinking, because, as she said, "He who has most thread spins most cloth." Even now she dwells with delight on the idea of having punished him, and talks of doing as much for her relatives who refuse her her share of inheritance. In any case she says she will cut down their vines and their grain.

She does not know that she was ever epileptic, but many times when at her work in the kitchen she has cut her hand without noticing it. She has had attacks of giddiness without cause, and has fallen to the ground in them; and finally she has on three distinct occasions shown that she did not know what she was doing by acts of unusual eccentricity, one being an attempt to light the fire with a note for 50 francs which she took from a drawer, and which her mistress only succeeded in snatching from her just in time.

She has no recollection of these acts any more than she was conscious at the time of performing them, and she relates them as they were told her.

Yet another case is that of a woman whom at first sight we took to be an occasional delinquent. She had but few characteristics of degeneration, only overhanging brows, a heavy lower part to her face, alveolar prognathism, and anatomical and functional left-handedness. She took part with her lover in an audacious robbery committed upon a dealer in second-hand articles: then tried to escape, but, when arrested, confessed everything (having, however, the stolen article in her hand). She declared that when released she would choose prostitution rather than crime. Her capacity was remarkable; her physiognomy pleasing. Her touch was dull on the left side, 3 mm.; her sensibility to pain normal, and normal also her taste and smell; visual field of left eye slightly limited. There was something virile and energetic about the woman. She had quarrelled with her father, and was filled with hatred for the lover who had been the cause of her misfortunes. Her rages were most violent, and because the prison-sister briefly reproved her she muttered, "One day I shall take her by the hair and throw her from the window."

This subject, who is a middle type between criminaloids and born criminals, had only one real attack of motor epilepsy, and that was caused by the deep annoyance of seeing her brother's mistress, who was also in prison, receive presents, while for herself there were none.

2. *Prostitutes*.—According to Parent-Duchatelet's statistics, the cases of epilepsy among prostitutes are as 0·98 per cent., which is higher than the figure which we found for minor born offenders, but lower than the average among the worst sort of female criminals. In Turin among 480 slightly criminal prostitutes we found 1·5 per cent. of epileptics.

But these figures as a whole do not correspond to the important part played by prostitutes in criminal anthropology, and we saw, moreover, that out of 25 women condemned for corruption of morals not one was epileptic, and only in one case, which was complicated by hysteria, did we find a true epileptic equivalent in the ranks of prostitution.

Here, then, is another of those contradictory facts of which we have met so many in the course of our work, but which becomes largely comprehensible when we reflect on the indecency, the lasciviousness, the semi-imbecility constituting the special character of prostitutes, as well as of the morally insane in the female sex (*see* following pages), and when we remember that the courtesan reproduces the atavistic condition of the primitive woman.

Seeing the passive and retrogressive nature of the prostitute one can understand how an atavistic return of moral insanity accounts for her appearance on the scene without the intervention of that cortical irritation which produces psychical epilepsy and leads to the graver crimes and the more striking cases of sexual perversity.

3. *The morally insane.*—In 1888 there were 148 cases of moral insanity in the Italian lunatic asylums, 105 being men and 43 women; that is to say, for 100 men 40·9 women. In the years 1886–88 there were 155 females and 274 males, or 55·6 of the former for 100 of the latter; and predominance of the male sex is more marked in Southern than in Northern Italy, just as we saw was the case with epilepsy.

	Men.	Women.	Out of 100 Men.
N. Italy	67	31	56·8
C. Italy	11	7	63·6
S. Italy (and the Islands)	27	5	18·6

"Moral insanity," writes Schüle, "shows itself in women especially during the first period of matrimony. They show an open aversion to their husbands. If they have children they treat them with undisguised indifference, and give them over carelessly to a wet nurse, so as to preserve their own beauty; and if their husbands do not gratify any one of their many caprices they revenge themselves by ill-treating their children. She declares herself neglected and ill-treated by her husband, and to revenge herself does not hesitate to calumniate him to her friends, and to reveal all the secrets of domestic life. She maintains always that she alone is right, and her fluency in inventing and misrepresenting is inexhaustible. She is extravagant, and levies small tolls on the accounts; she perpetually buys costly clothes, loves strange fashions, is extremely vain, and very anxious to appear young. If remonstrated with she threatens to commit suicide or to leave the family roof. She neglects to train her children, gives them a pernicious example of uncontrolled temper, and insinuates in them a hatred of their father. When such women become profligate they claim all possible license for themselves, and often threaten to enter a house of ill-fame, and yet are not rarely subject to a delirium of jealousy, in which they threaten their husband's life. When calm returns they retire to a corner and sit there brooding, suspicious and melancholy."

There is a more constant relation between prostitution and the commoner forms of moral insanity such as lead to confinement in an asylum. Here the symptoms are still anger and excessive hatred, but joined to these are obscenity and unnatural vices.

C. di B., who had lateral analgesia, cranial capacity greater than the female average (1445), and was epileptic, hated everybody who approached, even those who were kind to her: and one day she begged to be allowed to beat two dogs because it irritated her to see other people caress them.

C. di S. P. wanted to drive her own daughters to vice, and not for gain, but simply out of a perverted desire to give them pleasure. She was subject to unnatural vices, feigned a hundred maladies to avoid the necessity of working, and had created a positive association of calumniators among the hysterical women in her ward.

I knew a woman of high family, well-educated, and a poetess, who had led the most profligate existence, but nevertheless accused her husband of dissolute conduct with such plausibility, that she succeeded in drawing the attention of the authorities to him. In the asylum she boasted of her former profligate life, and twitted the matrons for having observed a different rule of conduct. She was already an old woman, but succeeded nevertheless in getting up intrigues within the asylum, then turned on those who had abetted her and calumniated them as she calumniated the medical attendants, thereby causing them the gravest annoyances. She composed magnificent verses on the beauty of platonic love, and on the very same day would resort to disgusting eccentricities of food—a perversion of appetite which was her only sign of madness.

Another poetess of great intelligence showed the same profligacy in her love affairs, of which she made shameless confessions to the men themselves. She was rich, but induced everybody to give her promissory notes, of which she always exacted full payment; and what she most desired in her intrigues was publicity, with its concomitant scandal.

Another woman, with all the characteristics of degeneration (enormous jaw and sinuses, but a great fineness of touch, 1·1mm.), had been sold by her mother to a man who honourably married her. From the very day of her marriage she poisoned her husband's life, accusing him before the syndic and the doctors of infidelity, even of incest. And when he wished her to undergo an operation for internal polypus, she maintained that he only desired it to kill her. She spent the whole day in idleness, only interrupted by excesses in drinking and profligacy, and by card-playing, the latter being resorted to by her for the purpose of divining the intentions of her husband and her lovers. Her habits and conversation in the asylum were most indecent. Like many persons of obscene habits, she also showed at times a desire for disgusting food; but she was clever enough before the doctors and judges to justify everything she did, and succeeded at last in getting her husband prosecuted.